Women in Control?

Women in Control?

The Role of Women in Law Enforcement

FRANCES HEIDENSOHN

CLARENDON PRESS · OXFORD
1992

Oxford University Press, Walton Street, Oxford OX2 6DP
Oxford New York Toronto
Delhi Bombay Calcutta Madras Karachi
Kuala Lumpur Singapore Hong Kong Tokyo
Nairobi Dar es Salaam Cape Town
Melbourne Auckland Madrid
and associated companies in
Berlin Ibadan

Oxford is a trade mark of Oxford University Press

Published in the United States
by Oxford University Press Inc., New York

British Library Cataloguing in Publication Data
Data available
ISBN 0-19-825 2552 1746419
Library of Congress Cataloging in Publication Data
Heidensohn, Frances.
    Women in control? : the role of women in law enforcement
/ Frances Heidensohn.
    Includes bibliographical references and index.
    1. Policewomen—Great Britain. 2. Policewomen—United States.
I. Title.
HV8023.H48   1992   363.2'2'082—dc20   92–25902
    ISBN 0–19–825255–2

Set by Hope Services (Abingdon)Ltd.
Printed in Great Britain
on acid-free paper by
Biddles Ltd., Guildford and King's Lynn

For Christina

ACKNOWLEDGEMENTS

In preparing and carrying out the research on which this book is based, I drew on the help and support of many people in Britain and the USA. Joan Lock was outstandingly helpful with advice and contacts, comments, and encouragement at all stages of the project. Mary Tuck, Lorna Smith, and Peter Southgate of the Home Office Planning and Research Unit gave advice at an early stage, as did Sandra Jones. Jo Campling proved, as ever, to be a true friend and enabler to writing by and about women.

Sabbatical leave from Goldsmiths' College enabled me to pursue research in Britain and the USA, and later, to write this book. My thanks to the Warden, Professor Andrew Rutherford, College Council, and Professor John Stone for this. Sue Balloch and Ed Randall covered my teaching cheerfully while I was away.

In the USA Debbie Lancaster was a wonderful guide and friend to me, as were Roseanna Sims and Marilyn Macdougall. I also received an immense amount of help and interest from Susan Martin (then at the Police Foundation, Washington, DC) and her colleagues, and from Darrell Stephens at PERF. Staff from the Police Departments of Boston, New York, Washington, DC, Dallas, and Bensalem were extremely helpful and hospitable. Among senior officials I should like to mention Deputy Superintendent Ronald X. Conway, Assistant Commissioner Joan M. Thompson, and Chief Maurice T. Turner.

My debts to academic friends and colleagues are immense. Mary Eaton was, as always, a constant source of advice, suggestions, and unfailing humour. It was particularly rewarding to be at the London School of Economics at the same time as she was. Paul Rock, too, was, as ever, kind and commented most helpfully on the manuscript. For comments, suggestions, responses to queries, and contributions from papers, etc. I am obliged to Meda Chesney Lind, Abner Cohen, Nigel Fielding, Nick May, Merry Morash, Robert Reiner, Kevin Stenson, Pat Thane, and Chris Wilkinson. I have been particularly fortunate in the financial and practical help

viii ACKNOWLEDGEMENTS

given to this study. Professor John Gunn and his fellow trustees of the Gibbens Trust at the Institute of Psychiatry provided me with an award at the outset; Mollie Weatheritt and the Police Foundation provided a grant which helped me to carry out the work in the USA. Finally, the administrators of the Morris Ginsberg Fellowship at the London School of Economics, by awarding me the Fellowship for 1991, gave me the opportunity to write this book. I am most grateful to them all and also to Professor Terry Morris and his colleagues in the Sociology Department at LSE for their welcome and kindness.

Sasha Shaw and Pauline Ryan of the Goldsmiths' College Library patiently assisted my quest for books and articles.

The first international conference on Women, Crime, and Social Control, held at Mt. Gabriel, Quebec in July 1991, was an inspiring event for all those who took part and was especially stimulating and challenging for me. My appreciation to all the participants and most of all to Marie Andrée Bertrand, Kathy Daly, and Dorie Klein who organized it. Lucy and Edmund Pereira of ABOS once more prepared my manuscript for publication with great skill and tact. Richard Hart was a most patient and generous editor.

This book represents, in part, my own tribute to the challenge and excitement which the United States offers to social scientists from elsewhere: so many central ideas and developments have come from there and its people are so open in welcoming and encouraging foreign enquirers. My thanks to Darril Hudson, Peter Bosch, and P. J. Baunach for introducing me to many aspects of America and American life-styles.

Most of all, I am grateful to all the women who agreed to be interviewed for this study. Their co-operation was essential; they gave it unstintingly, adding kindness and hospitality as unlooked-for extras. They remain unnamed by agreement; I trust that I have given their views fairly.

The task of completing this book was affected by additional responsibilities typical of university life in the late twentieth century. To those, especially in my own family, whose support helped me to write it, I owe a great deal. Christina Heidensohn accompanied me on my visit to the USA, checked text and references for me; Klaus Heidensohn advised me on the title, found me obscure references, and patiently watched repeats of *Cagney and Lacey* with me. Martin Heidensohn kept the music low and helped, with the others, to maintain my spirits. Since everyone has given me so much, I can only hope that they will find that the result is worthwhile. Of course, I must insist that I take full responsibility for what appears here.

CONTENTS

INTRODUCTION

SOCIAL scientists can learn much from the study of images. In the early 1990s, for instance, it was possible to collect a striking series of pictures of women from western mass media. Margaret Thatcher, Britain's Prime Minister for more than eleven years, resigned. World-wide she was shown not only departing in dramatic style, but her premiership was portrayed and analysed at length. A few months later, Edith Cresson became the first female Prime Minister of France. Between these two political events, women serving in the Coalition Forces in the Gulf War were depicted in combat gear and with weapons and also embracing their children as they left for the war. The most senior woman police officer in Britain claimed that she had been sexually discriminated against and was suspended while a disciplinary charge was brought against her. Fictional portrayals of women as detectives, especially in television series, are not new, but the 1990s saw new departures with films such as *Nikita*, *Blue Steel*, and *The Silence of the Lambs* in all of which the pursuing officer is a tough, armed female.

What all these have in common is that they show women in real or imaginary situations of control or command. Now these phenomena can be interpreted in many ways. Gun-toting women can be seen as male fantasy figures (indeed, this is the basis of the plot of *Blue Steel*) and close to forms of pornography. However, in this book I shall contend that these selected snapshots do record events and changes of a deeper and more significant kind. In particular, I shall argue that the part played by women in various forms of social control has altered considerably during the twentieth century; it has done so only slowly and jerkily, but the process continues and is now sufficiently notable to repay careful study. It is a process worth the attention not only of those interested in women and their position in our society and in the consequences of any shifts, but also of a much greater audience of those concerned about broader questions of social order and social change, about policing and law enforcement in all their forms, about equality and representativeness. Further, the study of women in any social institution inevitably raises questions about men as well; this is most certainly true of this project, and hence about wider issues of gender.

There are problems to consider about all these issues at many different levels. First and most obviously, it is necessary to focus on what roles women now play in social control and especially in certain key agencies. How far are these roles new and distinctive, how long have women been involved in them? What influences determined in the past, now determine, and may alter in the future, the level of women's participation, its range and significance? These themes are considered in Chapter 2. Few topics have been more discussed or caused more controversy in western (and some eastern) countries in the late twentieth century than that of crime and the policing of it. The extent of such debates has been matched by the growth of academic research on such issues. In Chapter 3 I outline some of these debates and those which are particularly relevant to the topic of this study. Are women effective as patrol officers? Are men? What is the impact of integrating police forces and departments? Does gender make a difference in methods of policing?

The following chapters outline the findings of my own comparative study of the experiences of women police officers in the USA and Britain. Drawing on a series of interviews, I suggest that the natural history of their careers can be understood not only as gender distinctive, but also as shaped by other factors, including the occupational culture of policing which, of course, itself involves gender influences but by a less direct route. Later chapters deal with the issues raised and the questions answered by the empirical work, as well as much broader topics.

Before moving on to look at the specific area of policing, and women's roles and experiences in it, I want first to explore the repertoire of concepts and techniques available to the student of such topics and to suggest how I have employed them. While such a presentation is a commonplace of sociological writing, it has a particular importance for this project for two main reasons. First, the range of concepts I discuss and use is wider and perhaps more idiosyncratic than is customary; secondly in part of what I set out to do I am trying to make connections and raise issues not usually raised in this way.

In this book I explore one small part of the experiences of some modern women. From their histories and accounts I wish to illuminate broader questions. In order to place this work in context, in Chapter 1 I outline some approaches to the study of social control and of gender and discuss how these might be used to help to answer the question implied in its title. As will soon be clear, none of the concepts and terms I suggest using is without either its problems or its critics. Nevertheless, I believe this to be an activity worth attempting. It would be possible to present my findings without preliminaries and outside any ongoing debates. But they do have a history and it is characteristic of the women I studied that they seek to make sense of their own careers in terms which relate to some of these. For, while these are academic considerations about theories and concepts, they do reflect aspects of lived and shared lives. Indeed, it is a notable feature of the themes of social control and of gender that they relate so closely to the everyday world as well as to formal social-science discourse.

As this book was going to press in July 1992 the claim of sexual discrimination brought by Assistant Chief Constable Alison Halford mentioned above was withdrawn, as were the disciplinary charges she faced. She accepted a settlement with the Merseyside Police Authority.

1

Social Order and Social Control

IT is a convention of social-science practice to define as early as possible in the project the terms one is using in it. With 'social order' and 'social control' there are considerable difficulties with this approach since distinctive meanings and interpretations abound. These are by no means always in competition or in conflict. Rather they reflect very disparate forms and usages applied by discrete groups of scholars to their own areas with little interest or awareness of what occurs elsewhere. This scene remarkably resembles that of Shakespearian comedies such as *As You Like It* or *The Tempest* where characters in another part of the forest or elsewhere on the isle obliviously engage in contemporary activities. In order to simplify a multiply complex and scattered situation I shall adopt and adapt the terminology used by Sinfield who writes of the 'social division of control' (1978: 138) and consider the sociological division of control first.

Sociological Division of Social Control

In his bleak and seminal study Stan Cohen points out that the term 'social control' has 'lately become something of a Mickey Mouse concept . . . In everyday language, that concept has no resonant or clear meaning at all' (1985: 2). He goes on to acknowledge that 'in the classical nineteenth century tradition of social thought, the concept of social control was near the centre of the enterprise', but concludes that this organic connection became weaker and weaker and hence 'the standard literature on social control probably *is* a little more irrelevant, misguided and foolish than it might be in most other areas of sociology' (1985: 5; emphasis in original). While this may be so for Cohen's purposes, which are to explore 'planned and programmed responses to expected and realized deviance [rather] than in the general institutions of society which produce conformity' (1985: 2), for the aims of this study I have found it necessary to range more widely and to acknowledge that there are gains to be made from airing some of the heirlooms of the sociological heritage. Four distinctive areas can be mapped out which can be mined for their conceptual treasures and insights:

1. The classical sociological 'core'
2. The new sociology of control
3. The new policing studies
4. The new sociology of welfare.

1. The Sociological Core

As Luhmann has emphasized, 'how is social order possible?' was *the* main issue for sociology in its classical phases in the nineteenth and early twentieth centuries. For Marx, order was achieved by the systematic exploitation of one class by another and by the appropriation of their labour; it was an enforced order which would, by inevitable historical processes, collapse under its own contradictions. Durkheim emphasized and first identified social solidarity as central to the maintenance of order and divided it into the mechanical form, characteristic of preindustrial societies, and the organic form in differentiated, modern societies, where cohesion is obtained through functional interlinking and division of labour. Max Weber saw social control in any society as exercised by legitimated authority. Legitimacy is derived from different types of social action: affective, traditional, and rational. These actions give motives for support for authority and a basis for his three types of authority: charismatic, traditional, and rational-legal. Each of these in turn produces different kinds of organizations. (The key concepts which I have harvested for use in this study are set out in Figure 1.)

2. The 'New' Sociology of Social Control

Janowitz argued in an article published in 1975 that the term 'social control' was properly applied only to self-regulatory, not coercive, forms of control. Its original use was to describe self-control, not the use of power by one group over another. While this may be an exaggerated, and refutable, view of this concept's history, it is certainly true that the classical sociologists were

Type	Key concepts	Agents	Gender
1. Core sociology	exploitation solidarity authority legitimacy	ruling class social systems social processes	—
2. New sociology of control	dispersal of discipline internalization inclusion	penal institutions asylums soft control	√
3. Police studies	professionalism militarism	police state	√
4. Sociology of welfare	oppression patriarchy integration	welfare system family voluntary sector	√

FIG. 1. Models of Social Control

concerned little, if at all, with the formal, coercive agencies of control. However, already at the time when Janowitz wrote and increasingly since, a 'new' sociology of social control has developed which has focused particularly on the patterns and changes in social control in pre- and modern western societies. In the works of Michel Foucault and of Scull, Ignatieff, and Cohen (1977, 1978, 1985), the disciplinary institutions of modern societies, the penitentiary, the asylum, community punishment are all excavated to reveal trends, particularly the dispersal of discipline and the dynamic nature of social disciplining.

For the sake of clarity, I have placed these two notions of social control as polar opposites. One depicts order as maintained consensually by means of central social institutions and the agreement of citizens. It is, of course, a paradox that all the classical writers considered that modern society had failed to remain ordered as a result of its transition from pre- to industrial society, and that all, while their diagnoses and solutions differed, did seek remedies. I have chosen to locate the coercive model of control in the work of the 'new' sociologists of control. Chunn and Gavignan see 'the conception of social control as organized repression [owing] an intellectual debt to . . . Tannenbaum . . . Lemert . . . labelling theorists . . . radical deviancy' (1988: 108). While their terms do not differ very much from mine, I consider that they give the infant control theory too many godparents and ancestors. Foucault is a (the?) major source of inspiration for much of this work and it is particularly characterized by its historical awareness and specificity, while the various varieties of deviancy theory were almost always ahistorical. Moreover, while deviancy theorists wrote about repression and stigmatization, they did not, with some exceptions, examine the agencies which brought these about. On the contrary, they continued the 1960s trend to research and to write about deviants—the nuts, sluts, and perverts approach to sociology—rather than the controlling agencies. Chunn and Gavignan go on to criticize the concept of social control, arguing with other critics that it is ahistorical and determinist, with a marked tendency for 'every thing and therefore nothing [to] count as an instance of repressive social control . . . the controlled, then, are passive robots at the mercy of a carceral apparatus which expands almost daily' (1988: 112). They complain, with some justice, that 'radical theorists tend to assume that any "control" is in and of itself bad or unjust' (ibid.), and that no sense of agency or model of interaction between controlled and controllers is allowed for in that model.

Nor, of course, is it within many versions of the consensual model which does not include any notion of a negotiated form of social order. Historians have been particularly harsh in their criticisms of both consensual and coercive models of control and have also elided the two models. Mayer has questioned the widespread attribution of bad faith to social reformers in social-control studies, their 'primary concern to demonstrate the falseness of reformers' good intentions' (1983: 20). He suggests further that key questions about 'who, why, how and how well' cannot be easily answered about social control. For example, little consideration is given to how effective controls were or why, if middle-class interests were being served, there was so much conflict over the aims of so many of them. Stedman-Jones makes more vehement attacks on the coercive concept, asserting that 'there is no political or ideological institution which could not in some way be interpreted as an agency of social control' (1977: 165). While all these authors' doubts have some substance and include key insights to which I shall return, they are, from the perspective of this study, somewhat beside the point, indeed they themselves prove another, central point. These schematic categories can prove helpful in stimulating debate or in merely providing frameworks through which the central topic can be viewed in perspective. We shall need to look at women in social control in relation to coercion and consensus in formal and informal spheres and at their dynamic interrelations. It is perhaps surprising that these modern critics do not observe the lack of gender as a dimension to control theories. (Chunn and Gavignan do consider some related topics.)

3. The New Policing Studies

Systematic research on policing has a relatively short history, although its volume has grown dramatically in modern times (Reiner and Shapland 1987). Further, the waxing of such volumes has not simply been crude accumulation: modern studies of policing have been deeply diverse and have involved major debates about, for example, the origins of Britain's 'new police' in 1829 and the degree of legitimacy achieved by them later in the nineteenth century (Reiner 1985). This detailed perusal of policing historically, procedurally, and even philosophically has considerably added to our understanding of what policing is about, what role police officers play in maintaining law and order in a modern state. Brogden, Scraton, and others have emphasized the conflicts between police and the working class and suggest that social-order maintenance in Britain has owed much in the past to colonial modes and, increasingly in modern times, to militaristic ones. A large body of work has emphasized the importance of professional skills in the maintenance of order (Reiner 1985; Fielding 1991; Johnson et al. 1981) while others have stressed, for instance, the checking of incivilities and minor disturbance as the keys: the so-called 'broken windows' hypothesis (Wilson and Kelling 1982).

4. New Sociology of Welfare

In a thoughtful paper published in 1980 Higgins noted the growth in interest 'in the relationship between social control and social policy' (1980: 1). She suggested then that social-control theories applied to social policies were revealing many controlling aspects of welfare institutions. She suggested three then current reasons for this development: the growth of (i) Marxist thought, (ii) urban studies, and (iii) radical social-work critiques. In the decade following this article new force has been added to its message by a series of other contributions, notably from feminist analysts but also from new right theorists and from critics of child care policies (Parton 1985), racism (F. Williams 1989), and community care.

This brief excursion through the scenic heights of the sociology of social control has given us the chance to collect and order some of the useful concepts which are on offer for analysis. It is worth stressing that I see these concepts in a neo-Weberian fashion; that is, they are ideal types, guiding taxonomies, lists, or models, which are only useful for as long as they help to illuminate a place, a person, or a problem; they cannot fully describe and categorize human experience, which I take to be much more complex, diffuse, and elusive than cheerfully clear categories may suggest. With some concepts already to hand to further the project, I shall now turn to survey the social division of control and to map out its various aspects.

The Social Division of Social Control

Social control can perhaps most helpfully be conceived in terms of its public and private dimensions and whether it is sustained by formal or informal means. Obviously, the categories are neither completely rigid nor completely permanent. Churches may operate in both the public and private domain. Ecclesiastical courts, operating canon law, used to try cases in pre-modern Britain, yet most of their sanctions have now been abolished and it is in the moral sphere that religion has most salience today. This taxonomy is neither comprehensive nor exhaustive and is here to provide an initial framework for later analysis.

The Sociology of Sex and Gender

One key modern development that has had a significant impact on our understanding of social processes and institutions has been the (re-)discovery of the sociology of gender. A trend report suggests that 'the study of gender is an important means through which sociology itself is being re-shaped' (Maynard 1990: 269). As Maynard points out in the article cited, gender perspectives have only been a mainstream concern in sociology for a relatively short time. A major research project on education and social mobility conducted in the 1970s and published as late as 1980 surveyed only male subjects, thus rendering it defective not only because it fails to cover the experience of women, but it limits the possible comparisons for males (Halsey *et al.* 1980). While gender studies are by no means secure yet in sociology, they have broadened and enhanced the subject. Four key approaches can be discerned which will be helpful:

1. Putting women in the frame
2. Studying women
3. Studying men and masculinity as problematic
4. Theorizing gender.

1. Putting Women in the Frame

These approaches reflect in some degree the phases through which gender studies and varieties of feminist thought have passed in their modern development. The first of modern 'second-wave' feminist writers emphasized the invisibility of women in a whole range of sociological studies and sought to remedy the gap by including women in work in the main fields of the discipline. Occupation and social class, education, politics, and crime have amongst other topics been re-viewed in this way (Crompton and Mann 1986; Deem 1978; Stacey and Price 1981; Heidensohn 1985).

Women's roles in law-enforcement and criminal-justice systems have also benefited from this approach. At least two kinds of studies can be discerned and are discussed below: equity studies and 'we can handle it out here' projects. Equity studies (Horne 1980; Feinman 1986; S. Jones 1986; Heidensohn 1989*b*) describe the entry of women into criminal-justice and control agencies and look at their comparative advance. What I have called 'we can handle it out here' studies are primarily focused on empirically based accounts of women's performance, especially as patrol officers, and on accounts of the attitudes of their male colleagues and the public to them (Bloch and Anderson 1974; Charles 1981).

While these projects can all be classified as aspects of the wider endeavour to render female action visible and to describe it, the impetus and the finances for such activities did not solely come from concerned feminist academics. Changes between the boundaries and within the boundaries of the social division of control outlined above played an important part. Simply put, in the 1970s in both Britain and the USA the official role and tasks of women in policing were altered, and, partly in consequence of this, their numbers rose. At about the same time, and not entirely unconnected with this, male recruitment and retention became a problem, in Britain at least. During the same decade major shifts were also occurring in personal social services which had profound effects on their social-control functions. In Britain, social-service departments were reorganized, the role of social worker was redefined, and a series of scandals put child protection high on the political and policy agenda (Parton 1985). In the USA decarceration, privatization of social services, especially for the mentally ill, and fiscal crises caused similar frontier fractures (Scull 1981; Warren 1981). I have stressed this history because it is important to note that, while the resources we can draw on to produce this account occur in diverse parts of different forests, they are never totally isolated or discrete. A strong new sapling may spring from seedlings cast by the most unpredictable birds or insects.

2. Studying Women

Modern students of gender did not remain content for long with the add-on approach. Painting women on to a male-primed and outlined canvas palls as quickly as painting by numbers as an excitement-generating activity. Many quickly moved on to study areas of human life, primarily, though not exclusively, the preoccupations of women, which had largely been left out of the sociological galère: housework (Oakley 1974), childbirth (Oakley 1980) amongst many others. It is in this area that some of the most interesting researches from the point of view of this present project have been conducted.

Focusing on women's experiences, and listening especially to their voices, revealed a catalogue of distress, which was distinctively gendered and had long remained 'hidden' from public gaze. Domestic violence, sexual harassment, child sex abuse, and rape have all been delineated as well as the oppressive effect which fear of such crimes has on women and the restrictions on their freedoms which it imposes (Stanko 1985 and 1990; Hanmer and Saunders 1984; J. Edwards 1987). Work in this field has not been merely descriptive or empirical. Writers have also attempted to move on into our third category and to theorize about the reasons for the existence and persistence and tacit coherence of such gross violence in civilized societies. Rape as a means of social control has been propounded by Brownmiller (1975), who argued that it is more widespread in more militarized societies. Walby (1989: 224–5) argues that male violence towards women forms one of six 'patriarchal structures which together constitute a system of patriarchy'. She later makes a most telling point: according to 'Weber's definition of the state, legitimate coercion is its monopoly. Does, this make violent men part of the state apparatus?' (1989: 225). She concludes that it is necessary to 'abandon the notion that the state has a monopoly of legitimate coercion in a given territory'. This is a bald statement and one to which I want to return. At this stage, I merely record it and suggest that it should probably be modified to acknowledge that the state may grant implicit licences to some people (mostly males) which give them a degree of authority and legitimacy in the use of coercive power. The clearest example is over children. It is, of course, significant that such 'licences' have been increasingly revoked and questioned in modern times.

The study of women has filled canvases with innumerable vivid figures as busy as in a Brueghel painting. Impressions of action and bustle are in some senses, nevertheless, misleading. There are still considerable gaps unfilled in the study of women's experience. This is hardly surprising given the short period during which work has been conducted. A further problem is undoubtedly the modest resources available for funding research. The gaps are, however, of a systematic kind and are important for our purposes here. While, for instance, women's experiences as victims of crime have been charted extensively, their roles as perpetrators are still much more obscure. Little has as yet been done on women's own violence (Heidensohn 1991b). Even the categories of studies of women in law enforcement noted above are light on women's own accounts of their experiences; they contain indeed disproportionately the perspectives of the male colleagues of policewomen. In this present study, therefore, I have concentrated on exploring the experiences of women in policing and on giving them a voice.

3. Studying Men and Masculinity

'It may seem strange to describe the study of men as a "new" area' (Maynard 1990: 282). After all, the earlier phases of gender work outlined above were directed at redressing the perceived imbalance in sociology in which so much had been written about men. In almost all such writings, however, men were treated as 'people', their experiences as 'society', and their masculinity never rendered as problematic. Effectively, this has made men as invisible in certain kinds of sociological accounts and explanations as women are in others. It also leaves gender a fractured concept. Walby has pointed out that histories of women's struggle for suffrage in

Britain focus on their actions and gloss over those who opposed them.

Those opposing the demand for the vote for women were not passive, but rather active participants in a battle . . . they banned women from attending political meetings . . . and forcibly ejected women from these meetings. (Male) police arrested protesters; (male) magistrates convicted protesters. . . . We cannot understand the suffrage struggle unless we understand the nature and extent of the opposition to feminist demands by patriarchal forces. (1988: 223)

There have been some developments in this area, such as the work of Hearn (1987) and Seidler (1990). This is still a relatively modest contribution to sociology and, as Maynard (1990: 284–5) has pointed out, can raise some difficult issues. 'Masculine' studies need probably to be linked to wider issues of gender rather than to stand on their own. For this present study, for example, I have found it necessary, although my focus is on women, to consider men's perspectives in some detail. Much has been written in the sociology of policing about the macho cop culture (Reiner 1985; Holdaway 1989) yet its existence has been rather more readily *justified* than properly *explained*. Even a highly sophisticated account such as that given by M. Young, which benefits from being that of both a long-serving police officer and an academic anthropologist, slides over these issues, taking far too much for granted.

The police world has *always* allocated priority and respect to male categories and symbols, finding it difficult to contend with the linking problems of gender, *simply* because masculinity has historically held the prime position and is deferred to and understood . . . In the task of controlling the street-visible activities of the predominantly male 'dangerous classes' the female has *logically* been excluded. In effect there is no real place for a woman in this world. (1991: 192–251)

Young's argument is that women are structurally excluded from policing, and he is clearly describing both his own real, lived world of police and that shared by many women officers. But gender is not unproblematically part of structure, nor are the police an ancient institution, nor are either structures or the police unchangeable. The unquestioned assumptions of *An Inside Job* are all the more curious since, elsewhere in the book, Young exposes other myths as social constructions: crime rates and the centrality of the role of the uniform beat officer (ch. 5). In these riveting descriptions, Young makes clear that, whatever their ingenuity at constructing crime figures, his former colleagues were hardly highly convincing in their policing roles. One is inevitably driven to ask why officers who are so cynical about and subversive of their role should so determinedly cling to it. A conceptual gap exists in this area and explanations will be sought later in this book. The problem can best be summarized as the gendered claim to sole ownership of the rights to social control.

4. Theorizing Gender

'Gender' refers to the socially constructed characteristics of masculinity and femininity. In all societies, expectations differ as to gender roles and they also alter over time and within cultures, differing by class, ethnic group, etc. Many explanations of gender formation are essentialist, relying on biological characteristics of the sexes to account for the traits of adults. Such approaches are by no means novel: Freud was perhaps the most notable contributor to them in an earlier era. More recently theoretical concern has been with first exploring the *constituents* of gender, both masculine and feminine, and assessing how far assumptions which have been taken for granted can be tested. Secondly, there is a problem of where gender fits into general social theory: are gender divisions all-pervasive? How are they explained? Can they be understood in terms of other distinctions, class or race, for example? (Giddens 1989: 710). If, on the other hand, gender is itself a, or the, most significant variable, then its operation has to be accounted for in some way. As Giddens's summary makes clear, mainstream sociology has only reached the dawn of such theorizing. Effectively only feminist scholars have made progress beyond this point. Most, although not of course all, theorizing of gender has been attempted by feminists of various persuasions and in fact it is probably in their epistemological contributions that feminist writers have made the most significant advances. They have, especially in some forms of feminist thought, presented the most radical challenges so far made to assumptions about gender so that, even if theoretical explanations of gender are not fully developed, some of the key questions have been posed.

Feminist Perspectives

Carol Smart, in a sharp critique of contemporary, 'cul-de-sac' criminology, takes Harding's framework of three feminist social-science perspectives and discusses their applications and limitations for the study of crime and deviance (Smart 1990: 77ff). Harding's categories are (i) feminist empiricism, (ii) standpoint feminism, and (iii) postmodern feminism.

All these approaches have in common that they see their subjects from a feminist, a woman-centred, perspective, but they differ in how these are achieved. Feminist empiricism, for instance, Smart links with 'adding women in' and with only minor threats to conventional studies (Smart 1990: 78) while standpoint feminisms are more engaged in, and spring from, struggles against women's oppression. These approaches differ in their concern with gender. Feminist empiricists are 'on the whole' committed to the study of men as well as women, whereas standpoint feminists are by definition most unlikely to be so (Smart 1990: 81). Smart underestimates, I believe, the potential of feminist empiricism. She classifies some of my work under this heading and thus, of course, I cannot be said to be an unbiased judge (1990: 78). Not only can it be presented more easily in the conventional discourse of social science, but it is in practice from those using this approach that some of the most innovative work has come. Postmodern feminism is the term used to describe the fractured, multiply-split approach engendered by the collapse of sisterhood and Marxism (Smart 1990: 82). While the approach I shall take in this study will be that of feminist empiricism, as must already be obvious in this chapter, this project is, methodologically at least, postmodern; the collection of concepts, approaches, and theoretical essays is inevitably fragmented and disjointed. There is no classical unity of form, grace, or explanation which I can confidently anticipate imposing. The point, for the moment at least, is to accumulate and speculate.

Gender and Control

My account above of classical and new concepts of social control indicated the absence of gender from them. Sumner has heavily criticized Foucault for consistently avoiding mention of gender. He carefully notes a series of points where Foucault's vision fails and yet where the logic of gender analysis seems inevitable and would have proved illuminating (1990: 30–5). Sumner concludes that Foucault failed to see that disciplinary power is gendered and that 'one fundamental structural feature of modern censure and social regulation [is] . . . its masculine character' (1990: 39). This is a significant and innovative contribution, but it is one of very few to consider the gendered nature of social control in this way. Scull, Cohen, Garland, and others who have used Foucault's work extensively do not tackle this issue at all.

Feminist writers of almost all persuasions have addressed this matter and have focused particularly on male oppression of women in public and private settings and through both formal and informal agencies. Many empiricist feminist criminologists, for instance, see the criminal justice system as oppressive of women as both victims and perpetrators of crime. S. Edwards argued (1984) that women were medicalized and infantilized by the courts, Adler that rape victims were harshly treated despite supposedly protective legal changes. The Dobashes were among the first to point out that domestic violence was a crime that went largely unpunished, while men believed they had a right to chastise and discipline their wives (1979). In a more recent work, S. Edwards draws on extensive observations of police work to show how, despite reforming policies, police values and structures help to victimize women twice over: first they suffer violence and then there is the failure to punish the perpetrator (1987). Most of this work relies on fairly simple categories of male/female in explaining the accounts. In particular, inequality between men and women, especially economically and politically, is seen as the explanation for male dominance and female submission.

Similar accounts have been used to explain sexual harassment, especially in the workplace, as a device to ensure dominance. Sexual abuse in the family by fathers and other male relatives has also frequently been redefined as not primarily sexual behaviour, but rather power-related activity, which ensures patriarchal dominance in the household. Stanko explores these issues with characteristic verve in an essay in which she looks at crime prevention and reducing the fear of crime. Fear of crime, much stronger in women than men and in older than younger people, is in itself a control device in our society. As Kinsey *et al.* have pointed out, it acts as a curfew for many women, especially those in uncivil inner-city environments (1986). Stanko recognizes that

Crime prevention from a feminist perspective necessarily includes a direct challenge to men's dominance in all spheres of everyday life . . . In part, this means challenging traditional notions of masculinity . . . [promoting] women's economic, sexual and political independence. (1990: 181)

The key theme of this extensive range of work is that female victimization by males is an important aspect of their oppression, even in advanced democratic societies.

In my own earlier work I suggested that these, as well as other more benign institutions and processes, operated as gender-divided controls to inhibit the potential of female criminality. I argued that gendered social control worked at several levels:

1. in family constraints, limiting women's scope and horizons by loading tasks on to them and restricting their freedom;
2. in the forms of violence and its threatened use indicated above;
3. through the giving and taking of reputation and good character;
4. via the mass media which exhort women to be good *women* but make no such claims to influence male virtues (Heidensohn 1985).

The earlier works all tend to assume that violence is used by males against females and that domination and subordination are the respective goals. Their primary focus is on the constraints caused by violence and its attendant fears, and on formal agencies such as the police and the courts. I did try to suggest that a series of other social institutions were also involved in producing female conformity (for which I was trying to account). I also stressed that women themselves were involved in some of these control processes: as editors of women's magazines, for example, or in the caring professions, and that women themselves might have a high level of commitment to social control because disorder could prove more damaging to their lives. In short, then, with few exceptions, existing work on gender and social control assumes that men carry out control, that they control women. What still remains largely unexplored is the use of gender as a mechanism for social control (although there is, for example, a literature on gender assumptions in welfare systems and their effects, see above). I shall argue, for example, that 'masculine' and 'feminine' ideal types of control can be identified in formal and informal agencies and that recent years have seen significant shifts in their development. Women's role in social control and as social controllers has also been largely ignored until recently. It is to a preliminary account of what I take to be that role and its development that I now turn.

Past Experiences

As I outlined above, some writers seem to suggest that history only records women as the oppressed and men as their oppressors. A significant exception to this generalization is Pitch's essay on key social changes in politics and welfare in Italy in the 1970s and 1980s. In this she argues that:

the peculiar position of women *as women* . . . makes them crucial in the production and management of social control in contemporary Western societies. Their work, both within and outside the family—in the context of a changed family and of different policies of social control—as well as their new public and political presence as collective actors has led them . . . to play pivotal roles in the definition, construction and management of social problems. (1985: 113)

Her thesis is based on experiences in Italy which may not have exact parallels in other societies, but she does make telling points which have not been picked up elsewhere. First, that women have become more involved in making and implementing social-control policies, and secondly, that, in many cases, they have sought this role by organizing and lobbying. She points out that 'actual policies of social control . . . are often fragmentary, heterogeneous, ambivalent. They must be seen as a terrain of struggle and antagonism' (1985: 128). She acknowledges that many groups of women in Italy have sought increased state intervention in a number of areas—heroin use, rape, care for the mentally ill, for example. This phenomenon she relates to women's resistance to the conventional burdens of domestic care and control and their objection to the (re-)privatization of social and moral problems. Pitch also notes that the style of many modern forms of control is 'feminine'. Italian penal policy, for example, has been altered by the extension of 'feminine' educators from female to male prisons. The women's movements Pitch describes in Italy do not have US or UK equivalents in modern times, but her emphasis on the very active role consciously sought by women in Italy in social control is an important contribution to the development of this area. In practice, women's role in all forms of social control has been complex and subtle. It underwent some crucial changes, especially in the nineteenth century, and it is clear that in certain areas distinctively feminine and feminist strategies for social control developed.

Women have always and everywhere played some part in the maintenance of order in society. Their position in the family in socializing the young and supporting and caring for both dependent and independent adults form the core activities of order maintenance, summed up in the phrase 'the hand that rocks the cradle rules the world'. Morality and values are frequently described as what 'we learnt at our mother's knee'. With monotonous regularity, outbreaks of deviant behaviour are attributed to failures of maternal care and supervision. The key point about the exercise of this female participation is that it occurs, and should always occur, within a male-dominated framework. Proper families have fathers *and* mothers.

In the same way, the vast majority of posts in the welfare system which, *inter alia*, ensure conformity through providing services preventing distress, etc. (Higgins 1980), are staffed by women. They are the majority of teachers and social workers and over 90 per cent of nurses (OPCS 1991). Yet, as Hearn points out, women are here acting as agents for men and to mask and soften some of the system's harshness:

capitalists are employing men to manage women to work in sensitive areas of economy and society. In turn these women care for and control other men and other women as patients, clients or whatever. *Women act as the agents of men*. (Hearn 1982: 192)

Much of Hearn's paper deals with developments in the nineteenth century and while he emphasizes the male framework in which semi-professional female welfare workers always work, he also outlines some of the developments in that era when radical and often feminist women sought to establish or take over a series of socially controlling enterprises.

Many historians have pointed out the strong ties between first-wave modern feminism and Victorian evangelical religion. Indeed Banks places religion alongside the enlightenment and socialism as a 'significant factor in the development of feminist consciousness'

(Banks 1981: 14). She acknowledges that this is surprising, given the 'woman's place is in the home' philosophy of Protestantism. What is perhaps more important for our present purposes is that women, inspired by Christian revivalism (and also given access to structures and to the public domain), joined, founded, or ran a vast series of charities, interest groups, and other activities many of which quite clearly had a socially controlling purpose. As Prochaska puts it in his history of nineteenth-century women's philanthropy, while women's 'sphere widened so too did their sense of mission' (1980: 2).

Pioneering work by Victorian women in the education of their own sex, the setting-up of schools and colleges, and the training of teachers is well known and documented. This activity, together with that in the founding and developing of modern nursing by Florence Nightingale, could in some interpretations be seen as coercive social control, but this is over-stretching the concept somewhat. Of greater interest for our purposes are the four areas of nineteenth-century philanthropy in which, Prochaska shows, women were particularly prominent and active and to which they made distinctive and sometimes innovative contributions. These were visiting the poor, visiting institutions, prisons, and penitentiaries, and moral rescue work (1980). Visiting the poor was an old, even an ancient tradition, but Victorian women gave it a new saliency and through it laid the foundations of forms of welfare and control agencies. Ellen Ranyard, for example, set up a Bible and Domestic Female Mission to bring scripture, moral principles, and practical guidance to the poor of London (Prochaska 1980: 127). It is clear from the innumerable accounts and records that these activities all increased very markedly during the nineteenth century and that women increased their participation in them. (Prison-visiting is something of an exception; this declined after the Gladstone Act.) Equally clear are the social-control principles and practices espoused by those who undertook them. Their basis was very often religious—Josephine Butler and Octavia Hill were both deeply-committed Christians. They often also believed that they as women had a moral *superiority* which they could bring to welfare work and public life. Thus Ellice Hopkins, a tireless moral rescue campaigner, wrote, 'it is the woman who is the conscience of the world' (1884: 37).

Much of their work was specifically directed at women, and it has sometimes been caricatured as middle-class ladies bountiful 'interfering' with the poor. But, as Pat Thane shows in a survey of gender and welfare provision between the 1880s and 1940s, the picture was much more complex. Middle-class volunteers were conscious of the dangers of over-officiousness (and Prochaska (1980) quotes the numerous handbooks issued to guide them). Thane also points out that working-class women 'time and again cited "ignorance" as the cause of their problems and praised the "education" they received from welfare centres' (1992: 10). It is nevertheless clear that the moral enterprises on which many Victorian women were engaged were either of a socially controlling, order-maintaining, or a morally coercive kind. Stronger powers were not usually available to them.

Women were very active in a series of nineteenth-century campaigns designed to alter their society in both the USA and Britain. What is significant about such campaigns is that they all focused on serious moral improvement: the abolition of slavery, the introduction of prohibition, and the suppression of vice. Women also became involved in suffrage campaigns; this was often as a result of their other activities which had produced political networks and exposed political power to them (Musheno and Seeley 1986). The founding of the Ladies' National Association for the Repeal of the Contagious Diseases Acts by Josephine Butler and her colleagues in 1869 is a classic case-study of mid-Victorian female action. 'By 1882 it boasted ninety-two local committees, making it one of the larger charities run by women in the second half of the century' (Prochaska 1980: 206). Not only was the National Association a campaigning body aiming to repeal the system whereby women could be forcibly examined and forcibly treated for venereal disease if they lived in garrison towns, its members also did rescue work for 'fallen' women. Moreover, they also attacked the double standard of morality which deemed the prostitute the sole source of infection and her clients somehow passive and therefore excused from sanctions and control. In the USA in 1875 Susan Brownwell Anthony launched a 'Social Purity' campaign against prostitution and for political rights (Musheno and Seeley 1986: 244).

Some accounts of women's early participation in law enforcement diminish its importance, complexity, and innovativeness. Feinman, for instance, declares:

Women reformers in the United States followed the pattern established in Europe: they were at first mostly upper class, white and traditional. They focussed on dealing with women and children, attempting to isolate them in homes for the purpose of moral restoration. They did not seek to change the social order, but rather, to preserve it. (1986: 7)

Yet historians of women's role are increasingly recording a much more complex and subtle situation. Rendall, for example, notes that Maria Stewart, a freeborn black woman, was lecturing to mixed audiences in Boston on anti-slavery as early as 1832, and that the Grimké sisters were insisting that black women should be able to attend the all-female Anti-Slavery Convention in 1837 (Rendall 1985: 250). Slavery and race were of course contentious issues for American women of the progressive era, and religious rather than revolutionary convictions underpinned most abolitionists' views, but it is the variety of such views, the radical and interventionist nature of some of them which is notable. Rendall observes that women's philanthropy and moral reform movements followed similar patterns in the USA and Britain, although welfare issues seem to have predominated in the latter, women's rights in the former.

Moral rescue movements in the USA developed on somewhat similar lines to those in Britain (although without the spur of the campaign against the Contagious Diseases Acts). In 1834, after public hostility to earlier attempts, the New York Female Moral Reform Society was founded, 'aiming in the long term at a morally pure world, in the short term . . . for the reclamation of individual prostitutes' (Rendall 1985: 260). They also expressed hostility to male behaviour and proposed ways of limiting it. A network of some 445 auxiliary societies was founded. Both their volunteers and those of the many voluntary charitable bodies founded in early nineteenth-century America adopted the practice of visiting the sites of their concern and dealing directly with—what we should today call—their clients. Thus it was that respectable and well-to-do women visited the poor in their homes and hovels, bars and bordellos, and trawled the streets to rescue prostitutes.

This hands-on approach was not the only distinctive feature to develop in both nations around the 1840s and 1850s; also notable were 'the claims made by women to a share in institutional authority, as their voluntary role appeared to be displaced by the intervention of the State' (Rendall 1985: 264). In other words, assumptions about the doctrine of public and private spheres, the one male, the other female, but subordinate to patriarchal authority, need to be tempered with caution. Not only did women seek work in the new public services, they also sought to use and influence these for their own sex. 'Many women evolved a conception of the role of the woman citizen, using her new political rights above all to direct the resources of the state to the relief of need, to make it a "welfare state"' (Thane 1992: 11).

In the USA women were admitted earlier than in Britain to employment in prisons and reformatories. The women's Prison Association was founded in the USA in 1845 and set up half-way houses for women, who could be directed to them from the courts. Eliza Farnham, a penal reformer who followed Elizabeth Fry's precepts, was matron of the women's section of Sing Sing from 1844 to 1848 (Feinman 1986: 37). (US campaigns were more successful than Fry's in Britain: as Fox remarked, all that Fry had 'asked of Parliament for her women in 1818 was granted by Parliament—in 1948' (Fox 1952: 29).) While it is true that Christianity, often of an evangelical and fervent kind, was usually the basis for nineteenth-century philanthropy and rescue work, it is clear that women did pose several challenges in doing this work. Josephine Butler was abused, attacked, and vilified for her campaigns. Prochaska cites many vivid accounts of rescue work in which women, armed only with Bibles and prayer, sought to recover women by seeking them out on the streets or actually in brothels or dens. They handed out tracts or 'liability cards' with lists of local refuges (1980: 192–4). Some of the descriptions of tactics employed in gaining entry to brothels and the trust of prostitutes sound close to modern policewomen's stories. It is clear that the campaigns against the Contagious Diseases Acts were premised on sexual equality before the law (Petrie 1971) and the whole rescue movement 'wanted nothing less than the regeneration of English family life through the transformation of the relations between the sexes' (Prochaska 1980: 217). A notable characteristic of the rescue movement was that female reformers sometimes made *men* their direct targets. Ellice Hopkins, for example, founded the White Cross Army in 1883. Only men were to be recruited, to be pure and to forgo foul language and indecency. There were branches in the Army, the Navy, and all over the Empire. While none of this was revolutionary in intent, it does suggest a more complicated and interesting picture than Feinman outlines.

By the end of the nineteenth century, therefore, women were playing an increasing, in some ways the leading, part in certain kinds of social control. While some were fronting traditional activities, others had very much chosen their sphere, felt that they as women brought special qualities to it, and had in several areas invented or developed their own new roles and tasks. These activities involved working-class as well as middle-class women and even, as Prochaska shows, children, predominantly girls, who supported voluntary work with contributions (1980).

Of course, the fact that large and growing numbers of women were engaged in these tasks does not make them of gender significance *per se*. There are other more interesting aspects. First, it is clear that male and female roles in such work differed considerably. Women set the agenda at various levels and undoubtedly ordered new priorities. Men were involved in the campaigns against the Contagious Diseases Acts, but in a different way and in a separate body. A very distinctive feature was that most of the work was 'woman's mission to women' and designed to cross class boundaries and develop gender-based links and networks. Indeed, commentators have suggested that such networks formed an effective basis for the suffrage movement and later campaigns (Rendall 1985). In the course of these activities, women discovered or developed many techniques which we now recognize as 'soft' forms of social control: social casework, multi-agency approaches, social fund-type loans and repayments. What is probably more important is that, in the pursuit of what could be seen as coercive goals—the moral reordering of society, the suppression of sin—they used the only techniques available to them, ceaseless careful work, close to homes and hearths, with women and children and at the most fundamental level.

It is possible to describe this situation as one of gendered social control. Almost all formal social control was still in the hands of men at the end of the nineteenth century (although Thane (1992) points to growing participation in political activity). Women were, however, increasingly involved in informal actions, public and private, and had new skills and interests, new to them and to society. Much of what they did focused on other women and children. Most important of all, women's activities were conducted within a framework of traditional gender relations. Women might patrol to rescue prostitutes, only policemen might arrest them. It was this situation, which some women sought to remedy in the early twentieth century, which began the slow and stately dance that changed the role of women in control. This had not been the specific aim of women before this, but some of them had already had ambitious dreams. As *The Magdalen's Friend* declared in October 1860, 'It is for the Bible women of the nineteenth century to penetrate the moral gloom of our cities and to regenerate society with the antidote to all impurity' (1860: 201).

Earlier in this chapter I cited the queries raised about evaluating the effectiveness of social control (Mayer 1983; Stedman-Jones 1977). It is curious that female, feminine, and feminist interventions in control were and remain extremely likely to be considered and tested, often against some vague male bench-mark. Rescue societies counted and claimed many reclaimed successes (Prochaska 1980). Some second-wave feminist authors have been harsh in their judgements on these pioneers of women's social intervention:

first wave feminists embraced women's capacities as mothers and moral guardians of the home to make the public sphere more accountable to women's interests. In efforts to raise the age of consent and to limit or eliminate prostitution, for example, reform-minded women unwittingly assisted the state in incarcerating large numbers of girls and young women for 'immoral behaviour' in the years just before and during World War I. (Daly and Chesney-Lind 1988: 509)

I have mentioned earlier analyses, such as Hagan's and my own, which point to the different degrees and different kinds of social control to which men and women are subject. In his Canadian study Hagan found high-school girls 'over-socialized—over controlled' and thus less likely to be delinquent (1979) and focused on the family as the prime setting for this self-renewing cycle of conformity. In my analysis I particularly stressed both the distinctive and additional pressures on women and women's own heavy involvement in a whole range of control activities (Heidensohn 1985: 163–77) and concluded that 'A great variety of institutions and customs comprise the "system" that keeps women in their place' (Heidensohn 1985: 192).

The purpose of emphasizing these comments is to pin-point both an ironic success story and also to highlight a crucial dilemma which will regularly recur throughout this book. It is inescapable that women's involvement in social control has often been outstandingly successful, if by success we count the curbing of vice or crime, or the reduction of public disorder. Some projects, most notably Prohibition in the USA, in which women were heavily involved, went spectacularly wrong. But others, as the above comments suggest, not only met their own targets, but also helped to alter recorded crime and disorderly behaviour amongst women but not men. In an interesting analysis of male and female crime rates in Toronto from 1859 to 1955 Boritch and Hagan found a decline in female rates substantially greater than in male rates and conclude that 'low rates of official female crime relative to male crime is rooted historically in structurally differentiated processes of social control' (1990: 587). They focus on the efforts of women reformers in providing alternative institutions for young women, enforcing new, tougher laws. They are, however, much less severe than Daly, Chesney-Lind, and others, arguing that:

To paint women reformers and their social control efforts only in these terms and with these consequences, however, is to see only one side of the picture; a side that under appreciates the success of the reformers' contribution to the overall and long-term reduction in the criminalization of women while young, single males continued to be a primary target of control efforts in the form of public order arrests, the dramatic decline in the female public order arrest rate signalled parallel developments. (1990: 591)

Women in control can thus be compromised: they may participate in the oppressive 'protection' of their own sex, in the most literal sense adding insult to injury. Even if their efforts do not achieve their goals, they may still be seen as 'tainted' because they have accepted the aims of a patriarchal, repressive system and possibly given it legitimacy. These are the perpetual dilemmas posed by weighing idealism against realism and they have a peculiar poignancy for women because no truly separate sphere exists for them to which they can withdraw to make concrete the moral reformers' ideal of a pure, uplifted world. These dilemmas and the conflicts they caused haunted the early days of women's policing in Britain. It is to those early days we shall turn in the next chapter.

Before we make that journey, I should briefly like to review the argument so far. My main task in this book will be of the kind described as 'postmodern', to describe a fragment. That fragment is formed from the related experiences of groups of late twentieth-century women involved in law enforcement. It would be possible to present those accounts boldly and without context, uncut diamonds in no polished setting. However, in order to achieve greater appreciation of these accounts, I do believe that they have to be situated in context, and placed within a frame so that they can be seen clearly. I have tried, for example, to show that social control is a problematic concept, and a reflexive one, which still has potential despite its flaws. History is very important as background: women did not suddenly enter policing in the early twentieth century from nowhere; they had at least half a century of increasing participation in public life in which many of them had sought to control social ills through voluntary action, and through increasing use of state agencies. Women saw this as not only their work but work to which they could bring unique feminine virtues and, particularly, sisterly sympathy. Some ventured to deal with male deviance, especially of a sexual kind.

There were many differences between women, as there continue to be. It is part of the postmodern condition that we recognize diversity and make no claims for the existence of a single category of womanhood. Class and race, age, marital status, and education could divide women.

Women's experiences are the focus of this study, but the context is more diffuse and fragmented. It includes various ways of considering social control and attempts to explore gender in its numerous forms. So far my goal has been to suggest that these forms all need to be questioned and explored. Thus I have already pointed out that male 'ownership' of social control tends to be taken for granted, leaving women as perpetual strangers, invaders in the field. It is salutary to remember that 'Gender relations and constructs of masculinity and femininity are not symmetrical but are based on an organizing principle of men's superiority and social and political economic dominance over women' (Daly and Chesney-Lind 1988: 504). Even while writing this, I am also reminded that I have already rejected the simple model of 'woman' as passive, accepting, and non-resistant. Women have always resisted, sought ways to take something for themselves, constructed new ways of doing things. Not all women, of course, and for those who did make their target social control in some form, the effects of this were more often felt by other, often young and poor women. Yet I do not think we can make progress by pretending that uncomfortable things do not exist. 'Denial of deviance' is an acknowledged strategy of female as well as male offenders who reject stigmatization. A form of it can sometimes flourish in relation to 'good' women who have sought power and positions of control. In this fragmented, refracted world it is best to know and to consider:

Previously the emphasis was on women gaining equality with men within existing social institutions, but today feminist thought emphasizes a new vision of the social order in which women's experiences and ways of knowing are brought to the fore not suppressed. (Daly and Chesney-Lind 1988: 498)

While in considering the role of women in social control I shall focus particularly on the formal disciplinary structures of society, and on the police in particular, I have tried to indicate briefly here that control has many dimensions and occurs in many arenas. '"Social control" should not be seen as unidirectional, but rather as the final result of conflicting interests, demands and activities' (Pitch 1985: 112). On our analytical agenda, therefore, are listed formal and informal agencies, public and private dimensions and gender in all of these, since it is not confined in its operation to any single sphere. Practically, however, I shall use the example of women in policing as illustrative of these issues. As the next chapter shows, groups of women, and some male supporters, themselves decided that informal privately-funded moral rescue work was an insufficient sphere for them and would not achieve their aims of the moral improvement of society. Quite consciously and determinedly they set out to enter an agency of control in which women did not work and whose ethos was distinctively of the masculine gender.

2

Women in Policing and Policing Women

IN 1910 Alice Stebbins Wells was hired by the Los Angeles Police
Department in the USA; in late 1915 Edith Smith was sworn in and
given arrest powers in Grantham in England. There are other
claims to both titles, but these two women are generally agreed to
have been the first proper policewomen in their respective countries
(Horne 1975; Lock 1979). Notable parallels exist between developments in both countries: women organized and campaigned in the
USA and England for women police, women themselves actively
sought office. For much of the twentieth century, women were a
tiny minority of officers in both nations, confined to specialist
roles, and this was, on the whole, what the campaigning pioneers
had sought. As we shall see in later chapters, many of the problems faced are shared by female officers in both countries as are
the policy issues concerning women on patrol, in public order situations, in handling violence, or in equal opportunities.

Many differences are nevertheless apparent. Women in England
organized and lobbied much more vigorously for women police
than in the USA, and the First World War gave a particular occasion for experiments and also caused some of the conflicts which
afflicted the campaign. Further, the battle to achieve women's entry
was much more prolonged in Britain and involved politics and
politicians to a remarkable degree. Entry was far less initially contested in the USA, yet the world which women police gained once
they were established was every bit as precarious.

Subsequent history also has its divergence and convergence. In
both countries the 1970s saw the rapid merger and 'integration' of
women into policing. In Britain this was due to central directive
and to anticipated legislation on sex equality; in the USA there
were also key changes in the law, but a feature of the American

scene was the remarkable number of lawsuits brought by individual policewomen to challenge recruiting and promotion practices as discriminatory.

Part of the purpose of these comparisons will be to explore, through looking at two related but separate systems, the importance of gender as opposed to local and occupational cultures in the forming of the experiences of women police. I shall therefore begin by looking briefly at what has been called Anglo-American policing. What is its character? Its origins? Are there one, two, or many systems? What kinds of men were recruited originally? How far are things different now? I shall go on to consider the origins of women in policing in both countries, later developments, and what impact these have had as well as the conclusions to be drawn.

Comparative Study in Policing

Serious academic studies of policing are relatively fresh growths in the intellectual garden: 'Until very recently neither historians nor social scientists appeared to recognize that police existed, let alone that they played an important role in social life' (Bayley 1985: 3). This is partly, at least, because, as Bayley himself points out, policing is a routine mundane activity and also 'because it is morally repugnant. Constraint, control, and suppression are undoubtedly necessary in society, but they are not pleasant' (Bayley 1985: 6), practical problems are also formidable. This situation has altered dramatically in the late twentieth century, as résumés of research cited elsewhere in this book will show. As a result, comparative studies of policing have become both attractive and more feasible.

Catherine Jones, in urging the necessity for the comparative study of social policy, a more fully-developed field than that of policing, insists that it has three merits: (a) better understanding of the home environment; (b) broader ideas and 'lessons from abroad'; and (c) wider case material which can further 'the development of theoretical constructs' (C. Jones 1985: 4). Maureen Cain, writing more particularly about criminology, suggests that comparison can eliminate silly and premature generalizations, and 'enhance the vision of the stranger while adding it to the vision of the outsider' (Cain 1991: 13). There have been numerous comparative studies published in recent years and Mawby has classified these into three main areas of work which we can label as international comparative analysis: overall comparisons of two or more countries; a focus of policing in one specific country; and a comparison of particular issues related to policing in two or more countries. (1990: 6)

This book falls into the third category. Studies of women in policing have previously been in one country (S. M. Martin 1980; S. Jones 1986; see Chapter 3 for a survey) and usually then of one department or force. International comparisons have been of a descriptive kind. Owings's (1925) book is described as 'a survey of the development and status of the female police movement' and catalogues the dates of women's entry into policing in various countries and their respective numbers at the time of publication. Horne's modern text includes a similar, though brief overview (1985: 7–24) as well as some comparative references in the main sections which concern women in policing in the USA. Horne draws on an earlier survey by Sherman (1977). Sources for these authors were published material or correspondence with police authorities. These reviews all suggest common, early twentieth-century starting dates for women's entry into policing, similar specialized tasks, with the focus on work with women offenders, juveniles, and in rescue and protection, and a very modest percentage of officers who are female even as the twentieth century draws to its close. Horne also notes that 'there is no clear-cut, international consensus concerning the utilization of women in law enforcement' (1980: 24). Comparative studies have not yet yielded empirically based studies of women in policing and those studies so far achieved do not use conceptual models to explain differences or parallels between countries as do other studies. It is my intention in this study to fill some of these gaps.

What is Policing?

Before I describe policing in the USA and Britain it is vital to give some attention to the meanings of police and policing. This is not just, this time, for the routine reasons given in any piece of social research for defining terms, it is also because what constitutes policing is a contended area in the field as well as in police studies. Debates about this have a particular resonance for this study: they bear on the foundation histories of the police, especially in Britain, and they also have significance for the role of women in policing.

Whether women can police or can be police, and who decides this, has much to do with what constitutes policing and the characteristics of a 'proper' police officer.

In the most comprehensive and analytic survey published to date, Bayley asserts that the word

police is used in this book, [to] refer to people authorized by a group to regulate interpersonal relations within the group through the application of physical force. This definition has three essential parts: physical force, internal usage and collective authorization. (1985: 7)

Mawby, on the other hand, stresses a broader notion of the police: 'an agency which can be distinguished in terms of its legitimacy, its structure and its function' (1990: 3). By legitimacy he means 'some degree of monopoly within society' while structure implies organization and specialization and 'finally, function implies that the role of the police is concentrated on the maintenance of law and order and the prevention and detection of offences' (1990: 3). Bayley characterizes police organizations as 'public, specialized and professional' (1985: 52) and 'the unique characteristic of police [as] that they are authorized to use physical force to regulate interpersonal relations in communities' (1985: 103). These definitions have already made explicit one conflict about the nature of modern policing, common both to the USA and to Britain, and inherent in its origins in both nations. This is described by Bayley as 'an acute tension between law enforcement and servicing' (1985: 219). One broader view of policing, related perhaps to the origins of the word in Greek and Latin terms for the state and its power, emphasizes 'maintaining law and order' and 'preventing crime' (Royal Commission on the Police 1962). The narrower perspective is that of crime fighters whose key symbol is the use of physical force 'force is the main symbol of authority and power' (Smith and Gray 1983: 87).

The origins of this 'acute tension' lie in the earliest dawn of modern policing when police organizations were first set up. Choices then made were to some extent arbitrary and not inevitable; other paths might have been followed. To take just one example, which has been carefully explored by Reiner, a fully-fledged 'alternative' model of policing to the one eventually adopted in Britain flourished: 'a conception of crime, order and control which was more alive to the interpretation of politics, law and social justice with criminality than was the later science of the criminal'. In the work of Patrick Colquhon, who favoured a professional police force, such ideas were most fully expounded, and they would have resulted, had they been achieved, in a system of 'General Prevention': 'the answer lay more in the field of welfare than penality, and even the police were conceived primarily in these terms' (Reiner 1988: 274). With these debates in mind we can now turn to the contended questions: how did present-day systems of policing develop, and what has happened to them since?

The Origins of the Police

The year 1829 is regarded as a key, the key date, in Anglo-American police history. In this year Robert Peel introduced the Metropolitan Police Act in the British Parliament, and in September the first recruits began walking their beats in London. This was the culmination of a series of failures to legislate and set up new police; at least eight previous abortive Acts, enquiries, and committees had failed. Depending on one's historical perspective (see below) one can stress as antecedents for this historic move the breakdown of the old local constable and watch systems, and their inadequacy in dealing with a burgeoning urban industrial society or the threat of public disorder: there had been the anti-Catholic Gordon Riots in the 1780s and the massacre of Peterloo in Manchester in 1819. The USA was also a turbulent society at this time with the particular problems of a new, frontier society, expanding its boundaries and drawing in migrants with diverse backgrounds.

By 1830 the London force numbered 3,300 men, and with various changes, by 1839 boundaries had been set which were to last it for a century (Critchley 1978: 57). More importantly, the 'new police' had already begun to be a model for many imitators. 'London's Metropolitan Police . . . was the first modern police force in a nation with representative government' (W. R. Miller 1977: p. ix). Miller highlights a number of novel features which distinguished London's new police: preventive policing, co-ordination and collective effort, pervasiveness and visibility (ibid.). As he points out, a delegation from New York visited London in 1833 to assess the new force and eventually after 'a decade in New York marked by social disorder and increasing discussion of adopting a

London-model police force' this was finally achieved in 1845 (Miller 1977: p. x). (Although Boston had the first preventive police in 1837, their numbers were small and there was no continuity between night and day watches.)

Many real and symbolic features of British policing were adopted in the USA: Chicago police imitated their uniforms; US police still often wear 'blues' as do the British, a colour chosen because 'the choice of blue uniform rather than red emphasized their difference from the army' (Styles 1987: 18). Until 1857 New York Police were armed only with truncheons like their colleagues in London. Other US cities and industrial areas followed the 'preventive' model. Nevertheless, it is clear that divergence from the Metropolitan template occurred at an early stage so that it is possible to note the differences which had developed in two major areas before the end of the nineteenth century: the respective *styles* of policing and the *organization* of police.

Organization is the simplest matter to contrast. No one seems to know how many police agencies there are in the USA: 'estimates of the number of law enforcement agencies vary widely between 20,000 and 40,000 (the Department of Justice . . . list 19,691)' (McKenzie and Gallagher 1989: 6). Many of these agencies have overlapping jurisdictions. In addition to city police departments 'there are state police, sheriffs and the Federal Bureau of Investigation as well as numerous local organisations'. South Carolina has 245 county, city, and municipal police departments and a further ten state-wide law-enforcement agencies; within the boundaries of the capital city, the District of Columbia, there are more than twenty-five agencies (McKenzie and Gallagher 1989: 27). Despite varieties of emphasis, most commentators agree that it is the federal, dispersed nature of the American political system and the form of local political organization which has determined this complex pattern: 'the complexity of the relationships between local, state and federal government in the USA has led to a multitude of solutions to jurisdictional difficulties (and) fiscal problems' (McKenzie and Gallagher 1989: 7). Bayley explains the lack of centralization in the US system as due to 'traditions of local self-government in policing' (1985: 69) and the lack of violent resistance to the formation of the Union. There was, of course, military occupation and police centralization after the Civil War, but local interests reasserted themselves afterwards. Monkkonen attributes the process to the developing nature of American local government which

in the last half of the nineteenth century began to provide a growing range of rationalized services—police, fire, health and sewerage—which previously had been provided on an entrepreneurial basis by various organizations . . . (1981: 55)

Politics clearly played, and still play, a vital part in this fragmentation. In 1857 the Metropolitan Police Act for New York created separate forces for the city of Brooklyn and other districts. These new police were commanded by commissioners and the whole exercise was a political ploy to break the Democrats' hold over the city (W. R. Miller 1977: 17–18).

In marked contrast, some forty-three forces control policing in Britain, a number that declined markedly during the century (from 125 in 1960 to 43 in 1964). They are characterized by the fact that 'Nowhere . . . is there the slightest duplication of police authority. . . . Their powers are identical and they exercise a territorial jurisdiction that is distinct and exclusive' (Smith 1960: 305–6). Rationalization and consolidation have proved possible in Britain, unlike the USA because of different political and, in part, policing cultures which are also relevant to the distinctive form and style of policing.

Banton, in an early comparative study of policing (1964), suggested that Britain's cultural homogeneity explained most of this variation. Miller, in his detailed comparison of the London and New York police in the nineteenth century, argues that while the former were 'modern' in Bayley's (1985) terms at an early stage, that is, public, specialized, and professional, this process took longer to achieve in New York and was much more contested. London police were more bureaucratized, more truly Weberian in their use of impersonal authority, whereas 'police discretion was part of New York's "netherside" . . . which allowed policemen to choose their own means' (1977: 141). Inconsequence, force was used much more frequently, plain-clothes detectives accepted more readily, and antagonism to 'disreputable' minorities, especially Irish immigrants, more acceptable. Of course, the major difference in democratic control and accountability between the Metropolitan Police and that of New York was, and remains, that the former is directly accountable only to the Home Secretary and hence not to any locally elected representative. In this it differs from all the other forces in Britain, too, and this clearly had an impact in the development of policing in London and the rest of Britain. The first commissioners, Rowan and Mayne, deliberately selected not only ordinary working men as recruits, and paid them modestly, but they also encouraged the selection of *strangers*, men who would be to a degree detached from their local community and thus able to exert impersonal authority (W. R. Miller 1977: 27). In marked contrast, Miller suggests, a combination of the political 'spoils' system and residency requirements in New York 'made the patrolman into a local figure probably known to his neighbours before he joined the force' as against 'the London commissioners' concern to prevent "improper connections" between policemen and local residents' (1977: 30). Provincial forces, on the other hand, had a different pattern. Steedman shows that after the 1856 Act local recruitment was relatively high (1984: 74). At the same time she notes that constabularies skilfully used the employment situation, both locally and nationally, to recruit, to mould, and to manage those recruits whom they retained, until they had created the peace-keeping force they wanted. Hence there was an expressed preference for former farm workers who could bear the loneliness of night watches (1984: 71) and against soldiers 'because they saw drinking as part of institutional life' (1984: 70).

The *sequence* of events in the history of Anglo-American policing is not usually doubted; the *selection* and the *interpretation* of these events are, however, highly contentious issues. This debate, or at least some of its key aspects, is relevant to this study for a number of reasons. As we shall see, the very existence of conflicting interpretations of the foundation story shows both its importance and the necessity for caution and scepticism. And if there is no authorized version of Genesis, if that does not seem too blasphemous a comparison, then the roles of Adam, Eve, and serpent can all be re-examined as problematic, contingent, and conditionally allocated. Moreover, since all the disputants agree that origins influence later and even contemporary developments, it is important to grasp at least some of the possibilities. Further, we shall also later be considering the entry of women into policing; this subject has received much less scholarly attention than that of the founding of the 'new' police and understandably, perhaps, generated far less debate. It will thus be instructive to set the two accounts beside each other and to use the one to throw light on and increase the understanding of the other.

Philips (1983) succinctly summarized the process from the perspective of historians:

Recent work done on the establishment and functioning of the early police forces has added greatly to our knowledge of this area of change, and, it is to be hoped, has destroyed for ever, the idea of a simple, linear progression from 'bad' old parish constables and watchmen to 'good' new uniformed police forces. (pp. 61–2)

His contention is that the orthodox accounts (Radzinowicz 1948–69; Reith 1956; Critchley 1978; Stead 1977) are 'Whig' views of history with even Radzinowicz displaying 'a simple linear view of reform as progress' (1983: 52). The Reithian view was 'that the modern British police force was the best possible type of police, and that his job as historian was to chronicle the efforts of the noble reformers who struggled to get such a force established in the face of blind, pigheaded obstruction' (Philips 1983: 53). Philips then goes on to outline major contributions to reappraising these versions based on both careful, detailed histories and on quite different interpretations of history which are in varying degrees Marxist or sociological. In a lucid and most helpful chapter, Reiner has summarized the two sets of arguments, which he calls the 'cop sided' and the 'new revisionist' views, and has then presented a synthesis. His outline involves the answers to some ten questions, ranging from (i) 'What was the source of the need for a new police?' to (x) 'what model of historical explanation underlines this explanation?' (Reiner 1985: 1).

As Reiner points out, revisionism 'is in many respects merely an inversion of the traditional approach'. Thus, while traditionalists see opposition to the setting-up of the new police as wicked or misguided, revisionists, in Reiner's phrase, when 'confronted with apparent periods and pockets of working class consent to policing, regard this as manipulated, a brittle skin over a bubbling cauldron of resentment' (1985: 32). Revisionist approaches have, Reiner agrees with Philips, improved the depth of understanding of the nature and the roots of policing. From our perspective here, a number of his synthesized conclusions are worth stressing. First 'both the orthodox and revisionist approaches assume a "fit" between the type of police system and the control requirements of an industrial or capitalist society,' but this leads Reiner to point out that 'even if some police force is seen as necessary in the last analysis, it does not follow that alternative lines of development were impossible'. He goes on to suggest some of these, drawing on the richer, more problematic scenarios depicted by the revisionists. There *might* have been a different police authority (i.e. not the Home Secretary) for London. Military policing could have been an option.

Once it is conceded that *the path of development was not tightly predetermined*, then our perspective on all the other questions shifts. Above all, the ideas and arguments of contemporaries assume a new significance as independent sources of influence . . . while these ideas and arguments are related to class position, and broadly limited by structural constraints generated by the political economy, they are not fore-ordained by them. Nor are people's strategies necessarily the best for their interests. (Reiner 1985: 33)

In producing his synthesis of both perspectives, Reiner makes several crucial statements. One that 'the emergence of professional policing in Britain . . . was surrounded by acute political conflict'; secondly that, while there was working-class opposition to police, they 'did gain increasing acquiescence from substantial sections of the working class, not only as a result of "soft" service activities, but in their "hard" law enforcement and order maintenance functions' (1985: 47). Further, he concludes that although police reformers were successful in creating a tradition (*sic*), 'policing is embedded in a social order given by structured bases of conflict, not fundamental integration' (1985: 47). Debate continues: Brogden (1987) extended it to include colonial policing, especially the Royal Irish Constabulary, and was challenged by Styles in the same volume (1987). In an iconoclastic analysis of policing as observed during his own career, Young consciously espouses the revisionist view and links it directly to patterns of modern policing:

For over a century . . . [the] system of power and control has primarily been directed towards the protection of property and to prevent assaults on the individual . . . [as a result] . . . there is now a specifically created police culture of the dramatic, which incorporates illusion, praxis and imagery as part of a well-directed social production. (M. Young 1991: 1–4)

To sum up, it will help to take forward this particular enterprise if we note that:

1. Nothing can be taken for granted about the nature of the modern police, who they are, why they choose to be, under whose command, since their origins were highly contingent on political expediency, and a variety of other influences. It is possible, indeed fruitful, to explore a range of other possible outcomes which could have occurred.

2. The teleological myth of an inexorable future predetermined and programmed to produce a modern constable from a Saxon tythingman, borsholder, or head borough (Critchley 1978: 1) is just that: a myth. Reality has a far more complex and devious trajectory.

3. The founding myth has, notwithstanding, been immensely powerful in making sense of, and justifying, subsequent events. If the threat of the 'dangerous classes' justified the new police in the 1820s, a similar notion can be used today: 'police culture . . . rejoices in an enhanced belief in . . . mythological archetypes of good and evil . . . series of interlinking metaphors of chaos and inhumanity are generated to maintain this dramatic mode and ensure that the agenda for control remains firmly with the system' (M. Young 1991: 4). (Young is not the only former police officer to refer to the sustaining myths of the police. Holdaway, describing his work at Hilton police station, declares that 'the tales, allegedly based on personal experience, may seem trite and at times fantastic—just talk between policemen. But such talk is essential if their world is to retain any semblance of order' (Holdaway 1983: 154). See the discussion of Bittner's work below.

4. Where carefully prepared histories are available of the early days of policing, it is remarkable how negotiated, how contested an issue it remained and what a variety of devices were deployed to neutralize and sustain it. Steedman maintains that nineteenth-century provincial policemen in England had a neutral, passive role; they 'actually did very little, in the public eye except walk around and watch' (1984: 6). It is central to her thesis that unpromising recruits were finally made into policemen by a variety of processes which differed between areas and between London and the provinces (1984: 160–2). A two-way system was at work, understood by policemen and masters 'that in the mid nineteenth century policemen were

not important' (1884: 163; original emphasis). Exploring the origins of Anglo-American policing suggests that this should lead us to predict no single final or finite outcome of its history and that the holding of simple, equilibrium-reinforcing, mythical notions may have been more important sometimes than challenging them.

Later History

Histories of policing in the two nations commonly record recent convergence, yet past divergence. Reiner, and many, save the most ardent revisionists, argue that in Britain there was a prolonged period of police legitimacy, from 1856 to 1959. Throughout that period, in this view, consensus policing flourished, whereas 'in the US by contrast, the more free-wheeling and aggressive style of policing evolved not as a consequence of social divisions, but the political integration of American society as something approaching a property-owning democracy' (1985: 52). Unlike Banton and other sociologists who point to socio-cultural factors in the achievement of this consensus, Reiner argues that the consensus was socially constructed, was the product of conscious choices, and was highly contested, needing seven critical policies for its achievement (1985: 52–61). In outlining the development of policing in Britain and America, McKenzie and Gallagher highlight key differences between British and American policing, notably that

order maintenance with added public service has, for various reasons connected with historical, social, economic and legal factors, been the paradigm for analysis of policing in England and Wales, whilst that of the USA has, for similar reasons been typified by a more legalistic approach—law enforcement with an added social role—compounded by a multifaceted, complex, nonsystem. (1989: 175)

They also argue that, when compared on organizational as well as philosophical/legalistic dimensions, British policing is growing more like the American version, for which it once, ironically, served as a model. Organizationally, they point to the setting-up of the Crown Prosecution Service and to plea bargaining, philosophically to the Police and Criminal Evidence Act. Other authors have commented on the modern 'downfall' of the British police in the eyes of the public: related to corruption and bribery scandals, the decline of the 'service' role, the increased politicization of the police, and the alienation of minorities, especially young blacks

(Reiner 1985: ch. 2). All these sound remarkably like Americanizing tendencies. The important difference is that US police never enjoyed a 'golden age', mythical or not, so scandals and public disorder such as occurred in the 1960s and 1970s were not quite as damaging as they have been in Britain. On the other hand, two major features stand out in late twentieth-century US policing. First, it remains an astonishingly fragmented enterprise, all attempts at consolidation having foundered on the rock of democratic sentiment; secondly, recorded crime rates in the USA, in the ghettos and inner cities, remain remarkably high.

Most writers on policing group Britain and America under one heading in their classificatory schema. Mawby places them in the same categories in his framework, even though he acknowledges that British police are normally not armed (1990: 30). Miller notes key differences between police in London and New York, but also that the London police were altering as he wrote and growing more similar to those in New York. In comparing the particular aspect of police that I propose to do, I want to note these parallels and these important distinctions. In their institutions of law enforcement Britain and the USA provide an invaluable example of a ready-made comparative research situation and a device for exploring the considerable range of possibilities which can stem from one plant grown in different climates and conditions.

The Entry of Women into Policing

As I have already suggested, a comparative examination of the entry of women into policing in the USA and Britain reveals that this process had common features in both countries. Moreover, the events and their antecedents were markedly unlike the founding of the respective police forces proper about a century earlier. Susan Martin, in her study of the role of women officers in Washington, DC, distinguishes two phases in the early history of women in US policing: the specialist first phase and the latency period of the 1930s. A similar distinction can be usefully made for Britain. I would add further stages to Martin's: first, a preliminary phase:

1. Moral reform, rescue, and matrons (1840–1910/15)
2. Specialists and pioneers (1910/15–30)
3. Latency and depression (1930–45)

4. Informal expansion (1945–70)
5. Integration and afterwards (1970s to present)

While the history of the origins of female participation in policing is quite distinct from that of male, it is equally true that the course set by the pioneer policewomen determined the direction and form of the enterprise for many years to come, as did the founding fathers of policing. The history of women in policing has yet to be subject to a revisionist analysis, although two articles have attempted some work of feminist reclamation on the British pioneers (Bland 1985; Radford 1989). There is one full-length academic study of the British experience (Carrier 1988) and a history by a former woman officer (Lock 1979), a number of reminiscences from the pioneers (Wells 1929); Owings 1925; M. S. Allen 1925; Wyles 1951) and short sections in general histories such as Critchley's (1978: 215–16) or the few texts on women in policing (Horne 1980: 26–30) and criminal justice (Feinman 1986: 80–7). Britain is more fully covered than the USA. In the research papers reviewed in Chapter 3 historical backgrounds often preface the findings, but they all for the most part draw on Horne and Feinman for their accounts. As the story is so different from that of the main police it is worth much wider attention. Fascinating in its own right, especially in the British version, it is also a highly instructive tale, laden with messages and symbols about the nature of social control, of gender, and how these were (re-) constructed to include a novel role for women in the early twentieth century. If the narrative of the new police can be construed as an epic western, in which PC George Dixon emerges as the good guy, after defeating all the bad characters in town, to maintain the peace for a century, then women's entry into policing is a version of *The Secret Garden* in which some uppity women laid siege to a male preserve and gained admittance, only to find themselves regularly being excluded from most of the garden's primary activities for more than fifty years.

Moral Reform, Rescue, and Matrons

Rightly, in my view, Feinman begins her version of women's role in US law enforcement with a description of the nineteenth-century women's moral rescue movement, especially the introduction of prison matrons. (Aspects of this were touched on in Chapter 1.) In 1845 the Women's Prison Association and the American Female

Moral Reform Society succeeded, against much opposition, in having six matrons hired to supervise women prisoners in the gaols. Their primary aim in their associations and in this project was clearly moral rescue:

although they were concerned with homeless and drunken women, their prime interest centred on eliminating prostitution . . . arguing that police matrons were necessary to prevent sexual abuse and attacks upon arrested and incarcerated women by policemen and male prisoners and to protect young girls and first offenders from hardened women criminals. (Feinman 1986: 80–1).

This impetus spread with several major cities recruiting matrons. As Feinman notes, 'The police matron movement coincided with the professionalization of social work, and many women applied social work concepts and methods to their matron duties' (1986: 81). This move resulted in turn in 'many reformers . . . pushing for appointment of women professionals who would work in the streets with prostitutes, runaways and delinquents' (ibid.). Some women were appointed to these outdoor tasks: in 1905 Lola Baldwin, secretary to the protective group, the Travellers' Aid Society, was taken on as a 'safety worker' at an international exhibition in Portland, Oregon (ibid.). Her duties were to protect women and girls from harassment, but also to stop women and girls pursuing men.

After the exhibition closed, Baldwin was retained by the city government as director of the Department of Public Safety for the Protection of Young Girls and Women.

Neither she nor the police department wanted women to be called 'police-women', because neither wished to associate women with the concept or job of policemen. The women, called 'operatives' or 'safety workers', considered themselves social service workers. (Feinman 1986: 81–2).

There was also pressure in England for the appointment of matrons to attend women prisoners in police stations. This pressure came, as in the USA, from the alliance of evangelical, temperance, and moral reformers who had already been heavily and successfully involved in voluntary work, as we saw in Chapter 1. Carrier records for instance (1988: 7) that Louisa Twining was one of the instigators of this project. Her career was typical of middle-class Victorian reformers. She became secretary to the Workhouse Visiting Society in 1858, wrote manuals and memoirs on the topic, and became a

Poor Law Guardian in 1884, having helped to form the Society for Promoting the Return of Women as Poor Law Guardians in 1861 (Prochaska 1980: 180). She gave evidence to the Royal Commission on Education in 1860 and made clear her view that women should be involved in staffing all aspects of institutional care:

how could men alone be fit judges of what went on there? . . . Results would be far different if the influence of women of feeling, and education were introduced . . . and [would] help to counteract the fatal effects of life in an institution and in a mass for girls. (Rendall 1985: 268)

These events indicate the strength and the widespread pressure of women's moral reform and voluntary efforts at the turn of the century in both the USA and Britain. Not only were such movements and activities very prevalent, they had also achieved considerable success, with women playing an increasing part in the growing welfare systems of both societies. Paradoxically, however, this very success led to raised expectations and consequent frustrations as these women found themselves limited in power by their lack of enfranchisement and of proper paid employment. Some of them had, however, learnt a great deal about achieving certain goals and had found a value system which could support such actions. 'Evangelical religion provided a model for association and a powerful imagery which embodied and gave strength to the particular qualities of womanhood' (Rendall 1985: 322). Thus was formed both the seed-bed of first-wave modern feminism and the template for its first strategies.

In sketching the background to the earliest days of policing by women, I have deliberately stressed the *moral basis* for the pressures which built up in support in both nations. Carrier, in what is still the only full account of the entry of females into law enforcement in either country, focuses on the equal-opportunities aspects of the movement: 'the employment of women as police officers has to be seen as part of the expansion of women's employment in many areas of work' (1988: p. xvi). Yet as he himself points out, the move was precisely *not* like the opening up of other professions to women which happened at about the same time:

Unlike for example, women doctors and lawyers, policewomen were at first claiming to be doing a different job from that of the men, or at least, to be doing it better than any man, because of the very fact of being female. (1988: p. xxi)

Indeed, the first policewomen were volunteers and moreover, it can be argued, as Carrier himself does, that 'the entry of women into police work, far from liberating women from the traditional female stereotype, can be seen as an anti-feminist step, designed to protect the traditional view of family life' (1988, p. xxi).

Both Bland and Radford (1985 and 1989) in articles on the topic focus solely on the social-control aspects of the development and are very troubled by its implications. Bland argues that police-women became involved in control *over* women when, as femi-nists, they had wished to protect them *from* men (1985: 23). Radford uses the history as a warning against any compromise with patriarchal institutions in modern times (1989: 44–5).

Moral pressure in the USA for women police also developed with rescue and protection moves. America's first woman police officer was Alice Stebbins Wells, appointed to the Los Angeles Department in 1910. Wells conforms exactly to the reformer model we have already observed. She had a degree in theology and had been in church-based social work. She 'felt that social workers engaged in preventive and protective work for women and children would achieve better social results if they had police powers avail-able to them' (Horne 1980: 28). Her work was specialized in its focus on women and children and targeted public and recreational places where they might meet and be 'at risk'.

Alice Stebbins Wells was, in a dual sense, a missionary. She sought and used her police powers quite evidently for protective, gendered work. She thought there was 'a real place for women police officers, without whom a protective work for women, chil-dren and the home could not be developed, both the public and the Police Department accepted the innovation as right and need-ful' (Wells 1932: 15). Her second missionary stance was to *prosely-tize* very widely. She toured the USA and later abroad, urging the appointment of women officers in all police agencies.

One other strand from the (pre-)history of women police, espe-cially in Britain, needs to be woven into the emerging design, and it is one around whose role then, as now, there is controversy: feminisim and militancy. Joan Lock begins her history of *The British Policewoman* appropriately with a crash, caused by a stone flung through the window of the Home Office in 1909 by Mary Allen (Lock 1979: 11). Allen later played a prominent part in one, the more radical, group of women police (the Women Police

Service). She went to prison twice for suffragette activities and
spent time on hunger strike while inside. Nina Boyle, first a member of the same group as Allen, had also been engaged in the campaign for votes for women as a supporter of the Women's Freedom
League. (Lock 1979: 14–15). As Radford observes, the Women's
Freedom League (which had broken away from the main Women's
Social and Political Union in 1907) 'is another part of women's history that has been overlooked' (1989: 18).

Their activities included monitoring courts and recording the
gross inequalities in sentencing and the systematic failures of the
criminal-justice system to protect women from male violence. As
part of their strategy for reform they began to argue for women to
be recruited to all parts of the criminal-justice system, including
the police. (Radford 1989: 22–5). Radford stresses the League's
concern with male violence to women, but their publications
emphasize 'protection' in the moral sense. What is radical is their
wish to have women protecting women, since men cannot be
trusted, 'man is the prevailing danger' (Boyle 1915: 727). Suffrage
was also a background factor for some of the US women police, in
Chicago, for example (Lock 1979: 151). The campaigns for
women's 'suffrage were more politically complex in the USA than
in Britain'. Some areas, Wyoming and Utah, enfranchised women
with 'little campaigning and very little opposition in the 1860s'
(Grimes 1967: 7). The Civil War and enfranchisement of black men
later split the movement. It did not generally adopt the same tactics as did the British suffragettes. Opposition to votes for women
tended to come covertly, from big businesses, who secretly supported anti-suffrage groups because they feared the attack on drink
and low-waged employment which might come from empowered
females who had temperance links and sought to introduce protective legislation (Banks 1981).

I have emphasized the (pre-)history to the employment of
women police because I believe it aids our understanding both of
how this was achieved and also what character those police had.
This background was totally different from that which preceded
the 'new police' of the early nineteenth century. Then the climate
was one of concern about public disorder and rising crime, the aim
to bureaucratize and professionalize (in England and Wales), to
assert official vigilantism (in the USA). Popular support was sig-
nally lacking in both countries and had to be effortfully attained

over many years in Britain and politically manœuvred in the USA. Policing had been of a quasi-amateur kind and was held to be increasingly ineffectual. (Whether it was or not is, as we saw, still a contentious topic.)

A century later women's roles had substantially changed in both societies. Women had already organized and engaged in many activities, such as philanthropy and in campaigns against slavery, drink, and impurity. They were still campaigning for the vote. Many more women worked outside the home and had begun to enter, especially in the USA, professions hitherto barred to them. Initially, at least, women police can be seen as daughters of the tide of feminist evangelicalism, propounded by moral reformers who, whether they believed in feminism or in feminine superiority, sought to protect and sometimes to police their own sex.

Specialists and Pioneers

Because of the quite distinct organizational character of the countries we are examining, the arrival of women in policing had very different impact. In Britain's more centralized, unitary system of government the state was consistently involved throughout and Home Secretaries, MPs, and civil servants expressed their views incessantly and copiously. Numerous committees considered the issue and it took a Royal Commission in 1929 finally to achieve women's entry. In the USA there was no comparable central activity, nor was there any 'concerted opposition to policewomen in the US' (Horne 1980: 30). Instead, there was a strong policewomen's movement, led by Alice Stebbins Wells, based on the International Association of Policewomen which Wells helped to found in 1915.

Achieving the appointment of women as police officers in Britain took more than fifteen years, absorbed numerous organizations, of central and local government, the police, the Army, the Church, Parliament, the press, the public, as well as a remarkable array of groups who sought this end persistently and campaigned and politicked for it. The story is worth telling in its own right and has no real parallel in the USA. Nevertheless, the outcome for the role of women in policing was remarkably similar in both countries, a curious symmetry which we can find repeated in later events.

Carrier's account (1988) of the whole history is based on the original sources (and including government papers) and is remarkably detailed and precise. In what follows I have drawn out the key events which have relevance for later developments and for modern policing. The First World War provided the catalyst for women, and their male supporters, who wished to see women as police. At the outset it provided the occasion for a truce for those women who had been campaigning for the vote and who suspended this while hostilities lasted and turned to war work.

While the outbreak of the war was the immediate occasion for recruiting women police volunteers, this was by no means a new idea. A delegation of women's groups had already approached the Home Secretary in June 1914, before the war began, and there had been a conference. Owings notes that the vigilance and purity movements were behind this pressure and that their aim was 'the appointment of "women police constables with powers equal to those of men constables in all country boroughs and the metropolitan boroughs of the County of London"' (Owings 1925: 4–5). In continuing their rescue and support work with refugees, both Margaret Damer Dawson and Nina Boyle came to the conclusion that women police should be appointed to offer protection to women and girls. War had brought enormous social change. Thousands of men were congregated in army camps, women were working in munitions and in novel occupations. Refugees had flooded in from Europe. Dawson and Boyle were already recruiting volunteers, known as the Women Police Volunteers, in 1914. All were volunteers, but received some training and had the permission of the Commissioner of Police of the Metropolis to patrol (Lock 1979: 20).

Within a very short time a conflict emerged within the Women Police Volunteers which had significance for the movement to promote women police and is a telling illustration of issues in relation to women in control. In November 1914 three of the volunteers went to work in Grantham. They agreed to do so under orders issued by the General Officer commanding the area. He had imposed an all-night curfew on Grantham women and the volunteers were required and agreed to police this, and thus became involved in controlling women for the sake of men (rather than their own) and for public order. Boyle was outraged, the movement split with Dawson taking the vast majority of members with her into the renamed Women Police Service (Radford 1989: 34–8; Lock 1979: 28–9; Carrier 1988: 4).

The Women Police Service volunteers proved very successful and

popular, though not with all official authorities. In 1916 they were
contracted by the Ministry of Munitions to provide female police
to handle the policing of munitions factories where thousands of
women were now being employed (Carrier 1988: 56 ff.). Women
Police Service volunteers wore uniforms and were often of middle-
class background with good education. Their work was clearly
control and protection of women and children. In doing this they
did not shirk what might be thought of as intrusive or prescriptive
activities (Lock 1979: 62). Lock declares, 'there is no doubt they
were Mrs. Grundys' (1979: 67) but notes also that the experience
of enforcing the double standard of morality radicalized Damer
Dawson so that by the end of the war she was attacking hypocrisy
and injustice to women: 'they talk as if men were innocent angels,
helpless in the hands of wicked women' (Lock 1979: 90).
Throughout the war Damer Dawson had persistently used all her
skills and address to achieve a more permanent and institutionalized basis for policewomen. It is clear that she sought an independent body of women to do specialized work with women and
juveniles and that the officers should have the full status of sworn-
in constables (Carrier 1988: 46–8). Meanwhile, volunteers were
widely used in many parts of the country, but they had rivals.

Another body also set up women patrols, and for similar purposes during the First World War. The National Union of Women
Workers of Great Britain and Ireland (later renamed the National
Council of Women) launched the Voluntary Women Patrols. They
too aimed 'to influence and if need be, restrain the behaviour of
men and women who congregated in the neighbourhood' of camps
and to safeguard 'our girls from the results of the very natural
excitement produced by the abnormal conditions now prevailing'
(Radford 1989: 30). Their patrols were not initially in uniform,
although they did wear arm bands and carried identity cards with
an authorization from the Commissioner. They too were widely
used during the war.

At the end of the war the munitions police were disbanded and
the demand for wartime patrols might have seemed to have faded,
but supporters of women in policing were determined to persist.
Prostitution and protection were once again major social issues.
Moreover, women had proved themselves effective in policing and
Chief Constables, and some other policemen, who had had experience of the women patrols had changed their initial hostility to

support (Carrier 1988: 98). As a consequence of the (all-male) police strike of 1918, Sir Nevil Macready became Commissioner in London and very shortly set up a year-long experiment of recruiting women into policing. The Metropolitan Police Women Patrols (under the charge of a former Voluntary Women Patrols member, to the chagrin of Dawson and Allen) went on patrol in February 1919. They wore uniforms and had warrant cards, but they still had no powers of arrest and their work was specialized and focused on women and girls: 'although there existed a force of women police under the orders of the Metropolitan Force, this force was still in an anomalous position until their status and conditions of service were made equal to those of men' (Carrier 1988: 87). A Home Office circular (February 1919) also encouraged local police authorities outside London to appoint women police and by September of that year 34 out of 129 boroughs and 8 out of 60 counties had done so, with a total of 311 officers in post (Carrier 1988: 109). In 1920 a parliamentary committee sat under Major Baird to consider women's role and status in policing. They took extensive evidence and recommended expansion and establishment, but official inertia prevailed.

Worse was to come. In February 1922 the Geddes Report proposed savage cuts in public expenditure, including the abolition of the women patrols in London. A formidable battle ensued. Two full-scale debates took place in the House of Commons with Nancy Astor, the first woman MP to take her seat, taking a leading role. Deputations of the great and the good saw the Home Secretary. Public support was enlisted at public meetings and the Archbishop of Canterbury scathingly attacked the proposals (Carrier 1988: 126–7). After much political manœuvring a tiny 'nucleus' of patrols was saved and given somewhat better terms, the title of constable, and powers of arrest (Lock 1979: 146). The Bridgeman Committee in 1924 recommended that provincial police forces should appoint women officers, but the Home Office was, as ever in this matter, coy about local autonomy. It took another seven years, a *cause célèbre*, and a Royal Commission to achieve full status for women police.

The Savidge case was one of the pivotal scandals on which reform in British politics all too often hinges. Its significance for this narrative is that it provided the final stage in this cliff-hanger and in doing so rehearsed so many of the themes of consequence of our tale. In May 1928 Sir Leo Money, an elderly writer, and Miss Irene Savidge, a young, single woman, were arrested in Hyde Park and charged with indecency by two patrolling (male) officers. Next day the magistrate dismissed the case and criticized the police's handling of it. Questions were asked in Parliament about the matter and an experienced officer, Chief Inspector Collins, was deputed to make investigations. In the course of these he handled the questioning of Irene Savidge so disastrously that further questions and publicity ensued and a tribunal of inquiry was held. A key matter was that whilst Inspector Lilian Wyles had been sent to escort Irene Savidge to Scotland Yard for an interview, Wyles had then been ordered out by Collins who saw her in the presence of his male Sergeant. A majority and a minority report were produced by the inquiry; both insisted on the need for female police to be present at such interviews. The case and the tribunal received immense publicity and most reports supported the case for women police and for more of them (Lock 1979: 157–63; Carrier 1988: 190–202). Once again the arguments for women in policing, for their role in 'morals' cases, for their special qualities, had been rehearsed. The Metropolitan Police came badly out of the affair, only Lilian Wyles emerging with modest credit; Collins, though he was 'exonerated, received no further promotion' (Wyles 1951, 196–7). However the most important outcome of the scandal was the appointment of the Royal Commission on Police Powers and Procedures.

As Carrier points out,

although the Report [of the Royal Commission] was essentially concerned with the questions of procedure and the judges' rules, it can be interpreted as an important document in the history of the development of the movement for policewomen. The recommendations from this Royal Commission were to have a marked effect on the acceptance of women as police officers, in the sense that they gave added impetus to the campaign by the women's organisations for the issue of statutory regulations. (Carrier 1988: 213)

This Critchley considers to be the Commission's only contribution of any value (1978: 201). The initiative was still with the pressure groups and their allies and supporters. Women had been enfranchised at last on the same terms as men and fourteen were elected to Parliament in the 1929 election.

Lobbying persisted into the 1930s and finally Regulations were issued on 7 October 1931 which gave 'all attested policewomen uniform conditions of service, pay and pensions' (Carrier 1988: 241). Women MPs and their male allies, women's organizations, especially the National Council of Women, had continuously and formidably lobbied to achieve this goal. It was in many ways, however, a curious victory. Police work for women was still defined, and was to remain until well after the Second World War, as a specialist field, mainly confined to moral and sexual matters and inevitably making female officers complicit in the control of their own sex in ways in which men's behaviour was not controlled. The impetus for the female policing movement had come from women themselves, from a very large, diverse, sometimes antagonistic range of organizations who formed (and also broke) improbable alliances across class, age, politics, and views on feminism to press their cause. This was a remarkable and curious phenomenon and raised some interesting possibilities: of independent women's policing, of all-female police, of novel styles of policing and control. In achieving their aim, the women's movements had to surrender their own role and with it their particular approach. The future of women in policing lay henceforward within the established, unwelcoming, overwhelmingly male and masculine forces.

Women's entry into policing in the USA did not meet any obstacle so at once granite-like in structure, nor as productive of repelling memoranda and minutes as the Home Office, nor as tirelessly and resourcefully negative. The circumstances of the First World War, while they did stimulate some female police recruitment (Horne 1980) did not involve such far-reaching military and civilian mobilization nor hence the perceived peril to morals and military discipline. The British case is thus both wholly characteristic and quite exceptional.

Yet it also exposed factors which were common to both settings. These can be summarized under six headings:

1. *The Moral Basis for the Movements*. Both in the USA and Britain women's entry into policing was vigorously promoted by groups formed for moral protection, and sometimes feminist, causes who did so to attain social purity, rescue, and welfare goals.

2. *Volunteers*. Almost uniquely in the history of police, a group of citizens, in this case of women, sought to be police officers. Special

constables are the only comparable group in Britain. The first patrols were unpaid and their model and origin were the philanthropic bodies in which women had learnt to flourish, manage, and achieve some access to power. In the USA, Mrs Wells put herself forward as an officer supported by a citizens' petition.

3. *Proselytizing.* Supporters of women police and the pioneers themselves pursued their cause with missionary zeal, urging others to follow their example. Alice Wells was the archetype, but others followed suit, giving lectures, writing articles, and, in the case of Mary Allen, stopping the traffic in New York in monocle, breeches, and knee-high boots (Lock 1979: 150). In this role they were remarkably successful in gaining publicity and support.

4. *Opposition.* The strongest opposition in both nations probably came from the police themselves, both rank-and-file and senior officers. There was support, too, in and outside the police organizations and often from improbable sources. Tensions and contradictions were built up from the beginning which proved to be improbably robust. Thus, for example, both US and British police frequently alleged that purity, rescue, and protection work were not proper police work, unlike true crime-fighting and public order. Yet their own recent history had shown them eager to engage in just such activities. Storch has demonstrated how the Metropolitan Police gave such support to the Contagious Diseases Acts and to other attempts to achieve state regulation of prostitution to the extent that endangered their own organization (1977: 60–1). Miller illustrates the success of puritan-inspired 'Blue Laws' in New York and the concomitant interference in the leisure and pleasures of the anti-Sabbatarian Irish and German immigrants (W. R. Miller 1977: 158–66).

5. *Specialist Work.* In both the USA and Britain the movements for women in policing sought to establish the right of women to work with women and children. They wished to bring the feminine into control: to interview female victims and suspects, rescue children, and patrol and supervise doubtful public venues. General police duties were not their aim, though proper powers were. (It is clear, ironically, that there was some confusion over what preventive and protective work might mean and that interpretations varied considerably (van Winkle 1925: p. xvii).)

6. *Gendered Control.* Women sought in this period to protect their own sex. Sometimes this protection took primitive forms; sometimes, too, 'decent' men were the objects of their protection and 'wayward' women their target. In pursuing such paths some of the pioneers did confront the contradictions in their work and the ironies of the double standard. Yet they did not, at this stage, directly seek a mandate to police men on the same terms. Men and policemen would scarcely have countenanced that.

Latency

Once women's entry had been secured in the USA there was considerable expansion and confidence. In 1922 there were 500 female officers, by 1932 more than 1,500 (Horne 1980: 30; Heidensohn 1989*b*: 3). The Depression is blamed by Horne for the stagnation which then followed (1980: 31) but it is also clear that the terms on which women had entered US policing were insecure and a poor basis for expansion. 'The creation of separate women's bureaux had been a national goal of policewomen, but . . . this . . . tended to restrict and isolate policewomen from the rest of the department' (Horne 1980: 31). The separate 'Women's Precinct' set up in New York in 1921 and planned for characteristic protection and rescue work closed after a very short time for political and legal reasons (Feinman 1986: 85). Thereafter, in New York as in many other departments, women officers had no 'base', they were temporarily assigned and were often redeployed at short notice when a woman was needed for search or interview purposes (Mishkin 1981). Their entry was controlled by tiny quotas, and educational and age standards were higher than for men and promotion chances nil. In 1930 Massachusetts recruited women to the state police, but it was only in 1943 that Connecticut, the second state to do so, followed them (Mishkin 1981).

The formal position in Britain was, in this period, marginally better than in the USA since women had their own command structures and thus the possibility of promotion (up to Superintendent in the Metropolitan Police). But these were also Depression years in Britain and, in practice, little expansion occurred. 'By 1939 only forty-five out of one hundred and eighty-three police forces were employing women and a sixth of those women had not yet been sworn in. London now had about the same number they had reached in 1921' (Lock 1979: 172). Lock calls these 'the static years' and it is clear that the inheritance from the pioneer days was now too narrow. Specialist work was limited and, in restricting women to it, police practices meant that few women could achieve a career in policing, which was now becoming their goal, and none could become 'real' police.

Informal Expansion

The Second World War in the USA, as in the UK, gave some thrust to the expansion of opportunities for women. Marriage bars, requiring women to resign on marrying, were removed in England and Wales in most occupations. (But not in policing in Scotland, where they remained in force until 1968.)

Recruitment in the USA, which had been almost stable, rose after the war. In 1950 there were about 2,610 female officers, in 1960 5,617, and in 1970 11,234. Similar expansion occurred in Britain: 'during 1949–59 their establishment virtually doubled and continued to rise slowly during the 1960s. In 1966, for example, there were 4,000 women out of 95,000 officers' (S. Jones 1986: 4). More significantly, perhaps, in 1968 Indianapolis Police Department 'became the first municipal agency to assign women formally to patrol by delegating two women to traffic and patrol duties in 1968' (Milton 1972: 64). At its inception, the women police movement had been innovatory; by the 1960s the moralistic, philanthropic roots from which it had drawn its strength had withered or were transplanted into the fields of professional welfare. This time major changes came from outside the police for the most part, although individual officers in the USA did use the new climate, and the new laws, to alter their own and their colleagues' opportunities. A combination of a new approach to civil rights and of second-wave feminism shifted women's role in the police, that most conservative of control agencies, in surprising ways.

Integration

Once again it is necessary to remark that in the USA and Britain quite dissimilar policies and procedures have results in policing practices which quite closely resemble each other. By the mid-1970s both nations had enacted new laws or constitutional amendments which guaranteed the rights of women and minorities more firmly than before. In addition, a mass of cases and class actions in the USA and specific policy directives in Britain had altered the role of women police. Some six outcomes can be listed as a result of these changes.

1. *Integration.* Women police are now integrated into the mainstream of policing. They no longer have their own bureaux and most discriminatory recruiting practices are, or are being, removed. More problematic, of course, is their acceptance in practice by their male colleagues.

2. *Expansion.* Numbers of women recruited have increased in both systems although in only a few do they exceed 10 per cent of the total strength and scarcely any have achieved 20 per cent (Heidensohn 1989*b*; Adler 1990; Martin 1989).

3. *Decline of Specialist Policing.* Women's specialist work with their own sex and children has been replaced by the general policing role. There are signs, however, of it re-emerging elsewhere.

4. *Evaluation.* Partly because policing has moved into new territory, but also because of both caution and prejudice, these developments have been subject to a considerable amount of appraisal and evaluation.

5. *New Agenda.* Notwithstanding 3, above, it is clear that a 'new' agenda for policing has emerged which has some similarities with the old specialist tasks.

6. *Policing in Crisis.* In both the USA and Britain, policing is going through crises. In the USA this has more to do with concern over very high and rising crime rates, and fears about particular offences such as drug abuse and violence. In the UK it seems to be more directly related to the police themselves and their own performance.

In the rest of this chapter I want briefly to set out the legal framework within which most of these changes have been brought about and then the developments under each of these headings.

Title VII and After and the Sex Discrimination Act

Nothing better illustrates the differences of culture and the climate in which policing exists in the USA and Britain than does this topic. In the USA a mass of legal changes and a series of cases have altered women's position. A written constitution and a culture of political rights and high expectations aid this pattern. In

Britain, the Sex Discrimination Act 1975 did *not* exempt the police from its clauses and integration had to be achieved. Susan Martin (1980) suggests three main reasons for the changes which took place in the USA: legal developments in the field of civil rights, the crisis in policing, and the growth of the women's movement.

In the 1960s the American Civil Rights movement focused on racial discrimination and in particular on the denial of voting and other rights to black citizens. Campaigns, marches and civil disobedience, and voter registration schemes were organized. Students were amongst the participants as were many women. Later women's rights became an issue, not least because the leaders of the radical movements tended to be male and to be less than whole-hearted in their personal practices of equality and justice. In due course a separate women's movement was born and from it a programme for a new phase of women's liberation grew and flourished (Mitchell 1971).

Legal guarantees of civil rights were sought by the US protestors, not least because the USA is such a legally based culture and because the Constitution plays such a central part in the political culture. The Civil Rights Act 1964 (Title VII) made it unlawful for an employer to discriminate in recruitment, promotion, or other employment practices on the grounds of 'race, color, religion, sex or national origin'. In 1972 the Equal Employment Act extended the application of Title VII to state and local government (Potts 1981). Other statutes such as the Revenue Sharing Act of 1972 and the Justice Systems Improvement Act of 1979 limit Federal funding to programmes which are not discriminatory.

Such legislation is not merely symbolic. It has been widely used not only by individual women who sought to overturn discriminatory practices, but also by the central government and other agencies empowered to do so. In 1978 a female sergeant in the Los Angeles Police Department and her colleagues successfully sued to end sex-based selection criteria. Also in 1978 a female officer won a lawsuit to enable her to become the first woman detective in Philadelphia's history.

One reason Philadelphia and Los Angeles complied with the Brace and Blake decisions was that, in both cases, the US Department of Justice also sued for violation of the federal law prohibiting the allocation of federal funds . . . to any government agency that violated legislation prohibiting sex discrimination . . . the Justice Department was withholding $4 million in . . . grants from Philadelphia. (Feinman 1986: 93–4)

Use of the law by female officers in fact pre-dates the Civil Rights Act: in 1961 a New York Police Department officer filed a suit to enable her to take the sergeants' exam. She was eventually successful after three court cases and took, and passed, the exam in 1964 (Feinman 1986: 88–9). The 1970s saw a series of such legal challenges and, although not all were successful and some decisions were not complied with readily, an American Police Foundation Report was able to claim by 1981 that

various court decisions of the 1970s have virtually eliminated the use of height and weight requirements and physical agility tests. Consequently, female police applicants now face fewer notably adverse hiring practices. (Sulton and Townsey 1981: 21)

Positive Discrimination

Equal opportunities policies in the USA differ in at least one crucial respect from those practised in Britain: positive discrimination is not unlawful. Just what constitutes positive discrimination, also called affirmative action or sometimes reverse discrimination, is in itself a huge question (J. Edwards 1987: 4–27). For our purposes, I take it to mean the practice of favouring an individual or a group in some way in order to give them an advantage which might remedy past wrongs or injustices. Here it is important to repeat a point made earlier: policing in America is far more subject to direct, and more complex, political control than is the case in Britain. Most police departments are part of the local-government system of their city. As equal-opportunity policies have been a focus of US political activity since the 1960s it is hardly surprising to find them being vigorously pursued at least during the 1970s (Kirp et al. 1986: 159–68). There is evidence that in the 1980s 'the election and re-election of a conservative Republican president and the appointment of an anti-affirmative action attorney general have resulted in the reduction of affirmative action enforcement efforts on the part of the federal government' (Warner et al. 1989: 565). However, the same authors go on to insist that 'with the reduction of support for affirmative action programmes at the national level, the importance of local-level officials is enhanced' (1989: 566) and to demonstrate, in a survey of police departments in 281 US cities, that the presence of female political leaders in the civic administration did make a positive difference to the numbers of female police deployed (1989: 576). Such increases occurred 'only with a formal affirmative action plan' (1989: 576).

In a study of 'Gender Justice' in the USA, Kirp *et al.* (1986) point out that American action on equality shifted in the 1960s from a concern with gender-neutral processes, such as the recruitment criteria mentioned above, towards results. 'The result-oriented view of affirmative action became official policy during the 1970s' (1986: 160). The most famous case involved at this time was that of the American Telephone and Telegraph Company (AT&T) in 1973 which, under a consent decree, had in six years to fill between 50,000 and 100,000 jobs on a sex-preference basis (Kirp *et al.* 1986: 161–5).

Atkins and Hoggett (1984) have outlined four reasons why 'the implementation of positive action is very widespread in the US'. These are, they suggest,

the availability of the requisite statistics, the potential imposition of extremely high damages in discrimination cases; the powerful position of the Equal Employment Opportunities Commission in conciliating and monitoring out of court settlements; the power and willingness of the courts to make positive action orders. (1984: 55)

As they starkly put it, 'None of these factors is present in the United Kingdom.' There was, then, during the 1960s and 1970s a political climate which favoured affirmative action and legal mechanisms and remedies which made their pursuit possible and worth while in the USA.

While the police were rather less likely to be the targets of such suits and were particularly resistant to pressures to take positive action (Hochstedler 1984; Steel and Lovrich 1987) there were numbers of cases brought on behalf of women and of minorities.

In the particular case of police departments, the courts on occasion have enforced rather demanding requirements to increase the number of female officers. In some cities (such as Miami, Denver, Detroit and Buffalo) courts have ordered preferential treatment of female applicants to increase the representation of women in the police force. (Warner *et al.* 1989)

Whether as a result of direct legal sanctions, because of genuine commitment, or as a wise move, considerable numbers of US police agencies adopted equal-opportunities policies during the 1980s. In a survey conducted in 1981 of fifteen agencies, Hochstedler found that

affirmative action goals for women tend to be even more vaguely defined than those for minorities . . . in most agencies the urgency of affirmative . action is aimed at racial minorities, not women, and most agencies did not hesitate to admit that they were not expending much effort to recruit and select female employees. This inattention . . . is reflected in the absence of hiring quotas for females: not a single agency had employed such a policy. (1984: 239)

However, by the end of the 1980s many departments had set up detailed procedures to ensure equality and had employed full-time and specialist staff to promote and pursue such policies. During the research for this book I visited the Police Department of New York City and of the Metropolitan Police, Washington, DC, which did so (Heidensohn 1989*b*). Adler (1990) reports on a similar study visit and sets out the details of several such policies. She found only one instance of positive action for women, in promotion in Detroit (1990: 26–7). Such practices are more commonly pursued for the recruitment of black and other minority-group officers. During my visit to the Boston police they were recruiting under a consent decree which required them to hire one minority applicant for every white one (Heidensohn 1989*b*). Adler notes the considerable commitment to equality in many US agencies and, after setting out their features in some detail, concludes, 'It is unquestionable that American police departments with a firm equal opportunities programme have achieved significant progress for women, both in terms of their overall representation and, to a lesser extent, in supervisory positions.' My own findings (Heidensohn 1989*b*, 1990) suggest that she, and the equal employment opportunity officers in some agencies, are perhaps over-optimistic and that, notwithstanding the formidable arsenal of weapons at their command, the outcomes do not appear to be dramatically different from those in Britain. This we can explore when comparing integration and expansion in Britain and America. First, however, I want to look at the moves towards sex equality in Britain.

Equality and Opportunity in Britain

The United Kingdom has no written constitution, unlike the United States, and her citizens therefore live under the combined rule of ancient common law and statutes passed by Parliament. While Britain may present a legally unique phenomenon, it did not prove to be immune to the waves of social change which affected western nations in the 1960s and 1970s for civil rights and opportunities for women. In 1975 two Acts came into force, the Equal Pay Act and the Sex Discrimination Act. To over-simplify greatly, the former required that men and women be paid the same pay for the same work while the Sex Discrimination Act (SDA) made illegal three types of discrimination: direct, indirect, and as a result of victimization. While the armed forces were exempt from the provisions of the SDA, the police were not. Perhaps in anticipation of such changes, Sir Robert Mark, the Commissioner of Police of the Metropolis, disbanded policewomen's departments in 1972 and integrated women into general police duties, although some informal integration had also already begun outside London (S. Jones 1986: 7). Thus the legal framework in Britain was combined with central policy decisions which were resisted by police officers themselves and their representative bodies (S. Jones 1986: 9).

There have been very few cases brought under the Act in relation to the police in Britain, despite the fact that a number of discriminatory practices persisted long after the Act came into force. Smith and Gray (1983) found that the Metropolitan Police were operating an unlawful quota system in the recruitment of female officers. In her survey of a provincial force, Jones discerned a similar limit being used at a local level (1986: 46). The British police continued to use different height criteria throughout the 1980s; the Metropolitan Police abandoned them after various increases and decreases in requirements for both men and women (Metropolitan Police and Equal Opportunities Commission 1990: 18).

The Metropolitan Police did set up an Equal Opportunities Working Party in 1984 and issued a report on its collaborative exercise with the Equal Opportunities Commission in 1990 (ibid.). Whatever the merits of this approach, it is generally agreed that equal rights legislation and policies in Britain have neither the scope nor the legal support that they command in the USA (Gregory 1987). Indeed, in the 1980s it was the law of the European Community which had more impact on women's legal rights in Britain than did home-grown legislation (Brewster and Teague 1989). While the legal framework for equal rights in Britain has been much slighter than in the USA, some of the effects in practice have not differed so markedly.

Expansion

At one high point in the optimistic 1970s, Milton predicted that within a few decades, 50 per cent of all police officers would be women in the USA (1972, 185). A later assessment suggests, 'by the turn of the century, women will only constitute 10–15% of total police employment' (Steel and Lovrich 1987: 57). This estimate has proved to be more accurate.

In 1986 about 9 per cent of US officers were female and in 1989 around 11 per cent of British officers were (Adler 1990). Global figures conceal considerable local differences: in Detroit 20 per cent of officers were female and in the West Midlands 14 per cent were. What I found notable in my own research in 1988 was that New York, with its commitment to equal opportunities, had a female share of force membership very close to that of the Metropolitan Police (Heidensohn 1989b: 16–17, Tables 1(a) and (b)). There is no doubt that *absolute* numbers of women officers expanded in both countries after the legal changes discussed [although a study in Scotland seems to suggest a decline there (Centre for Police Studies 1989: 15)]. Numbers doubled between 1972 and 1979 in the USA. FBI figures indicate that in 1970 there were 5,617 female law-enforcement officers, by 1978 this figure was over 9,000, and by 1988, 30,000 (Sulton and Townsey 1981; Heidensohn 1989b). (It should be noted that the USA, in keeping with its own police traditions, does not have standard, centralized data as the UK does, and that these figures are based on surveys.) In Britain, there has been considerable growth. Thus in 1970 there were 3,621 female officers, in 1980 10,430, and in 1989 13,829. The numbers in the Metropolitan Police alone—3,406 in 1989—almost equalled the entire 1970 strength in the whole of England and Wales. However, as S. Jones points out (1986: 25–6), the introduction of the Sex Discrimination Act cannot explain expansion as the rate of increase in numbers was not dramatically greater at 78.6 per cent over five years than prior to the Act when it was 61.7 per cent for a similar period. Jones concludes a careful comparative analysis of data on male and female recruitment by claiming that 'the Act in itself has had comparatively little direct impact on the recruitment of female officers' (S. Jones 1986: 31). Other factors, notably a 'crisis' in male recruitment and retention levels, which was remedied by an attractive pay settlement, were of greater significance than the law. As she observes, 'What is of interest in the case of the police service is that this has happened almost in spite of legislation . . . which was specifically designed to disallow this' (S. Jones 1986: 31).

Integration

The most apparent, the most controversial, and the best-researched decisions taken in this field in the 1970s concerned integration. In both Britain and the USA policy seems to have changed fairly quickly and with relatively little preparation. (See Chapter 4 for an account of one experience.) In the USA the key issue was of women going on patrol, in Britain of abolishing the policewomen's departments and with them, apparently, the specialist work women had always done with women and juveniles. Indianapolis sent two women out on patrol in 1968 but the decision of Washington, DC, to deploy eighty-six women on patrol in 1972, and to evaluate their performance, is perhaps the best-known example (Bloch and Anderson 1974*b*).

No fewer than eight reviews of women on patrol were carried out in the mid-1970s (see Sulton and Townsey 1981: 13 ff. for a summary). Some of their findings are discussed in the next chapter. On the whole they were overwhelmingly positive and did not suggest that women should not go out on patrol (ibid.).

Women should now be able to apply for all specialist posts in the USA and for promotion on equal terms with male officers. In practice, achievements in both areas are still limited. In my own research, I found that women officers faced barriers to appointment as dog handlers, as mounted police, and as detectives. In the USA proportions of women in higher ranks rose after integration whereas in Britain they fell, since there the women's departments had had their own promotion and structure (Adler 1990). In 1990 the Metropolitan Police published a review which acknowledged that many discretionary discriminatory policies had persisted long after integration. A telling example is provided in the Dog Section where a dog sergeant will visit the home of an applicant for acceptance as a handler. Handlers are expected to have secure gardens and a suitable 'family atmosphere' for the puppy to live in for a year (1990: 41–2). The report concludes that there were dangers of discrimination and new procedures were recommended.

In 'Medshire' S. Jones found 'substantial qualitative differences in the way policemen and policewomen are deployed' (1986: 79). In particular, women were concentrated in administrative duties and not in detective or traffic work (1986: 56).

Despite major legal and policy developments which have directly affected the role of women in policing, it is still possible to describe the situation in both countries as one of only 'glacial change' (Walker 1985). These findings are also confirmed in a study conducted in a provincial force in Britain in the late 1980s (Hunt and Campbell 1991). Speed has appeared faster in the USA because, in some respects, the baseline was lower than in England and Wales. In researching police in both countries, I was struck by the marked degree of confidence and sense of achievement which characterized senior officers there. Adler confirms my view (1990). Caution was more evident in Britain. It was also true that older officers in Britain, who had been recruited before integration, expressed certain regrets about that process. Their objections focused on two aspects: one was the rapidity and lack of planning with which it had been carried out. Not only might they and their female colleagues have been better prepared but male officers should have been too. The second regret was for the 'special' work which they had done and for which they felt they had had special skills. This work they considered to have been of vital importance and that it should have been preserved in some way. Even nine years after integration Bryant found in a survey of two provincial forces that 'there was a significant number of women who would favour the re-establishment of a specialist department in both forces' (1985: 237). In a wider survey of five forces, Southgate found no overall consensus, save that nearly half the women sampled favoured a 'modified' as against a traditional or integrated role. This would involve full integration, except where violence was anticipated (1981: 163). In her 'Medshire' study, Jones used the same role-preference questions as Southgate had in 1977 and found 'quite a change in the degree of acceptance' (S. Jones 1986: 49): 58 per cent of the women in her sample favoured integration (though only 23 per cent of men did so).

In summarizing her views of the future in the USA, Adler con-

cluded that 'American police departments with a firm equal opportunities programme have achieved significant progress for women'
(1990: 31). This is particularly true in one way and one which cannot be matched in Britain for either males or females: the recruitment of minorities. Of US women officers 40 per cent are black or
Hispanic. Under 1 per cent of British officers are black or Asian
and the proportion of women is even smaller (Chief Inspector of
Constabulary, 1989). Departments such as Washington, DC,
employ a majority of black officers and most of their female
officers (82 per cent in 1988) are black. Several prominent police
chiefs in the USA are black.

My own conclusions were that while US *outcomes* did not differ
substantially from British, there were features of the US equal-
opportunities position which would give it more mileage than the
British. Amongst these were political, legal, and cultural positions
which had been highly favourable and would continue to be mod-
erately so. Others, and this is borne out, *inter alia*, by Steel and
Lovrich (1987), include later expansion and being in the south or
west in areas which continued to expand (Heidensohn 1989*b*).

Nevertheless, there is a huge, if shadowy presence which hangs
like a miasma over this whole matter. Since the 1970s, all manner
of indicators have suggested fine weather and a fair passage for
women in policing. In practice, the ship is still in troubled waters.
In article after article, in every interview I conducted, it became
clear that the attitudes of male fellow officers were crucially determining factors in policewomen's lives. Harassment and abuse were
reported in the interviews I conducted. M. Young catalogues
horrific tales of abuse and gross nicknames (1991). Reviewing this
material belongs properly to the next chapter, but its appearance
does suggest that life runs in curious and repetitive cycles. We
began with the story of women's entry into policing. Feinman's
conclusion for the 1980s would be as apt for 1918.

'The limited progress made by women in law enforcement is a
result, in part, of continued covert and overt resistance by their
male colleagues' (1986: 92). It is to anatomize that resistance that
we shall turn in the next chapter.

3

The Role of the Modern Police

I HAVE already pointed out that research on police and policing is a recent and fruitful addition to the academic orchard. Indeed, mushrooms rather than fruit might be a more appropriate analogy, since work on these topics has grown so rapidly. Introducing a collection on the British police, Holdaway noted 'the relative dearth of research' (1979: 1) yet 'within less than a decade' was able to mark 'its contemporary irrelevance . . . a great deal of interest is evident among academics' (1989: 55). The situation is described by Reiner and Shapland as 'an efflorescence of writing and research about the police . . . Books and articles . . . are now being published at a breath-taking pace' (1987: 1). There has not merely been an expansion of quantity: 'academic writing on the police has been one of the more successful accomplishments of British criminology' (Downes and Rock 1991). Nor is this purely a British phenomenon; Bayley observes 'the upsurge of scholarly interest recently in police in the United States' (1985: 5) and that 'neglect of the police role has changed dramatically during the last decade' (1985: 4).

Such abundant growth has causes, costs, and consequences. In the USA Bayley relates the 'upsurge' to the police's 'propulsion into the foreground of social confrontation . . . the attention of scholars may follow the dramatic currents of politics more closely than they would happily admit' (1985: 6). In a more schematic treatment of modern British writing on the police, Reiner divides the history of modern British policing into three phases: consensus, conflict, and controversy and lists major studies for each period.

Perhaps the most immediately striking aspect . . . is the explosive growth of work on the police in the 'conflict' stage . . . The growth of work on the police during the 1970s . . . is an evident reflection of the politicization of policing as an increasingly partisan issue, more and more central to political conflict. (1989: 9)

The research agenda and, indeed, the much wider agenda of all serious writing about police and policing, has been determined in a situation of flux, division, and disillusionment. Crucially, too, much of the funding and all of the access comes from official bodies concerned to improve a situation perceived as critical (Weatheritt 1989: pp. xv–xvi). Dangers in this approach are not only those of incorporation but also of altering priorities: not merely can we ask questions but are we asking the right questions?

When one surveys the mass of modern research, it is evident that many interesting questions have been asked even though there are still unexplored areas. 'We know most about officers on the beat, little about senior officers, black officers, women officers and specialist officers' (Downes and Rock 1991: p. x). In short, research and writing on the police has focused on certain key themes and groups which have been extensively studied, while others remain relatively uncharted. It is my aim in this chapter to review those aspects of general studies of the police which seem apposite to my central motif of women in policing and then to survey those studies which do bear directly on that topic. What we shall find is that the literature on women in policing tends to be separate from 'general' (i.e. on men) studies of police and is a kind of subgenre of its own with certain unusual characteristics. In conclusion I want to draw out the main issues to be explored in the subsequent chapters on the experiences of women police. Surveys of police research rarely mention women, except as victims (Weatheritt 1989; Reiner and Shapland 1987) yet the study of women in policing, and the related issues of gender and control, need to be situated in the wider context of policing today.

Two topics stand out from police research as highly relevant and as having a direct bearing on women's position in policing: the nature of policing and the occupational culture. Debates and conclusions about both are highly relevant to our purposes; after all, what police officers are supposed to do, what they actually do, and how they do it are highly germane to questions about whether women are proper persons to be police officers, while notions about the macho occupational culture of policing are crucial to problems of harassment, obstruction, and the progress of women in policing as well as to the experiences that women, and others, have as victims of crime or otherwise as the 'consumers' of the criminal-justice system. In considering this literature I shall inevitably concentrate on American material, especially for some topics. There is, for example, no British equivalent to the range of US studies of women on patrol. It is nevertheless interesting to observe how, on the first two themes, research has been closely intertwined.

Distinctive Definitions: The Nature of Policing

Earlier in this study, I have indicated some of the definitional problems which beset the study of policing. These are not merely academic concerns in the pejorative sense. A former US police chief,
James F. Ahern, was one of many practitioners to address what he
called 'three important myths' in public understanding of the police
mandate and police activity. 'Myth number one is that the police
devote the preponderance of their time and resources to combat-
ting serious crime' (Ahern 1972: 141). (The other two were that
crime was fixed and measurable and that the police alone could
lower crime rates.) More recently, senior police figures have sought
to challenge popular misconceptions about their role, to redefine it,
or to argue that police capacities were ineffectual without the co-
operation of the public or other agencies.

Modern empirical work, as well as various detailed historical
studies, have raised, and sought to answer, some of the key questions in this area. What do the police do? How much do the roles
of different forces, grades, and specialists differ? What distinguishes
police work from other kinds of activities?

Maureen Cain was an early contributor to debates about what
constituted policing.

That the police exist to maintain social order appears incontrovertible, but
it is in fact a meaningless statement . . . order from whose standpoint? . . .
[The police] see themselves as protecting the mass of decent, respectable
people from the few who are neither decent nor respectable. (Cain 1979:
21)

She notes 'the opposite view . . . of the police [as] agents of a
dominant power group, enforcing its standards and order in the
face of alternative sets of standard and definitions of order' (ibid.).

In a later review of sociological literature on policing she is critical of earlier studies which do not tackle definitions, and gives her own, which is a summary of the above: 'Police . . . must be defined in terms of their key practice. They are appointed with the task of maintaining the order which those who sustain them define as proper' (1979: 153).

However, Reiner points out that 'so broad a conceptualization fails to convey what is *specific* about the police within the array of institutions and processes charged with maintaining order' (1989: 3). He then cites as an example the pioneering US studies which emphasized the use of legitimate force and of coercion as the unique characteristic of the police (1989: 4). This view is succinctly put by Bayley: 'the unique characteristic of police is that they are authorized to use physical force to regulate interpersonal relations in communities' (1985: 103). In an analysis in the same work, Bayley attempts an international comparison of situations encountered by the police. He concludes that 'police work is overwhelmingly law-related . . . In the United States, two thirds to four fifths of the situations that can be unambiguously classified are crime-related' (1985: 126). Examining his detailed results, however, highlights the importance of traffic work in all but one department. In Britain Bayley found a different position, 'a clear preponderance of non-crime-related situations' (1985: 127).

Such observations have had considerable impact on both academic and policy debates about modern policing. One review of such studies declares, 'data from many of our largest cities, and from small and medium-size cities, show that general-duty police officers spend from 70 to 85 per cent of their time with non-crime-related matters' (Johnson *et al*. 1981: 17). In fact, results of such studies are more complex and capable of various interpretations. Cumming *et al*. certainly found that more than half of public calls to the police were for aid in personal problems and situations; their analysis led them to give their article the title of 'The Policeman as Philosopher, Guide and Friend' (1965). Banton, in a comparative study of five US and Scottish police departments and forces (1964), distinguished two aspects of the police role as 'law officers' and 'peace officers' and emphasized the importance of the latter, especially in the homogeneous 'socially dense' society of Scotland. He concluded that in the more distant, formal relationships prevailing in a society such as the USA, law-enforcement demands would prevail. Bayley came to the opposite view:

Not only do intimate associations maintain discipline, but they also provide social services to their members. As informal relations erode, people must turn to the state for these services . . . (thus) as societies become more industrial and urban and less agrarian and rural, police will deal with more service and fewer crime-related requests. (1985: 131)

Cain's comparison of rural and urban forces in the 1960s suggested similar counter-intuitive findings. She found that two to three persons were proceeded against for an indictable offence per uniform constable in the city force whereas with an average ranging from 7.2 to 3.75 per head in the country, 'each rural constable appears to have more crime work than his city colleague' (1979: 70–1). Cain attributes this difference to the differing conceptions of their roles and their *sources of legitimacy*. 'The rural man did not define his task purely in terms of crime . . . a way to express and conceptualize this [is]—peace-keeping, symbolic or representational function, value maintenance' (1979: 70–1).

In some of the earliest observational studies of police behaviour, Bittner described the characteristics of peace-keeping on skid row, at the most disorderly edges of American Society.

Peace-keeping procedure on skid row consists of three elements. Patrolmen seek to acquire a rich body of concrete knowledge about people . . . They tend to proceed against persons mainly on the basis of perceived risk, rather than on the basis of culpability. And they are more interested in reducing the aggregate total of troubles in the area than in evaluating individual cases according to merit. (1967: 714)

Bittner decided, unlike Banton, that peace-keeping and law enforcement cannot be separated because 'peace-keeping occasionally acquires the external aspects of law enforcement' (1967: 714). In his account of police procedures in the 'emergency apprehension of mentally ill persons' (1967), Bittner argues that the police pursued a special role in peace-keeping, containing elements of 'control and support in a unique combination', and specifically refutes the contention of Cumming and her colleagues that such police officers are 'amateur social workers' (1967: 714).

Yet just such a role appears to be expected from the police by the public. In a 1970s survey conducted in Essex, Punch and Naylor (1973) concluded that the British police were a 'secret social

service' since the majority of calls (between 50 and 70 per cent)
were for services and not crime related. Hough (1985) suggests a
proportion of approximately one-third service and one-third 'crime
incidents' attended by police patrols in another British study and
there seems considerable support for this view in the British literature (Heidensohn 1989a: 136–7). Indeed there is much evidence of a
resistance to this type of work from serving officers who recognize
the tasks and their volume but resent them. Smith and Gray made
extensive observations of both uniform and CID officers at work in
London; they report on the value system in which 'good arrests' of
'good villains', i.e. serious criminals, was viewed as real police
work, while domestic disputes were 'rubbish' although they also
note the stress in the CID on investigation (1983: 346–54).

Other, especially some more recent studies have added depth and
uncertainty to our understanding of the nature of police work. In
an account of patrolmen (sic) in three police departments in
Southern California, Michael Brown found that

57 per cent of the incidents observed in all three departments are calls for
service. Patrolmen in these departments are involved in crime-related incidents slightly less than a third of the time: 31 per cent of all incidents
observed involved either the apprehension of felons or the investigation
and suppression of crime. (M. Brown 1981: 138–9)

Brown argues that 'the need to provide services and the desire to
control crime conflict to the extent that a patrolman views his role
as largely one or the other' (ibid.). Joanna Shapland has reported
on two local comparative studies of policing in Britain. In the first
(Shapland and Vagg 1988) 'potential crime' messages received by
the police made up some 43 per cent of calls in a rural area, and
54 and 61 per cent in two urban ones. The remainder were split
between 'social disorder' (around 20 per cent), roads, and 'personal
services' (Shapland and Vagg 1988: 37–8, Table 3.7). From research
on a second project on commuter towns, she and Dick Hobbs
insist 'that the police are almost the one remaining all-purpose
emergency service and that because officers themselves perceive
this, they respond to any incident requiring a fast response because
injury might occur' (1989: 21). In trying to draw out conclusions
from the first survey, Shapland and Vagg comment on the diversity
of problems which the public saw as matters of concern, noting
indeed that there are many publics as well as many problems

(1988: 64). Uncertainty, some incoherence, and debate they see as present and future characteristics:

The task of policing, its mandate, and its priorities are essentially undefined. There are a large number of different audiences for policing by the police . . . each audience has a different view of what police priorities should be and, necessarily, sees a different mixture of what the police actually do. . . . The result of this indeterminacy is that there can be no permanent resolution of the task of policing and its control. It is and will always be a constant political debate. (1988: 191)

Such caution is not characteristic of a number of other studies whose authors are not merely sure that they know what the police do, they appear equally confidently to be able to prescribe what the police should do. The problem with these approaches is that they contradict each other, save over the 'service' role of the police. In a now classic study of police in a range of different communities, James Q. Wilson distinguished 'maintaining order' from law enforcement, and assigned personal service as the task of the patrolman, giving primacy to maintaining order. In later writings he emphasized the need for police to deal with 'incivilities': vandalism, public drunkenness, vagrancy. The key argument is that disorder breeds social breakdown and that this in turn leads to higher crime rates. Wilson does not see social service as a suitable job for the police and advocates this being hived off and privatized as 'Emergency Services, etc.' (Wilson 1968: 5).

On this point, Kinsey *et al*. 'whole heartedly agree', but they otherwise oppose Wilson's approach. They favour policing priorities being given, as they do not feel they are at present, to crime control of both serious and 'minor' crime, within a framework of public accountability and minimal policing (1986: 205–6). What is notable about their 'left realist' critique of Wilson's conservative position (Kinsey *et al*. 1986: 80–1) is that despite arguing that contemporary policing is ineffective yet heavy-handed, they end by supporting a traditional view of policing, 'that the police are necessary and that a minimum level of coercion is an inevitable feature of social order' (Kinsey *et al* 1986: 215).

Coercion is the common theme, then, of a wide range of studies which seek to show what police officers do, what they wish to do, what the public, the authors, or their superiors expect them to do, and even what some of their critics would like them to cease to do. The importance of this debate for the theme of this book lies in the elision which is frequently made: *coercion* requires *force* which *implies physique* and hence policing by *men* (S. Jones 1986: 146–62; M. Young 1991: 191–252). This is to over-simplify the issue greatly: it is not just the supposed centrality of the use of physical force to the police role which is alleged to exclude women from performing it, but a whole series of other connotations to do with the use of force, self-presentation, authority, danger, and vulnerability (S. Jones 1986: 146–62). However, to use arguments about coercion and force in this way seems to me fundamentally to misconstrue them and especially their gender implications.

It is perhaps not surprising that such misapprehensions do occur, not least because one of the classic formulations of the role of the police is Bittner's paper 'Florence Nightingale in pursuit of Willie Sutton' (its subtitle is 'A Theory of the Police') (1967 and 1990*a*). In this article, Bittner argues that criminal law enforcement 'is something that most (police) . . . do with the frequency located somewhere between virtually never and very rarely' (1990*a*: 240). Having established that police rarely, if ever, engage in law enforcement and that on the other hand they frequently and competently perform acts of social service, Bittner argues that they nevertheless carry out such tasks in a very different way: 'even though what they actually have to do often could be done by physicians and social workers, the service they perform involves the exercise of a unique competence they do not share with anyone else in society' (Bittner 1990*a*: 251). This uniqueness, he holds, resides 'in their capacity for decisive action . . . *The policeman and the policeman alone, is equipped, entitled, and required to deal with every exigency in which force may have to be used, to meet it*' (Bittner 1990*a*: 256; emphasis in the original). This begs, of course, numerous questions: Where does the mandate derive from? Is it essential? What of other groups who may have partial mandates? What of citizens' own rights? What about legal challenges? Bittner then, so to speak, 'cops out' by massively qualifying this assertion: 'I am *not* saying the police work consists of using force to solve problems, but only that police work consists of coping with problems in which force *may have to be used*' (Bittner 1990*a*: 256). Force thus becomes not the defining factor of policing but the limiting case, the exception that is meant, somehow, to prove the rule. In his conclusion in a telling reference to his title, Bittner mentions 'an illusion'.

Believing that the real ground for his existence is the perennial pursuit of the likes of Willie Sutton—for which he lacks both opportunity and resources—the policeman feels compelled to minimize the significance of those instances of his performance in which he seems to follow the footsteps of Florence Nightingale. Fearing the role of the nurse or, worse yet, the role of the social worker, the policeman combines resentment against what he has to do day in, day out with the necessity of doing it. And in the course of it he misses his true vocation. (1990*a*: 263)

The paper concludes with a proper attack on pretence and its presumed immunity; it cannot therefore come amiss if I point out that nowhere in the paper does Bittner refer to the fact that Florence Nightingale was a woman, and British, he only describes her as 'the heroic protagonist of modern nursing' while Willie Sutton was a man (and American) and 'in his day a notorious thief' (1990*a*: 264).

My purpose in dwelling on this paper is to show how difficult (near impossible?) it is for a noted authority on policing to sustain his argument about the unique, coercive nature of the police mandate. Not that the case is refuted, it is rather that it remains unproven, with a status more akin to myth than reality. Massive research on all aspects of policing (although much of this tends to focus on the visible, vulnerable figure of the patrol*man* (*sic*, usually) who is bound to be at the sharpest end of police work) has not been able to provide overwhelming evidence to support this case. A study of policing in New York is probably typical, and salutary. Three precincts of the City were studied, including one with high crime rates, in order to explore

the dynamics of potentially violent encounters between police and public . . . Its major conclusions are: 1) violence, even verbal aggression, is relatively rare in police work; 2) most conflict is dampened by the arrival of the police, leaving little scope for the use of defusing tactics. (Bayley and Garofalo 1989: 1)

Most authors writing on police work agree on the banal ordinariness of most of it, the relative absence of glamour, drama, or violence. Police officers seem to be distinguished by their legitimate use of coercive powers. Whether this has to do with the innate characteristics of their work, with the historic origins of policing, the discretion allowed to officers, with the traits associated with policing, or even with traditions or myths, are issues which have yet to be proven. For the moment all I wish to do is to stress that research on policing, which has largely covered patrol work, has sketched out its nature, called attention to changes in its trends to the diverse expectations of citizenry, constabulary, and critics and generally left us with far more questions raised than can with certainty be answered. With practically no exceptions, all the work I have cited omits two considerations. First, Anglo-American policing (in some instances, all policing) is treated as a unity, yet there is a major and relevant distinction: US officers are armed while British ones are not only not armed, but only a small proportion are given firearms training. Secondly, the 'police' discussed in these studies are police*men*, even though some of them cannot have been. Yet gender has been shown to be of great importance in one area of police studies, the area which has attracted most attention, even notoriety. Unusually, of course, the gender is masculine and the area we turn to next is that of the occupational culture of policing.

Occupational Cultures of Policing

All occupations develop some kind of sustaining culture consisting of shared meanings and traditions. The occupational culture of the police is distinctive in a number of ways: in its character and persistence, in the amount of research enquiry to which it has been subject, in the role it is alleged to play in supporting or preventing change in police organizations. All these are of great importance to the central theme of this book; indeed in them may be the reasons for the form which women's role in law enforcement has taken.

The Characteristics of Cop Culture

'The occupational culture of the police has found reference points in virtually every publication about policing' (Holdaway 1989: 55). Another former policeman depicts it thus.

The police organization I have described can be defined as forming a primarily masculine domain where metaphors of hunting and warfare predominate. Categories of prestige, power and status are allocated to tough, manful acts of crime-fighting and thief-taking. Tensions experienced in these battles and conflicts with antagonists both inside and external to the organization have created a rigidified and defensively aggressive world. (M. Young 1991: 191)

He attributes the creation of this closed world to the police's need to have structures and limits which separate them from the rest of society. Much of his book is taken up with describing the dishonesties of police culture which overtly praise uniform patrol work, yet denigrate it. It also supported in the 1960s (and apparently still did in 1981) a breath-taking system of counting crimes which would render virtually all such recorded figures invalid. He describes visiting a 'clear up squad' detective:

Both he and I understood these statistical truths were a relative commodity, for the success of the unit was always measured in terms of its 'clear-ups' for the record of detections. The resulting cynicism manifest in our exchange, I would argue, occurred in part because of an unspoken acknowledgement of the obvious complicity which some chief officers and senior detectives play in this scrabble for an acceptable crime figure, for many have engaged in similar practices themselves as they have struggled up the hierarchies. (M. Young 1991: 367)

Danger, authority, and results are the three key factors which Skolnick identified as forming the 'working personality' of the urban police officer. For this very influential work he drew on his own and William Westley's studies of police and public attitudes. Westley argued that officers responded to public hostility and threat with aggression and violence. This in turn escalates into further threat and tension and makes the police secretive and self-protective (1970: 49). Skolnick developed this further in his explanation of how policemen are formed:

The combination of danger and authority found in the task of the policemen unavoidably combines to frustrate procedural regularity. . . . Danger, typically yields self-defensive conduct, that must strain to be impulsive because danger arouses fear and anxiety so easily. Authority under such conditions becomes a resource to reduce perceived threats rather than a series of reflective judgements arrived at calmly. (Skolnick 1966: 44)

Westley (whose research, although published in 1970 was based on his 1951 Ph.D. dissertation) gives a detailed description of police-recruit socialization by older officers which bind them through secrecy and loyalty (1970: 144). There are, however, a number of possible criticisms of these accounts. First of all, one can query whether cop culture can be as purely *reactive* as Westley and Skolnick assert. Even if it was so originally, for instance in the earliest days of the 'new police', the thrust of subsequent accounts suggests the *perpetuation* of the culture for reasons which have to do with internal factors. Secondly, it is by no means clear that the hard men on mean streets image, what Reiner depicts as 'the police officer faces, behind every corner he turns or door-bell he rings, some danger, if not of firearms at least of fists' (1985: 87), is either authentic or universal. There are more dangerous jobs than policing, and police work in the USA is considerably more dangerous than in Britain because of the widespread availability of firearms and their ready use. I have already pointed out that police do not encounter much violence even in a crime-ridden New York precinct and spend much time on mundane routine activities and on paperwork. Holdaway has also criticized the empirical bases of both Westley's and Skolnick's work. He points out that both in fact describe 'a vast range of diverse experiences encountered during the course of their routine work' (1983: 19), but fail to show how this is 'moulded in the course of routine police work' (ibid.).

In a later review of British research on the concept, Holdaway takes Reiner to task for 'glossing over the tenuous link between British and American studies' (1989: 67). Reiner does indeed try to integrate both the bases, the core characteristics of police culture in Britain and America, but goes on to give two classificatory typologies, one of the main features of cop culture, the other of the types of cop who operate in it. Key features in Reiner's framework include a sense of mission, isolation, conservatism, racial prejudice, and pragmatism (Reiner 1985: 87–103). It is not easy to see how these traits can be derived from the external constraints cited by Westley and Skolnick, and indeed Reiner warns against Skolnick who 'overemphasizes the degree of external compulsion in this' (1985: 88). As he points out, the police have sought to influence public perceptions of themselves. Moreover, they often appear to prefer danger, excitement, and hedonism to the dull reality of 'rubbish' work.

There appears to be considerable diversity within and between police cultures. Reuss-Ianni produced a study of schisms *within* the New York City Police Department where, she suggests, there is a split between two cultures of 'Street Cops and Management Cops' (1983). She focuses on conduct maxims as the key aspects of the street-cop culture. This is also the case with a number of other studies which have emphasized the part played by informal rules in the maintenance of the cop culture. Chatterton calls these 'working rules' and notes that they are distinguished from formal rules and can be continuously worked and reworked (1983). One of the most extensively documented descriptions of police cultures is that by Smith and Gray of the Metropolitan Police. Their account not only depicts the culture(s) of the Metropolitan Police but also considers its impact. They noted 'informally understood objectives and norms and showed how they influence the general pattern of policing and the detail of police behaviour' (1983: 336). As newcomers they themselves were expected to undergo initiation rituals. They found marked group solidarity, displayed in rapid responses to support calls to colleagues and also a preference for informal, peer-group sanctions as discipline (1983: 355–6). There was, however, more than one culture, or variation on the culture, in London. Smith and Gray found that the CID had, so to speak, their own in-house subculture. It took a particularly gross machismo form and was characterized by four elements: alcohol, violence, sex, and a lack of human sympathy (1983: 363–5).

Diversity *within* police culture is perceived by Reiner as 'distinct types of individual police perspective around the core elements of the culture' (1985: 103). He derives four types from a range of Anglo-American studies:

1. The 'bobby'—the ordinary copper
2. The 'new centurion'—the street-wise crusader against crime and disorder
3. The 'uniform carrier'—the lazy cynic
4. The 'professional'—ambitious and career-conscious

Disagreements may exist about the types of cop culture and about its sources, about its importance, about whether there is one 'core' type or many varieties, but there seems to be widespread agreement that it exists and that one of its major characteristics is the significance of gender to it. It is this which makes Young argue that women cannot be assimilated into it: 'Women who do breach the boundary to penetrate this masculine world can only ever be partially successful and will often have to subsume "male characteristics" to achieve even a limited social acceptability' (M. Young 1991: 193).

Once again, as with research on police work, many questions are left hanging. Self-evidently, cop culture is *not* always supportive and sustaining to police. Both American and British police have lived through major corruption scandals (notably in New York and London) in the 1960s and 1970s. Solidarity and group cohesiveness clearly aided these, and certainly helped to perpetuate them. Box has pointed out that the persistence of group norms and stereotypes may be counter-productive—it may be much *harder* for the police to achieve their allotted tasks or to adapt to change. It has been argued that cop culture is not strictly functional in the way some writers suggest, but rather that it represents something 'precarious—just talk' (Holdaway 1983: 154). What he describes is not so much a culture as folk-tales whose telling and retelling supports a 'social construction of policing' (ibid.). In quite different vein, McBarnet (1979) fastens on the legal framework and not the culture to explain police behaviour.

Women and gender do figure somewhat in studies of cop culture. Gender largely figures because of the need to account for its macho character. Virtually all accounts describe, sometimes with almost celebratory enthusiasm, the drinking, crude jokes, racism, and sexual harassment encountered and sometimes expected (Reiner 1985: M. Young 1991). What they do only perfunctorily is to analyse and anatomize it. Young himself neatly encapsulates the problem with his anecdote about suggesting 'to a group of colleagues . . . that there was no logical reason why the existing male/female ratios could not be revised (i.e. about 10,000 men and 111,000 women . . . about an hour later . . . a Sergeant queried: "you know, what you're suggesting would mean changing not just the police but the whole of the world"' (1991: 234).

Reiner concludes his review of cop culture by suggesting that its differing forms 'do not seem related to demographic characteristics such as ethnic group and gender' (1985: 106) although this is based only on American findings. He has more recently suggested that diversity in recruitment must be breaking down old subcultures such as those described by Young, Holdaway, Hobbs (1988), Skolnick, and Westley. In the next chapter I shall discuss the experiences of women in the cop culture and how far their lives were affected by it.

Research on Women in Policing

Most of the research on women in policing differs markedly from the rest of the academic exercise in this field. To begin with, the topic seems to be treated largely in isolation; the majority of major studies ignore policewomen, or indicate their presence in an aside. This may partly be a function of generation: the pre-integration 1960s were the period when some of the classic studies were carried out which have shaped research ever since (Weatheritt 1989). Grimshaw and Jefferson (1984) are 'asiders': their index contains thirteen references to women police officers, but these nearly all turn out to be citing situations involving women members of the public and police officers. Fielding (1988) contains an interesting discussion of the attitudes of female as well as male recruits (pp. 148–57) and M. Young (1991) has a lengthy ethnographic account of female police which is integral to his argument about the inappropriateness of police culture and organization for their allotted tasks. Bayley and Garofalo indicate that women officers featured in their study of police reactions to violence in New York, but they do not make clear how many or in what categories. Such integrated treatment of women officers is comparatively rare. Instead they have been the focus of particular kinds of research, distinguished in several ways.

Mainstream concerns do not, on the whole, water these creeks, nor is there much fertilizing flow-back. Walker has pointed out that

Police research . . . has neglected the effect of increased minority or female employment on the police subculture. The literature on the police subculture is still shaped by the paradigm developed in the 1960s. This paradigm views police departments as predominantly white and male, with both racial minorities and females seriously underrepresented and with females not assigned to routine patrol duty. . . . The changing profile of the American police officer renders this paradigm highly suspect. In some departments both the absolute number and percentage of minority officers have increased substantially. Is it even possible to speak of the police subculture, in the traditional sense of the word, in these departments? (Walker 1985: 565)

Just as the increased presence of women in police service has hardly affected policing studies, so too do studies of women remain detached, or even cause a diversion, from the central questions of the subject.

The question, for instance, of whether women form their own subculture within the police has scarcely been addressed. Martin (1980) suggests that they do not and that they concentrate on developing coping strategies to deal with the male subculture. Remmington (1981) also, like Martin, carried out a participant observation study on police for her thesis. She undertook this in Atlanta where various recent changes had left local police demoralized and disloyal. Most white male officers spent 'only a small percentage of the shift actually . . . on policing duties' (1981: 189). The group was divided racially and sexually, but remained solid in its 'cop' culture: the 'incorporation of women officers has effected little change in either the cohesiveness of the group or in its sense of isolation from the public' (1981: 187). But such accounts are rare, and exclusively American.

Indeed, not only is much of the research of women police American, it covers the whole range of such studies, such as they are, whereas British work has mainly focused on equal opportunities. The US studies are, like the British, policy led, there are numerous accounts of evaluating women on patrol, of how to achieve greater equality, and the rather bizarre subgenre of the attitudes of male officers to their female colleagues. At least two of these are solely concerned with male officers' attitudes to female officers (Hernandez 1982; Golden 1981). There are also a great many descriptions of projects on women officers' traits and characteristics, usually in relation to male officers or the job. Another unique US contribution has been a series of performance evaluations which have sought to assess women police's policing performance, usually at street level. These were obviously prompted by the integration policies of the 1970s. Almost all these studies cover very small numbers of respondents, those which use mailed surveys and similar strategies reporting extremely low response rates. What is not offered is perhaps at least as significant as what is. Few fundamental questions are put and indeed it has been argued that these studies have provided a convenient diversion from more central issues.

The obsession of researchers addressing the competence of women in policing as compared to male officers, as rationale for relegating them to clerical functions, has been detrimental to women as *well as to the police profession*. The consistent measurement of women, by the male standard, *distracts society's attention from the competence of male officers* and reduces society's ability to identify and analyse problems or formulate and implement solutions. The issue is not that policewomen are more or less competent than policemen, but that a predominantly male-oriented police system has failed to prevent, deter, or solve crimes that have been brought to their attention. (Bell 1982*a*: 119–20)

Bell's criticisms are probably more relevant for the 1970s, when integration, and the evaluation studies on integration, took place, and also for the USA. Performance research of this kind has not found a place in Britain, although US results are cited. It is more generally noteworthy that wider issues have not been addressed, such as ways of handling women, and minority entry into policing. Some police research has begun to take account of change (Fielding 1988 and 1991; S. Jones 1986) but far too much of it seems to regard the occupational subculture as an irreducible 'given', a non-negotiable Gibraltar. 'Longterm' glacial 'changes are not accounted for in most police research' (Walker 1985: 568)

Hunt, who participated in one of the patrol evaluation studies, has given a vivid account of her experience as a researcher/observer and uses this to analyse aspects of rapport in the research situation. While her article's primary purpose is to explore methodological questions in relation to gender, she also gives graphic descriptions of the nature of police culture and how she consciously achieved acceptance in it:

status and gender are the two most basic categories which define membership in the policeman's world. 'Real cops' must demonstrate particular 'masculine' characteristics associated with police work in the outside realm of the street and reject certain 'feminine' attributes associated with 'inside work' in the domestic domain. At the same time, the 'real cop' must identify with rank and file police in opposition to management. (1984: 283).

She deliberately acted in ways which created a distinctive identity for herself as a 'street-woman-researcher'. In order to achieve this she behaved in ways which convinced her colleagues that she was 'masculine'—by enjoying target-shooting, displaying a 'combat personality' in a fight, and by 'acting crazy' (1984: 290). Most of Hunt's observations are of her own behaviour or of male patrol officers and, in a sense, her study belongs to the section of this chapter in which I discussed research on the traditional cop culture. However, her most interesting remarks are the few in which she relates her own role reconstruction to the position of the women officers in the Department she studied:

some women in non-traditional occupations resist role encapsulation and actively negotiate new definitions of masculinity and femininity. Female police officers in Metropolitan's City, for example, are transforming the policeman's cultural order by constructing a new category of woman-cop in much the same way as the field worker. (1984: 293)

Of great interest, too, are her comments on the significance of gender in police culture. She insists that 'the policeman's world constitutes a symbolic universe permeated with gender meanings and this symbolic structure is preponderate over other factors which explain the behaviour of the police' (1984: 294). In consequence, Hunt explains male resistance to women in policing not as a result of behavioural socialization, but,

Policemen . . . oppose the 'moral woman' . . . because she represents the exposure of an informal world of policing on which masculine gender is based. In addition her presence signifies the exposure of the 'police myth' . . . which conceals the demeaning nature of the 'private' occupation and maintains the policeman's public image as a successful crime fighter. Symbolically, then, she reminds him that he can only achieve illusory manhood by denying and repressing the essential feminine dimension of police work which involves social relations, paper work, and housekeeping in the public domain. (1984: 294)

To Hunt, then, policemen object to women's presence in policing for exactly the opposite reasons to those given by M. Young (1991), Reiner (1985), and derived from the US studies such as Skolnick (1966) and Bittner (1990a). These authors all stress the hard side of policing, the cameraderie it generates and necessitates. Hunt, on the contrary, is arguing that policing is much softer an occupation than the cop culture allows, although, paradoxically, she gained acceptance in it by playing along with the toughness and the machismo. Like the other authors, she does not explore why policing should be such a notably gendered activity, especially when, as she insists, the reality is so far from the image. Certainly in my own study, especially in the USA, I found that female officers had gained just such insights as she offers and were often engaged in constructing new roles and strategies within the organization.

In the rest of this chapter I want to outline the research findings from Anglo-American research on women in the police from 1970–1990. I have grouped the studies under four main headings:

1. Personality and adaptation
2. Performance

3. Attitudes
4. Equal opportunities

These categories are inevitably somewhat arbitrary because they are often police-led, or by serving officers: studies of personality or attitudes often contain proposals for improving opportunities, but they do represent some broad clusters of concerns in the literature.

Personality and Adaptation

Earlier in this chapter I outlined some of the history of the concept of policing styles and particularly Reiner's synthesis of these. He is insistent that 'these typologies, constructed for different purposes and with reference to different police forces are remarkably similar . . . the differing orientations do not seem related to demographic characteristics such as ethnic group and gender' (Reiner 1985: 105–6). Yet there are analyses of policing by women which claim that their styles differ, while others do not find such differences. There is, in part at least, some lack of clarity about whether these 'police orientations and styles' (Reiner 1985: 103) are adaptations and responses to the work of policing or to the occupational culture. As my earlier discussion indicated, these two are seen as inextricably linked, the nature of the former causing the latter to develop and flourish. For females, of course, who lack the marks of affinity which entitle them to join the culture, dealing with its prior existence *and* becoming professional officers are discrete tasks. Reiner seems to run the two together in the passage cited above where he says, 'Nor is there evidence of significant differences in policing style between male and female officers'. 'Again, though it is plausible that raising the proportion of women in the department might alter the masculine ethos' (Reiner 1985: 106). Reiner cites two projects which are effectiveness studies from the Washington, DC, experimental series; these were designed to evaluate women's *performance*, against records etc., rather than their styles and adaptations. As we shall see, much research on women in policing is basically about how women cope with police*men* rather than with polic*ing*.

Perhaps the best-known and most widely-cited study is Susan Martin's observational account of women on patrol in Washington, DC (1979; 1980). Her empirical work was carried out in the same decade as the performance evaluations in the capital, but formed a separate enterprise. Martin enrolled as a special-reserve officer and observed male and female officers extensively, and she makes quite clear that the starting-point of her work was to interpret how women adapt to a male occupational culture. Women, she argues,

are excluded from the information exchange network and informal social life . . . Policewomen's behaviour is circumscribed by the stereotyped roles in which they are cast . . . which reminds women that as females they are sex objects, vulnerable to harassment, yet held responsible for the outcomes of the interaction. (Martin 1980: 157)

The deliberately ambiguous title to her book indicates her interest in 'the study of one such group of women "breaking and entering" into police patrol, an occupation traditionally reserved for "men only"' (1980).

She draws on the earlier work of Alice Hochschild, who had explored the experience of women who enter hitherto masculine occupations. Often they are 'tokens' and, initially, marginal. They face status inconsistencies between their gender and professional roles and they resolve these through techniques of role restriction. This is essentially a reactive strategy to cope with the rejection they encounter. At the extremes of adaptation, she suggests, are two poles which involve women becoming either defeminized or deprofessionalized (1973). 'Defeminized' women see themselves as different from other women; they become super-efficient, as good, or better than their male colleagues so that their competence comes to mask their femininity. 'Deprofessionalized' women, at the opposite extreme, do not compete with male colleagues, but accept subordinate status and concessions granted to them. Martin applied this typology to twenty-eight women patrol officers whom she observed while on the police reserve in Washington, DC. She described their adaptations as falling along a continuum which coincided with Hochschild's although she called them POLICEwomen and policeWOMEN. POLICEwomen focus on law enforcement, rather than service, show a high commitment to the job, even criticizing fellow female officers with males. Their careers are more like males' in that they wish to do specialist work and to be promoted. PoliceWOMEN, on the other hand, emphasize the feminine; a police-WOMAN 'accepts the men's invitation to function as a nominal equal while actually functioning as a junior partner or assistant and

receiving treatment and exemptions from work tasks appropriate
for a "lady"' (Martin 1980: 315).

It is important to remember that these represent the two 'ends of
a continuum and that many women will demonstrate some characteristics of both these role adaptions. Often they struggle to achieve
a balance between the defeminized and deprofessionalised roles'
(S. Jones 1986: 172). This advice is often forgotten and Martin's
typology is rendered merely, for example, as 'female officers tended
to adopt two principles of coping' (Potts 1981: 12). Of her twenty-
eight subjects, Martin placed four as policeWOMEN and only three
as POLICEwomen so that the majority were in between. Martin's
appreciation of her subjects is very much related to what might be
termed their presentational style. Jane (a short, black officer with
one year's service) 'does not have a convincingly authoritative or
imposing manner' while Ann 'rather than feeling hesitant in dealing with unruly male citizens . . . capitalizes on being female—her
policing style stresses her listening and interpersonal skills' (Martin
1980: 10). Martin is keen to emphasize the organizational reasons
which bring about problems of breaking and entering, rather than
individual or psychological ones. She sees two sets of variables as
crucial: one represented by organizational factors such as power,
opportunity, and the numbers of women employed, and second by,
culturally established sex-role norms. 'The women's interaction
with other officers . . . multiply the stresses they face in performing
their duties on the street' (1980: 157). And they still have to resist
the stereotypes expressed by males: 'I don't think they should be
on this job, not in uniform, not working with me. I want somebody who can back me up . . . I don't want someone I have to
back up' (1980: 92).

Martin's work provides a bench-mark for other studies of
women in policing and is frequently so cited (Potts 1981; Kay Lord
1986; Bryant et al. 1985; S. Jones 1986). She did find distinctiveness
in policewomen and their policing, but she attributed this to the
organization and culture of policing, and, of course, her extreme
POLICEwomen exhibited masculine styles, although the social and
self-reconstruction they must undergo renders doubtful the notion
that they experience policing in the same way as their male colleagues.

Remmington also carried out an observational study of police at
a time of change, in her case in Atlanta, Georgia, in the late 1970s,

when the Bureau had undergone changes both to their powers and to their organization as a result of both racial and sexual integration (1981: 5). Her observations covered uniform patrol and the work of the Homicide and Sex Crimes detectives (1981: 4). Remmington found, paradoxically perhaps, that women in the Atlanta Bureau had assimilated into the masculine ethos, but were not fully accepted into it, and yet their policing styles were distinct from those of the men.

Policing has had its effects upon the women who have joined the department . . . it can reach into all aspects of their lives. . . . Despite their inability to be assimilated into the group by the males and despite their own recognition of inadequacies in their job performance, the acculturation of the women into the policing world has caused modifications in their attitudes, behavior, and social relationships. (Remmington 1981: 200–1)

She draws a picture of women officers who, in a sense perhaps, resemble Martin's policewOMEN:

Women do not generally patrol in the same way as male officers. Many of the reasons for this may be in the protective attitude and behavior of their male peers who rarely permit them to police alone. But several women were observed who deliberately drove slowly to a potentially violent call. No female observed ever tried to find law breakers, by driving down dark alleys in the hope of locating some criminal activity for example. (1981: 199)

Such accounts, and they are extensive, suggest at first sight perhaps that southern culture produced a wholly 'feminine' female membership of the Bureau. Yet, at the same time, Remmington documents the low morale and mere token policing by the (mainly white) officers at the time of her study

Few white officers, either male or female were performing the prescribed duties in anything but a cursory manner. Their alienation from the hierarchy had been furthered by the recently promoted black sergeants many of whom have been enforcing the rulebook much to the chagrin of officers who had developed a style of policing which included many infractions that had often been overlooked by the white brass. The result has been a token policing effort by the uniformed officers. Their remaining work time is spent in . . . personal pursuits. (1981: 118)

These personal pursuits turn out to be sleeping or 'cracking', watching television or reading, or conducting illicit affairs (1981:

121–4). (Although, and this does say something about the role of women as 'observers' in the police, whether as colleagues or anthropologists, Remmington notes that her female informants reported 'there may be an uncommonly high rate of impotency among police officers' (1981: 123).) In short, she pictures a police service who are doing anything except policing. This situation she attributes to the appointment of a black police commissioner who 'had followed a course of reverse discrimination in hiring and promoting policies' (1981: 5). Indeed, she reports the Bureau's cop subculture as split along racial lines (1981: 119) and she argues that the masculine solidarity was stronger than ever, in part reinforced by the situation outlined above 'since shared knowledge and/or participation in acts that transgress the orders of the police hierarchy and in some instances the law, create deeper ties of loyalty among officers' (1981: 119).

This very interesting and rather neglected field-work draws our attention to a number of points (unlike Martin's, it is almost never cited in later studies—Allison Morris's (1987) is one of the few subsequent summaries to include it). Clearly, Martin's continuum of coping was only represented at one of its ends; further racial and other local political factors had marked impact on the policing situation and culture. Remmington also shows, more clearly than any other writer, that women may become part of the cop culture, yet nevertheless not act as 'real police' because of their gender, even though they are paying some of their dues in full with high divorce rates, social isolation, right-wing views, and 'hardened attitudes toward people and their impoverished lives' (1981: 202).

Interestingly, Remmington emphasizes, as does Martin, the differences in the use of weapons and force between American and British police. In the USA, Martin says, 'Women . . . could hardly have represented the moral authority of the state nor did they have the physical characteristics considered symbolically and practically important for the job' (1980: 20). Even in modern times 'the core of policing remains the use of authority in potentially violent situations in which males by virtue of their physical stature, socialization and society's assumptions are at an advantage' (ibid.). Machismo and force are, in Remmington's view, the keys:

it is not the authority element of the officer's role per se which precludes acceptance of women in policing at this time. However, the image of police authority as it has developed in North America was closely identified with physical macho power. Cross cultural research could be employed to examine the reception of female officers in other countries, such as Great Britain where physical force is not the primary image of police authority. (1981: 203)

In fact, four British studies do throw some light on the comparative issue. Only one (S. Jones 1986) involved observational work 'on patrol' although another one (Fielding 1988) was longitudinal and used a variety of techniques (pp. 212–13). Three were focused primarily on the impact of the Sex Discrimination Act 1975 in Britain (see below) and addressed the occupational culture question as an adjunct.

In the most recently reported study (S. Jones (1986) actually conducted her field-work some four years later), Fielding (1988) surveyed 125 recruits, of whom ten were female, who entered training in Derbyshire in 1979–80. The main foci of the study are training and occupational socialization. Most of the section on gender gives statements from male officers about WPCs (women police constables) and these graphically illustrate the power and persistence of the occupational culture: 'the early impact of occupational culture is such that it can provide a perspective on experience before the recruit gains direct experience' (1988: 165). While very few women are cited directly, Fielding insists that his female subjects were socialized into the police culture, accepted it, and did not manifest deviant adaptations. One senior officer offered what Fielding describes as 'a hard core "police perspective", and a *mark of the conquest of biography by the occupation*' (1988: 166). This is just as true of the young:

the female recruits put forward an attitude that is not so much complacent as matter-of-fact. . . . They are set to conform to what is required of them and regard the police mission as unproblematically defined by those who have come before . . . Their views are remarkably similar to the men's . . . novices operate with a high degree of consensus about the meaning of their status as employees of the police organization. The real controversies of employment in the police are largely shared by male and female employees. (1988: 167)

The group of women in this study was very small and although the research fellow involved was a woman, the main interviewer was male.

If American post-integration research focused on women police officers' effectiveness, the (much smaller) output of British studies has been concerned with measuring assimilation and this concern has led to an interest in cop culture and its persistence. Southgate (1981) surveyed female officers in five forces in 1977 and circulated a questionnaire (there were 680 replies, giving a 90 per cent response rate). Southgate suggests that three role preferences were available to women: the old, pre-1975 'traditional', a fully 'integrated', and a 'modified' role 'which gave women much wider duties than previously, but also took account of differences between the sexes . . . nearly half favoured a "modified" role; neither of the two extremes received majority endorsement, though there was a bias towards the "integrated" role' (Southgate 1981: 163). When asked to judge their own ability to deal with various police tasks as compared with male officers, 85 per cent or more felt they were 'better' or 'the same' at most tasks (1981: 164) and that they could cope better with traditional cases, such as child abuse. On the whole, however, Southgate found 'no majority support for a complete return to a social work role for policewomen . . . general police work was a far more popular option' (1981: 165).

Bryant and her colleagues surveyed WPCs in two provincial forces in order 'to examine the causes of the high turnover rate for female police officers' (1985: 237). They explicitly used Martin's formula in their analysis and conclude 'that many policewomen choose something approaching the (POLICEwoman) behaviour. *This is certainly the case amongst the leavers.* However . . . some of those who have become disenchanted with the work, for one reason or another, adopt something of the policeWOMAN's role (1985: 240). But the example they give is about social work rather than frivolous femininity (1985: 240–1). They do acknowledge the power of the occupational culture in forming policewomen's roles and quote one officer: 'policewomen must be prepared to be "one of the boys". There is no priggishness or being a "prude". However, this has to be balanced against not denying that you are a woman and not appearing "butch"' (1985: 240). This paper suggests that POLICEwomen may leave the service because they are frustrated by lack of opportunities, whereas Martin suggests that they are the ones who stay because they are ambitious and career-minded.

In her study, Sandra Jones aimed to explore the impact of the Sex Discrimination Act on the role of women in policing. She interviewed forty male and female officers and surveyed 354 by questionnaire in a single force. She describes in great detail the existence of a series of

beliefs and attitudes which underpin the way in which the policewoman's role is shaped within the organization. . . . What has become clear through this process is just how widespread and strongly held many of these attitudes are among both older and younger male officers, and often in the face of contrary evidence. (1986: 161)

Jones explores the copious rationalizations—she calls them 'ritual arguments'—given by male officers against women's full participation in policing and, interestingly, notes the counter-arguments held by the women, even though a minority sought a 'modified' role (in Southgate's terms) (1986: 160). She links her findings with Martin's continuum:

Many of the women interviewed for this study displayed these types of role adaptations to a lesser or greater degree . . . this is to some extent related to time of joining the service. Those 'traditional' women who most regretted the demise of the policewomen's departments . . . were more likely to display predominantly policeWOMAN characteristics. (1986: 172)

Within this group, who had joined the force before 1975, were a few POLICEwomen and they had *all* left the policewomen's department for other specialist work, such as the CID. It was younger women among whom 'POLICEwomen adaptations were more in evidence' (1986: 173) and while this made these women more similar to their male colleagues it was achieved at enormous personal cost.

Several small-scale US studies explore some of these issues and shed a little light on them. Wexler (1985) interviewed twenty-five women and observed their work. She proposes 'four role styles (of) dealing with male colleagues, neutral-impersonal, feminine, semi-masculine and mixed' (1985: 170). It is very noteworthy that 'the limited range of behaviours implicit to those styles with male colleagues *was not apparent in situations with other people* (i.e. victims, suspects, female colleagues)' (ibid.). Most (eleven) were 'neutral' and eight were 'semimasculine'. Wexler suggests that the 'neutral' style is innovatory both for men and for women; it was 'implicitly challenging the traditional views of women and of the masculine nature of policing' (1985: 754).

Kay Lord's larger sample study of 125 male and female officers gave some support to the notion that occupational culture is more significant than gender in the formation of attitudes since 'male and female officers' perceptions of women police officers were more alike than they were different' (1986: 89). Lester *et al.* compared thirty-three female state police recruits with thirty-one female college students. Using the Bem androgyny scale, they found the recruits to be more 'masculine' than the students but this was 'added on' to their femininity: 'female recruits appear to add masculine traits without losing any of the feminine traits' (1982: 359). At the same, their profiles were similar to male state police recruits on a measure of personal preference (1982: 360). The latter's femininity is not recorded. In seeking to establish how 'traditional' or otherwise women in various professions were, Kennedy and Homant found that their forty-four policewomen were significantly different from nurses on femininity and scored high on modernity. Their femininity scores were only slightly closer to nurses than to policemen (1981).

Policewomen's personalities remain elusive. Popular documentation and even fiction probably present fuller portraits. Most of this research turns out to be how policewomen adapt to policemen. It is by no means clear that results of US research, in itself very localized and surprisingly small scale, can be readily extrapolated to the British scene. Indeed, it may be that US researchers caught a snapshot picture of forces in flux rather than painting a serious portrait. The female 'nightwatch' still await their Rembrandt.

Performance

In the 1970s a flurry of research evaluating female police performance occurred in the USA. Within a few years, an almost barren picture of little or no studies which either included or acknowledged women's role in policing was transformed. I have located eleven of these and others are referred to in the literature. Their results are among the most widely quoted in all of modern police research (Horne 1985; S. Jones 1986; M. Young 1991; Steel and Lovrich 1987; Homant 1983): 'that women can perform the duties traditionally assigned to men and as effectively as the men. They also indicate that men are in no more danger with women as partners than with men as partners' (Feinman 1986: 95). They were for the most part prompted by policy changes and one because, according to Horne, 'the department set out to prove that women do not perform the job of general patrol as well as men' (1980: 104). Evidence from these reports has been used in court cases in the USA (ibid.) involving sex discrimination. For few pieces of social research could it be claimed that they were used so effectively in policy-making as these studies. In the words of the President of the US Police Foundation, 'Police Foundation research on women in policing in the early 1970s, along with changes in federal civil rights legislation and emerging case law, made a pivotal contribution to policing' (H. Williams 1989).

These reports have, then, a widespread and widely accepted status as 'facts' both in the USA and Britain. At least one writer on the topic regards the subject as closed:

Before 1972 there has been no study or experimentation concerning policewomen on patrol. Since then numerous studies have been conducted. . . . Hopefully, researchers will not waste any more time and money answering the question of 'can policewomen successfully perform patrol duty?' The answer to that question is clear and obvious. The results are in, and the facts are there. Policewomen can do the job on patrol. (Horne 1980: 105)

Yet, as the next two sections will show, despite this mass of 'facts', inequality persists, and it is recognized as a problem in both the USA and Britain (Heidensohn 1989b: Adler 1990). Further, one of the most robust features of the masculine police culture is its antipathy to the integration of women police in spite of such clear evidence of their achievements (Fielding 1988). At least one piece of research suggests that male officers' attitudes polarized when they worked with females; this was possibly due to generalizing attitudes from one female patrol officer 'to all other female officers' (Vega and Silverman 1982: 38). The answer may, then, be clear and obvious, but it has not been heeded by some of those to whom it might have most significance. Before I go on to discuss aspects of that situation which are indicated in research, I want to outline the key features of the evaluation studies and of the criticisms which have been made of them.

To begin with, it is important to remember some salient points. All these projects involved direct evaluation of women officers and comparison with male officers. Such direct appraisal of police effectiveness is most unusual (Audit Commission 1990). It is, for one thing, very hard to achieve consensus on indicators to measure. Indirect assessment of effectiveness, through the use of crime rates, clear-up rates, surveys of public attitudes, are much more commonplace (Kinsey *et al.* 1986). In recent years techniques of assessing effective policing in financial terms have become feasible because of computerization, and popular because of budgetary constraints (Johnson *et al.* 1981: 391–2; Audit Commission 1990: 12–13). In 1981, for instance, Johnson *et al.* could confess of the USA, 'After nearly a decade of police-community relations efforts, we may have a national inventory of programs, but we have very little in the way of properly evaluated programs' (1981: 391). An article which reviews eleven community crime-prevention evaluations and lists all their outcome measurement indicators shows that a range of proxy measures, such as crime rates and citizen satisfaction rates, were used, as well as vague ones such as 'social disorder' (Yin 1986: 299, Table 14.2)

Next, it should not be forgotten that the evaluations are overwhelmingly of patrol work and its close cousins in highway patrol. This is not untypical of much police research which has, unsurprisingly, focused on the visible, accessible aspects of police work. It does make some caution necessary, however, in that patrol is not the only kind of police activity; it is merely the only one where female performance was measured in this way. These studies are sometimes referred to as a series, but they are not a series in the sense that the World Series is, that is, they were not planned or co-ordinated in any way and did not share a common methodology, and while their purpose was to deal with police issues, the aims were by no means all the same.

In their assessment of these reports Morash and Greene (1986) list nine:

> Pennsylvania State Police Department (1974)
> Washington, DC (Bloch and Anderson 1974)
> St Louis (Sherman 1975)
> California Highway Patrol (1976)
> Denver (Bartlett and Rosenblum 1977)
> Newton, Mass. (Kizziah and Morris 1977)
> New York City (Sichel *et al.* 1977)
> Philadelphia (Bartell Associates, Phase I, Phase II, 1978).

In addition there is El Monte, California (Snortum and Beyers, 1983). (Sulton and Townsey (1981: 13–16) include a summary of eight of these.) Of these, the first, the best known, most compre-

hensive, and widely cited is Bloch and Anderson's (1974) comparison of eighty-six new patrolmen and eighty-six new patrolwomen
in Washington, DC, which found few differences in their actions.
Women made fewer arrests and issued fewer traffic 'tickets'. The
opposite finding occurred in St Louis, where women issued more
traffic notices. There were numerous other findings of slight gender
differences, e.g. women shoot less accurately (St Louis,
Washington, DC, New York), men had more complaints from the
public (Denver), New York citizens rated women as 'more competent, pleasant and respectful' than men; women in Philadelphia
were assaulted more often when making arrests. It is possible to go
on listing such minor differences, however some of the most
notable were not to do with policing but with its organization and
ethos. Thus the Pennsylvania study found supervisors 'reluctant to
assign female troopers to potentially dangerous situations and mid-
night patrol with male troopers' (Sulton and Townsey 1981: 15). In
Newton, Mass., 'Women performed better than men in certain
areas' but were affected by negative male attitudes (ibid.).
However, each study (with the possible exception of Philadelphia,
Phase II) finds 'some gender differences, but reaches a final conclusion that female and male officers are equally capable' (Morash
and Greene 1986: 231).

Morash and Greene in their paper go on to evaluate the evaluations. They question the fundamental premises of such research
on sex difference. It tends to focus on male-related variables and
on stereotypical and unproven links, e.g. that men are strong,
women emotional; gender is usually taken to be innate and
immutable, and finally differences within the same sex are glossed
over while differences between the sexes may be exaggerated. All
these have pertinence for the studies under current review as does
the separate one that policing is hard to evaluate (1986: 232–3).
They are very critical of many aspects of all the studies. Each item
on each study was rated by nine evaluators and the findings are
curious: they are heavily (male-)stereotyped, they do not reflect the
balance of real-life policing. Thus 35.7 per cent of the St Louis performance measures involved use of weapons and 43.9 per cent in
New York involved physical exertion (1986: 240). On the other
hand, paperwork was 'deemphasized by the choice of items' (1986:
242). They challenge particularly the picture of policing in these
studies. The impression is given

that actual and potential violence pervades the police work environment . . .
The presentation of a violence-laden police work environment is objection-
able on three related grounds. First it under-represents the bulk of police
work, which is associated with nonviolent and service activities. Second, it
compares women and men on an artificial standard—the ability to deal
with constant violent and confrontive behavior. Third, and most appropriate to our analysis, it lends credence to the idea that the underlying dimension to many of the evaluation items is conformity with the masculine
values of dealing with danger, a hostile citizenry, aggressiveness in action,
and physical powers. (1986: 243–5)

These authors do not take up some points made by other critics.
For example that some of the data is thin because few observations
were made, or that the women recruits were over five feet seven
inches tall (Washington, DC, study, Snortum and Beyers 1983:
37–8). Several studies covered only small numbers, e.g. only sixteen
males and sixteen females in St Louis, did not match them
(California), and suffered from certain observer effects (New York
and Washington).

   These studies represent the most concentrated effort so far
focused on women in policing. It is clear that these projects had
short-term, pragmatic goals and that their assumptions and
methodology can be queried. Inevitably, this throws doubt on the
validity and reliability of their findings. This is, however, not the
same as saying that these are disproved and that their general conclusion, that women are as capable as men at policing, does not
hold. If anything, Morash and Greene's analysis suggests that it
was quite remarkable that women stood up as well as they did to
the comparisons, given the many biases built into these studies.

   It is also salutary to end this section with echoes of two issues
raised at the beginning. First, this was in no way a national series,
rather a set of local, disparate projects. Where valid comparisons
are possible between departments, results might be rather astonish-
ing. They also include, particularly in the Washington, DC,
reports, was well as copious tables, a rich vein of anecdotal and
first-person reports which are amongst the first and the few in
which women police found their own voice. Snortum and Beyers
(1983) found a very marked difference in levels of policing activity
between Washington, DC, and El Monte with the latter having,
apparently, a much more hectic regime, with which women kept
pace. They conclude:

if we treated our findings in concrete terms, we might be drawn to conclude that EMPD policewomen can work circles around Washington DC
men. The safer generalization is that local work rates strongly affect local
performance. (1982: 42)

Finally it is necessary to stress that the findings of these studies are
now officially accepted as valid and US and British police pursue
equal-opportunities policies partly at least because of that.

Attitudes

There is one theme common to nearly all this research, that despite
the research findings outlined above, despite two decades of integrated policing, attitudes of male officers to women police continue
to be hostile and form the main impediment to their progress.

The limited progress made by women in law enforcement is a result in
part, of continued covert and overt resistance by their male colleagues.
(Feinman 1986: 92)

The traditional police attitude about the 'inherently' masculine nature of
law enforcement makes the prospect of having a female partner or
coworker particularly offensive to some male officers. (Kay Lord 1986: 85)

A substantial number of male officers have strongly impeded and resisted
women in law enforcement. (Horne 1980: 74).

Such views are not confined to North America:

it is the group values of the men that have the greatest effect on the
women in the Force. What women police officers say is amply confirmed
by our observations of the way in which they are treated. (Smith and Gray
1983: 374)

the behaviour 'prescribed' by the equal opportunities legislation is not
reflected in the attitudes of the majority of policemen and that, in reality,
informal practices which more closely follow those attitudes have a major
impact on the working lives of policewomen. (S. Jones 1986: 163)

The resistance to change means that the integration of women into the
police preserves challenges the status of male structures which are built on
a belief in and the prestige of 'real polices's' work. (M. Young 1991: 203)

There is very extensive documentation, which I have already discussed, of the strength and persistence of the occupational culture
of policing and its powerfully masculine character. This seems to
be at the core of the hostile attitudes recorded above and their

effects. Remmington, in her anthropological account of Atlanta, depicts the situation in innumerable vignettes and quotations and also analyses it.

the women's lack of impact in policing appears to be the result of two somewhat contradicting factors. The women have not affected the males' self image or police–public relations because they have not been accepted as true police officers . . . they have been acculturated into the group's behavioral and attitudinal patterns (but) . . . because they are not regarded as equals, the police group maintains its social isolation. (Remmington 1981: 187)

Theories about the origin of police cultures and their links to job characteristics or social environment were outlined above. Even if these can provide necessary and sufficient aetiological reasons for its formation, they do not explain the specific features of the reactions to women. Such theories are implicitly, at least, functionalist. They assume a fit between cop culture and the requirements of the police role. Yet, as Remmington so graphically describes, in Atlanta the policing culture was highly destructive: police did not police. It can be argued that these cultures, in so far as they alienate the agents of change, which women and members of minorities were once hoped to be, damage forces and alienate citizens.

Several research studies have documented male officers' values and attitudes as well as observing them in action. Jones's survey produced a great deal of information on all aspects of these attitudes; she found that there were two basic aspects to antipathy towards women, that policing is unfeminine, and that training women is uneconomic. She carefully points out the lack of validity of both views (S. Jones 1986: 132–7), but this, from other research, and from Jones's own view, since she calls these 'ritual constraints', seems not to be the point. Charles, in an observational and questionnaire study of a mixed class of recruits at the Michigan Police Academy, found male recruits denying the evidence of their own eyes.

As training progressed some male recruits denied the value of women in policing with increasing fervor, despite the fact that women are subjected to similar training methods and curriculum and pass these criteria in accord with pre-established requirements. (Charles 1981: 219)

Jones's study showed no great difference in attitudes between younger, more 'modern' recruits' attitudes and those of their older colleagues. Similar results are reported by Fielding (1988) and Vega and Silverman (1982) in Tampa, Florida, although the latter did observe that college education had a liberalizing impact on values, which were more negative than the women's own views of their competence.

There are many limitations to these studies. The most obvious is that while they offer graphic descriptions of prejudice and harassment they cannot account for the power of what are essentially myths. There are myths about policewomen, but they are derived myths. It is the myths *about the nature of policing which are critical*, as Jones (1986: 159), for example, makes clear. Violence and crime appear to be aspects of policing whose importance in policing is exaggerated, and this is used in turn to deny a role and legitimacy to women. This does seem to be a topic which should be more firmly on the research agenda. It is one of those where, arguably, it is men who are the true prisoners of gender. They it is who, in significant numbers, have joined an occupation believing, or in which they come to believe, that strength, size, and force are vital, only to find that this is not so. Much police research (Punch 1979 and 1983; Remmington 1981) describes varieties of police deviance and police boredom. Prisoners of gender have to pay their dues as do those who are in penitentiaries or who are guests of Her Majesty. I think there would be merit in exploring an idea which I derive from the accounts which policewomen gave me and which fits with the literature. That is that it is social control and social order at their deepest levels which male officers lay claim to and feel that they own. It is a profoundly gender-linked concept at all levels from informal family settings to governments of nation states. Females can be granted franchises on it, so to speak, but it is harder for them to challenge the core concept. It seems to be control over other males, where strength and size are so important apparently, that is least likely to be ceded. Yet one of the reasons why the history of women in policing began was because some women thought they could police their own sex. In doing so they found themselves drawn to the control of men as well. If traditional ways of policing had been overwhelmingly successful, there would never have been a challenge to their dominance.

In considerable contrast to these accounts, several studies report citizen satisfaction with policewomen as reported in the performance studies above. Winnand (1986) found that citizens were sophisticated and expressed preferences for strong male officers to handle violence cases and females to deal with rape. Shapland and Vagg report that 'Women officers and young officers only a short time in the service were as, or more, effective than the more mature men often pictured as ideal for such posts' (1988: 148). (This was in tasks where handling problems was crucial.)

Just one article from the material under review asks a challenging question, which any observer of the police might pose: are males suited to police patrol work? (Van Wormer 1981). Perhaps with her tongue in her cheek, she observes, 'One finds not a single article . . . with the title "Should Males be Placed in Patrol Work?" or "Are Males Doing a Good Job?"' (1981). She notes that men will be stronger than women, have supportive wives, and relevant military experience. On the other hand, there are six disadvantages with males: (1) they provoke more retaliatory violence; (2) they have poor Public Relations and social skills; (3) they are more brutal; (4) they do not accept female colleagues; (5) they overprotect women; (6) they have poorer educational records. Van Wormer's article is not perhaps a wholly serious one, but in asking an interesting but avoided question she has raised a more crucial issue than many more profound pieces do.

Equal Opportunities

The three areas of research which I have covered so far all relate in some way to policing. That is they explore whether women adopt different policing styles, what the impact of police culture upon them is, how effectively they patrol. There is a fourth category, to which a number of writers have contributed, which has as its main focus the implementation of laws relating to equality in both the USA and Britain. Almost all the recent British studies fit into this group. Strictly speaking, such work could be categorized as equal-rights or policy implementation research, but these are primarily concerned with the impact on police forces and on the causes, for the most part, of the gap between aims and execution. A number of studies indicate considerable concern about these issues; these are almost all studies commissioned with policy purposes in mind. (I have already noted the policy-related nature of much police research.) It is perhaps therefore not surprising that certain initial problems present themselves with these studies.

A Fair Cop and Fairer Policing

My heading for this section of the chapter is equal opportunities, and this title, or some variation, occurs in several book and article titles (*Policewomen and Equality* (S. Jones 1986) 'Equal Employment Opportunity and Female Criminal Justice Employment' (Potts 1981), 'Equality and Efficiency Trade-Offs in Affirmative Action' (Steel and Lovrich 1987)). Yet definitions and discussions of what equality means in policing are scarce; the respective legal frameworks, the Sex Discrimination Act 1975 for Britain, and Title VII of the Civil Rights Act, etc., are seen as the measure and the goal of what should be achieved. These are for the most part interpreted in terms of the *numbers* of women in policing, their attainment of higher ranks and of specialist positions (S. Jones 1986; Martin 1989). Less tangibly, reports of women's own histories of exclusion, harassment, and isolation are cited as evidence of policies on integration failing to work (Remmington 1981; Bryant *et al.* 1985). Yet what, for example, constitutes a good outcome in terms of numbers of women in a police service? I have described (Heidensohn 1989*b*) how the New York City Police Department were pleased with a figure of 11.3 per cent female officers and Adler (1990) commends US affirmative action programmes to British police forces even though the former had achieved under 9 per cent female presence by 1986 (NB this is almost certainly an overestimate of the national figure, given the way in which US departments are sampled. See Heidensohn (1989*b*) for a note on the low figures in small, and rural, departments).

Just what these policies may mean for modern policing can be interpreted in many different ways. Often they are presented in several ways in a single policy statement or research project. A joint report from the Metropolitan Police and the Equal Opportunities Commission is prefaced thus by the Commissioner: 'Equal opportunities is about equal consideration based on merit, fitness and capability; full opportunity and fair treatment for all. This not only affects employment practices but also our delivery of service to our customers—the public' (1990). There are at least six which are touched on the literature or elsewhere:

1. Keeping the law
2. Achieving a representative bureaucracy

3. Bringing a source of innovation and change into policy
4. 'Feminizing' policing
5. Undermining police tradition and 'proper policing'
6. Increasing opportunities for individual women and for women

1. Keeping the Law

Discrimination on the grounds of sex or of race is illegal in both the USA and the UK; this legislation applies to the police and they are therefore required to obey it. As S. Jones points out, while this is true for all social institutions affected,

what makes the police service unique is the . . . trust placed in the police to discharge their law enforcement responsibilities. It is justifiably argued that this carries with it certain moral obligations . . . one might expect the police themselves to be an exemplary role model for other organizations within society. (1986: 163)

This is a strand in some of the projects, although what is perhaps more noteworthy are the debates in Britain about exempting the police from the Sex Discrimination Act and the way in which such debates continued in various forms in which, *inter alia*, research projects are involved or invoked as part of the process (Southgate 1981). It is by no means unusual for police, especially through their representatives, to criticize and debate legislation (Reiner 1985). They are not usually, however, advocates of non-compliance with law.

2. Representative Bureaucracy

There have long been discussions about whether those who enter public service should be selected as representing the public from whom they are drawn and will have to serve, or on merit or other criteria. This is a much more live issue in the USA where far more public offices are subject to election. It has gained added resonance since the 1960s and the rise of racial divisions as preoccupations in both nations. For the police it has become a central concern because of the loss of legitimacy in the black community which they have sustained. Here there is a sharp difference between Britain and the USA. Men from ethnic minorities were 21 per cent of all male officers in the USA in 1986 and 40 per cent of all female officers (Martin 1989). In Britain the figure was 1.035 per cent (Home Office 1990). In some departments, Washington, DC, for example, black officers constitute a majority, as black people do in that city's population. Thus US police forces are more representative of that country's ethnic minority population, while British ones reflect the country's female majority composition less well and its black population scarcely at all.

3. Innovation and Change

Many commentators, especially in earlier reports, claimed that women officers would be a force for change in the conservative police structure. This seems to be based on the two ideas that integrating women was in itself a revolutionary step (Bahn 1984) and that women who chose policing as a career would be modern and innovative (Kennedy and Homant 1981).

4. Feminizing the Police

Ironically, perhaps, an argument sometimes proffered in relation to equal-employment opportunities in policing for women has to do with their supposed differences from men. Either they should be recruited because they have unique or superior abilities, such as interpersonal skills, which the police are in particular need of today (Smith and Gray 1983; Southgate and Ekblom 1984) or policewomen are seen to be the solution to the crises of modern policing. In particular, crimes such as rape, domestic violence, and child sex abuse have moved up the political agenda and are perceived as requiring higher recruitment levels of women officers (PACE in Britain does have that effect (Metropolitan Police and Equal Opportunities Commission 1990)).

5. Loss of Tradition

There is no doubt that these policies met enormous resistance from inside the police. While much of this was expressed in public debate, research has sometimes been used to attempt to justify not implementing equal-opportunities policies (Morash and Greene 1986). Larger questions about research are raised about this issue: 'equal rights' has to some degree in some US departments become a proxy for all kinds of discontents. Remmington's portrait of Atlanta illustrates this all too clearly (1981).

6. Opportunities for Women

The political starting-points for legislation in both countries lay in the political era of the 1960s when individualism flourished. Therefore progress in and into policing for women are ways of measuring the system's capacity to reform.

With all these choices possible, as well as various combinations open to them in focusing on equal opportunities, it is hardly surprising to find police and police researchers somewhat confused. What we find if we look at the main studies and reports is that they divide into distinct lists. On one lie a short series of historical accounts which describe in varying levels of detail the history of legislation and policy, and exhort or admonish the police to do better (Mishkin 1981; Potts 1981; Walker 1985; Bell 1982a). All of these outline policies and some of the legal cases. Only Walker attempts any kind of analysis of what he calls 'glacial change'. None report any original research, all rehearse some aspects of past history. In some part they seem to be contributing to the *legitimacy of the idea of women in policing*. The respectable antecedents of the history are meant in some way to alert readers to keep within the law. Some in particular over-stress the mark of affinity argument. 'Some have killed when they had no choice in the matter. Some [women] have been injured in the line of duty' (Mishkin 1981: 31).

Is It Working?

There is now quite a large volume of research aimed at finding out how forces managed as they implemented these policies. Some are substantial pieces of work, others much slighter and shorter. One very important point to register at once concerns data. Most authors of what I have called 'is it working?' research have pointed to the inadequacies of the basic information for monitoring whether the policies are working. No comprehensive statistics are regularly collected in the USA (PERF 1988). The Police Foundation has conducted two major surveys in order to get national data, although these are samples. Other data exist and yield valuable material. S. Jones (1986: 186) commented unfavourably on existing British statistics. There has been a slight improvement but the information could be both better produced and presented. It seems obvious that good statistical material should be essential as a minimum to monitor police performance.

British Studies

British research has been concentrated in this area and it is one in which, as I have already suggested, the outcomes are rather different from those found in the USA. There are also some slight advantages to research in Britain because there are fewer police forces and they cover much larger areas. Southgate (1981) surveyed the reactions of 680 women in five forces to the 1975 integration. His conclusions were fairly optimistic. Bryant *et al.* (1985) surveyed two forces and discerned a gloomier portrait in which policewomen were caught in a double bind: if they stayed on in the force, with or without children, they were regarded as unnatural; if they took a career break to raise a family they were wasting their training.

Wilkie's survey of the massive Strathclyde area in Scotland showed a very gloomy picture with women more demoralized than ever. Jones in her 'Medshire' study found, as did Smith and Gray, that the force applied an illegal quota on female recruitment. She also analysed those beliefs and practices which sustained this system. Her concept of 'equality' is clearly compliance with the law and she gives some attention to all six of the headings listed above. She does not say this, but the proper title of her book should be *Policemen and Inequality*, given her stark conclusions.

US Studies

Several US survey results show that women are not 'equal' in US policing because they are not hired in the same numbers and not promoted as easily (Hochstedler 1984; Townsey 1982). They also attempt to improve matters by suggesting, on the basis of the differences in achievement, what the most effective policies are. Hochstedler (1984) argues that there is conclusive evidence about having an affirmative action programme. She proposes what she describes as a 'feasible strategy for achieving affirmative action'. This involves:

1. Setting up a hiring quota
2. Setting high standards for recruitment
3. Applicants must not be 'ranked' in order
4. Choosing a combination of random selection and quotas for minorities

Townsey, who reviewed policies and practices (1982) for hiring black women, agrees. Steel and Lovrich have published articles based on national surveys. They also stress the value of affirmative action (Warner *et al*. 1989) and of having powerful female figures in local government as agents of change (Warner *et al*. 1989).

In sum, British and American experience is more convergent over women in policing than over race. The most successful US departments in attracting women achieve levels not seen here but they too have yet to make the quantum leap which Kanter considers crucial for establishment of a female stronghold in any organization. Much more is already being done in the USA to ensure that equal-opportunities policies are carried out.

Conclusions

Surveying the literature on women in policing I am struck by the idea that it already says quite a bit, but what it says is restricted to certain topics and certain voices. Most of the research has been done from a police perspective and/or a policy one, such as that of the Equal Opportunities Commission whose job is to monitor the Acts on Sex Discrimination and Equal Pay.

Innumerable questions remain unasked, let alone unanswered. In the next chapter I shall try to answer some of these and link with the wider output of police research of which this has not seemed a central area. Having experienced a stop-and-search procedure, it is now time to listen to some new voices.

4

Policewomen in Britain

ONE main purpose of the earlier chapters of this book was to set the scene for the characters whom I now wish to introduce, the female police officers interviewed for this study (further details of the methodology of this study are given in the Appendix). All my informants were serving or former police officers in England or the USA. The group was formed by means of a 'snowball' system of sampling and thus cannot be claimed to be a random selection. As I shall make clear, it was not my intention to seek a representative group in that way. Rather, I tried to give a voice to women who have, as will become clear, a great deal to say about police and policing, yet whose voices have been relatively muted.

Women's Voices, Women's Lives

It is a commonplace of a variety of feminist thought nowadays to say that women have lacked the opportunity to express themselves (Spender 1980). While language itself may be described as 'man made', specific constraints, such as poverty (Millar and Glendinning 1989), lack of education (Deem 1978), and the threat of violence (Hanmer *et al.* 1989) have all been indicted as particularly oppressive and silencing of women. It may seem therefore extremely odd even to suggest that women in the police, one of the more powerful agencies in modern society, are not able to be heard. There are, nevertheless, reasons for doing so.

First and rather obviously, women still form a fairly small minority in policing in the USA and Britain. Only in one or two US departments is their share approaching 20 per cent of sworn personnel, the average in both countries being nearer to 10 per cent. Moreover these officers are overwhelmingly in junior ranks, because they have in many cases only been recently recruited and because attrition rates are higher for women than for men (Martin 1989; S. Jones 1986). Secondly, for a number of reasons, women have felt less than welcome in the police. Even after integration, forces in Britain were alleged to be maintaining quotas for the entry of women: if so, these were, of course, illegal (S. Jones 1986; Metropolitan Police and Equal Opportunities Commission 1990). In the USA affirmative action programmes had to be pursued through the machinery of consent decrees, in a number of cases, in order to ensure the entry of women (Steel and Lovrich 1987). More profoundly, the strongly cohesive masculine ethos of policing has been widely cited as a barrier to the acceptance and the continuance of women in policing (see Chapter 3). Another effect has been that 'the police' are widely perceived to have heavily stereotyped views about women and their roles, outside as well as inside the service (Smith and Gray 1983; Siegel 1980). M. Young (1991) is only the most recent to recount, at great length, the range of abusive terms policemen use to describe their female colleagues, which, he assures us, the women often cheerfully accept. Categories in this culture are few and polar: policewomen are either dykes or sluts, it is not a rich and varied seam of folklore. It is hardly surprising, then, that women police have been careful about speaking out: stigmatizing labels are readily applied. Moreover, the macho culture still requires their loyalty. Lillian Wyles, one of the first female officers in London, wrote her memoirs in retirement and recorded the many slights and harassments she had received. She also recorded that, when she did have the chance to denounce in public Chief Inspector Collins in the Savidge Case inquiry, she did not do so because she recognized the demands of the occupational culture. The historian of British policewomen, Joan Lock, finds it 'curious . . . that while she appears to have lied for her colleagues at the tribunal . . . she chose to tell the truth (or agree with Miss Savidge's statements) in her book' (Lock 1979).

As the account given in Chapter 3 shows, policing research has, for the most part, taken one of three approaches to the role of women. In the first, women are completely ignored, even though the descriptions of the occupational culture are often replete with gendered explanations and terms. The second, much smaller category has almost exclusively appeared since the 1970s and is concerned with the effects of legal and policy changes made in those years. While performance studies remain exclusive to the USA, the broad categorization still applies. Finally there is a curious hybrid, research which is in practice about male officers but focuses exclusively, or as part of a wider project, on their attitudes to females. Even the studies which have women as their main focus (Horne 1980; Martin 1980; S. Jones 1986) contain extensive sections on the attitudes and behaviour of their male colleagues. More general 'post-feminist' analyses which feature sections on women cite far more male than female respondents in these pages (Fielding 1988; M. Young 1991; Johnson *et al.* 1981). In classifying these studies in this way, I do not wish to belittle them or to argue that they have not contributed to the discussions that I regard as important. On the contrary, as my use of them throughout this book makes clear, I value them and see them as an important part of the process of discovery, debate, and understanding, which I take to be the purpose of research.

The approaches to research from which one would expect the most in exploring women's roles in social control and law enforcement would thus seem to be the diverse group called 'feminist', that is those, whether radical or Marxist or liberal, which make women visible and central to the process of enquiry.

But, and it is quite a big but, the study of women as social-control agents does not fit as easily into the various feminist paradigms which have informed much modern research on women and from women's perspectives. However these paradigms are defined (Stanley and Wise 1983; Harding 1987; Daly and Chesney-Lind 1988; Smart 1990; Cain 1990), they generally have in common a radical, challenging approach to women's position in society. Women who are, in some way, 'part of the problem', who share, however meagrely, in the system of oppression are not, therefore, easily assimilated into feminist politics nor happily explained in the framework. Cain, for example, cites 'women who have positions as agents of social control' as an issue 'of particular professional concern' to her (1991). In spelling out this concern it becomes clear that she wants to ensure that women in such positions will use them on behalf of women and not oppressively. She does not here go into wider questions about their role. Indeed, these issues have made other feminists uneasy. I have already quoted the papers by Bland (1985) and Radford (1989), which deal with the formation of the first female volunteer forces in England and their plainly moral purity approach. That such concerns can seem anti-feminist by today's standards does not render them inauthentic, and to subdue the tones of those who expressed them is to be in danger of losing some part of that episode of women's history.

In Chapter 3 I discussed several studies of women in policing which might be described as feminist-empiricist in approach. Martin, for instance, aims to explore how women came into, and then dealt with, a modern American police department. Her title hints at a notion of deviance, even infraction, and the purpose of her book is to show how an occupation may be 'mastered' by women. However, she concludes by suggesting that it is the women who are mastered because their adaptations to their situation involve them in either losing their femininity or compromising their professional standards. What Martin (1980), Remmington (1981), Wexler (1985), and S. Jones (1986) all use or imply in their work is an equal-rights model for women; they assume that access to law-enforcement professions confers a benefit on women, and may well improve policing, which is neither a very successful social institution nor carries much feminine influence.

While my study develops themes raised by these earlier, pioneering works, it differs from them in several important ways. Most previous researchers (although not Southgate 1981 or Bryant et al. 1985) concentrated on a single force or department or, in Martin's case, one division in Washington, DC. I chose to try to make international comparisons between Britain and the USA for a number of reasons. First, as I illustrated earlier, both British and US 'new' police and women's entry into policing shared common, albeit different, roots. Yet the extensive discussions of the former pay little or no attention to the latter, although it seems at least probable that some of the debates about, for example, the acceptance of the new police, or the 'colonial' nature of some aspects of the police model, would be illuminated by such comparative consideration. Secondly, the history of women's role in law enforcement has marched broadly in step in both nations, except that the early British history is seen as having been more advanced (Sherman 1977), while the USA is perceived as being more progressive in recent times (Adler 1990). Such views are somewhat over-simplified (Heidensohn 1989b), but there is merit in contrasting the differing developments in the two systems, given their shared origins and the long-established pattern of exchanges of ideas and policies.

The choice of a variety of US departments was deliberate since all evidence suggests that there is considerable diversity in policing there and also in external factors which have had particular impact on the appointment of female officers. In my own earlier report (1989*b*), I was able to confirm the findings of Steel and Lovrich (1987) that departments in the south of the USA had had higher rates of recruitment than those in the north-east because they had expanded in the 1970s and 1980s when equal-opportunities policies were being pursued, and when these cities were enjoying a boom, unlike the north-east, which was in decline. Although in Britain there has been a tradition and a theory of local autonomy and, in particular, scope for considerable discretion on the part of the Chief Constable (Reiner 1991), in practice, central control has been considerable and local political influences far more limited than in the USA (McKenzie and Gallagher 1989). (The Metropolitan Police are, of course, a special case.) Interviewing officers whose local experiences might well differ gave an important, and relatively novel, dimension to the project, enabling comparison over a wide range of aspects. International comparisons give an added and, as far as I know, unique angle to this.

There are other points of substance too. In the status which the academic world and its professional and policy consumers attach to research, international comparative studies rank high (Stenson and Cowell (eds.) 1991). Small-scale, local projects have a much slighter cachet. Feminist scholars have often preferred the latter, mostly for epistemological reasons, but sometimes, too, for practical ones. In this study, I have sought to give the importance I believe the topic deserves by internationalizing it, while attempting to retain all the advantages of face-to-face interviews by the same person. Comparative criminology is coming at last into its own; I have urged elsewhere the importance of relating British experience to European (Heidensohn 1991*a*) and noted how, sometimes misleadingly, America is the only nation with which comparisons are made. While it is vital to develop the European side of comparative criminology, the USA is still a key part of any such analysis. It is the largest and most advanced western democracy and it also has extremely high crime rates, uses imprisonment heavily, and is thus seen as a 'forerunner' for many other countries. In the present case, the comparison is appropriate because of the links between the two systems, and the discourse which has developed in studies of policing which have, so far, largely excluded women's contributions. Fielding, in a note to an article using field-work material comparatively, has argued that in order to justify the view that 'the similarities implied by the term "Anglo-American policing" are more important than the differences . . . one must specify whether the aspect of policing one is examining is illuminated or obscured by this stance' (1988: 62). I hope to show that both light and lustre are thrown on this subject by this comparison.

Experiencing Interviews on Experience

The form and the process of interviewing in social research has come under considerable challenge in modern methodological literature. In his text on field research, Burgess notes, 'there is a considerable difference, between the interviews that are discussed in standard methodology texts . . . and the practice of interviewing' (1984: 101). The accounts which he quotes of 'different' interviews are of the unstructured type and many of the cited criticisms of objective and involved interviewing styles are from feminist writings (Oakley 1981; Finch 1984). Oakley described in her article a style of interviewing which involved her in close relationships, in some cases after the end of the project, with the women she interviewed. She also insisted that her own experience of motherhood enabled greater rapport to be established between her and the mothers in her survey. Finch also suggested that being a woman interviewer meant that the young mothers in her study of playgroups told her things they would never have raised with a man. It has become almost a cliché of feminist methodology that a reflexive, interactive style of interviewing is the only appropriate one to use (Roberts 1981; Bowles and Duelli Klein 1983). Indeed, Caroline Ramazanoglu has been highly critical of her own early, pre-feminist and male-standpoint research on shiftworkers in the 1960s:

the women generally saw the interview situation as an unequal one in which I had control. . . . There was no way that good interview rapport or a trusting relationship could be established when I was identified in this way and expected to reveal as little as possible about my self and my intentions. (1989 431)

Prescriptions about what constitutes an appropriate methodological paradigm are harder to establish than are the flaws in the old ones. Ramazanoglu attributes these difficulties to 'fundamental problems in the sociology of knowledge . . . Feminist sociologists are largely agreed on criticisms of the sexism of social science . . . the differences between them emerge however, in methodological innovation, in attempts to provide improved knowledge of social life' (1989: 432). Lorraine Gelsthorpe, on the other hand, in a discussion of these issues in relation to criminology, focuses on more practical, less radical concerns. It is not always feasible to share control of research between researchers and 'the researched' 'women who participate in other women's research [do not] . . . necessarily share their politics' (Gelsthorpe 1990: 92). In studying this literature one becomes aware of a formidable mass of warning signs about directions not to take and a set of directions which it might not be possible to follow. In constructing my own approach I tried to be as aware as possible of the strictures of fellow researchers while selecting the most attractive solutions from the work of others and, to some extent, improvising my own.

In accounting for my particular approaches I think there are four questions to which I need to respond: who controlled the research? Who set the agenda for the interviews? What were the settings and procedures? To all of them I can reply at a fairly simple level, but a fair account has to include indications of considerable negotiations and of shared work and also to conclude with some observations on research in a post-feminist world.

Who Controlled the Research?

The straightforward answer is that I did; it was my idea, clearly prompted by reading, debate, and interest in areas outlined above; I initiated it and planned it. The Police Foundation did provide me with funds to finance part of my visit to the USA and in return I wrote a report for them (1989*b*) on equal opportunities in USA policing. They specified requirements but did not edit or control my findings. This project was arranged only after the main plans had been made. However, co-operation from other key people was crucial and it quickly became clear that it was not hard to obtain co-operation from those whom I wanted to interview because the theme of the project touched a chord. Once I had sought and gained initial support and advice, other contacts were quite easily established. There were, however, significant differences between

Britain and the USA. In Britain my links were from one officer to one, at most two, other officers. In the USA, a series of key informants not only provided me with a great deal of help and advice, and told me about their careers, they also established links with other policewomen in their own area. As a result, they had considerable impact on the conduct of the study.

Who Set the Agenda?

Again, the answer is that I set the agenda (the informal interview *aide-mémoire* is in the Appendix). Nevertheless, there was considerable exchange and interaction between the women and me, some of which caused me to alter my approach in later encounters. As will become clear, *I derived the concepts which I have applied* to the lives of these women from what they told me. There was also, as Oakley describes, a considerable amount of interaction and responsive questioning, especially in the US departments. Thus questions were frequently raised about policewomen's uniforms in Britain: 'do they really wear skirts?' and the unarmed state of most British officers.

It is perhaps worth outlining here some points about my own status as they affected my role in the research (I have discussed these more fully elsewhere.) I am not, and never have been, a police officer. Indeed I do not conform even to today's more relaxed qualifications for entry as I am only five feet tall and far from athletic in build. In Britain I had the impression that my position, as an academic in a university department, was quite clear and not confusing (a relative of one officer had studied sociology and had read one of my books). In the USA, on the other hand, it was assumed on several occasions that I was a serving or former officer, and despite my explanations I was still treated as an informed respondent. What struck me most about negotiating my own role as interviewer and explaining my interest in them and their world were two things: the shared assumptions about women and the desire to express themselves. It became rapidly clear to me that I was conducting research in a post-feminist world. As two Australian sociologists put it, 'it would be plausible to propose that gendered subjectivities have assumed far greater salience for both sexes since the establishment of the women's movement' (Emmison and Western 1990: 244). This certainly proved to be the case here.

While the women whom I interviewed did not by any means give *the same* meaning to such notions of feminism, equal opportunities, sexism, etc., *they obviously recognized* such ideas and related them to their own experience, that of their colleagues, and to wider issues in the contemporary world. They thus readily identified and accepted the area which I wished to study and their own place in it. They also used and understood ideas such as the links between the public and the private and that 'politics is personal'. One of the more reserved of the senior British officers, for instance, made a point of stressing her single status and its consequences for her at a key stage in her career.

I was never home. I was constantly washing and packing and going. The male officers were of course, with their support service at home, always ready, you know they used to dump the laundry and pick up the clean and they were away, whereas I had to run my home, make sure that when I was away in the winter diabolical things didn't happen.

This is, I think, an important change which affects research on women, and indeed must affect all research. My own experience of empirical research more than twenty years earlier began in a pre-modern feminist era when the notion of studying women was itself puzzling and problematic (Heidensohn 1968, 1985) and, of course, theoretical constructs as well as defining categories were missing. We now, certainly as far as the advanced western countries are concerned, inhabit a knowing world. Women know they are interesting and they are interested in themselves.

It would be conceited if feminist social scientists or activists were to take total credit for this situation. While initial ideas and action may stem from them, mass media appear to be very much responsible for disseminating many ideas about contemporary women. The US crime series *Cagney and Lacey* about two female detectives in the New York City Police Department served as an instantly recognizable image of modern female officers and their lives. I asked American police how realistic the series was. While most women responded by agreeing with a Boston officer who said, 'that precinct is too busy, nowhere's that exciting even in New York,' they recognized its validity in tackling issues such as sexual harassment and discrimination.

Settings and Procedures

Interviews took place in almost every kind of setting; some were of my choosing, but many were selected by the interviewee herself. In Britain, where possible, I went to the woman's home and interviewed her there. Some interviews took place in the officer's own office and one in my home. All these were as requested by the women themselves. In the USA there were again variations with several taking place on police premises. It was very obvious on two occasions that the women officers were delighted at the opportunity which the event afforded them to claim some space for themselves in this way. In the USA there were several group interviews. These were set up by the women themselves and on all but one occasion there were convivial and celebratory aspects to the activities. I am quite sure that the participants enjoyed the events; they certainly told me that they did. This was not purely social either. In fact, not all of them knew each other well socially. The chance to compare histories, or reinforce each others' accounts was obviously valued, even though contributions varied in length. One aspect of the celebratory nature of the interviews was that twice a kind of party was set up, for which the officers had prepared food and brought drinks. All the interviews were taped (I asked permission to do this). I found it significant that interviewees themselves noticed the tape running out and helped to change it.

Perhaps I have in this account described the seduction or incorporation of a naïve researcher. Students of the police can be particularly prone to this disorder; Punch has graphically described how his assiduous ethnography in an Amsterdam police station failed to reveal extensive police corruption (Punch 1985) yet what the interviewees revealed to me was not flattering to the police and sometimes not to themselves. Some of what they shared had to do with dealing with difficult situations which could not be publicly acknowledged. One talked of extensive corruption in the USA, an officer in Britain described the shock there at the revelations of high-level corruption in the Metropolitan Police. Some may have set out to charm me; if so I think their efforts were because they and I were women and not because they were police officers. In short, while this was my project, I began it and it remains my own; it also became a shared endeavour with those whom I interviewed. My best evidence for this is the number of times that I have been asked when the book will be ready.

Concepts in a Career: A Career in Concepts

I have already alluded to some of the pitfalls encountered by others in conducting interviews with women. I now want to turn to some helpful perspectives which crystallize the approaches I took. Marjorie Devault has described in detail how she studied the talk of what she calls 'muted groups' of women on the subject of food and family meals and found that 'respondents spoke easily and naturally' and that from these discussions she was able to construct the topics of her research (1990: 99). As I indicated above, some of my US interviews were with *groups* of women. Initially I simply accepted this as a necessary hazard of planning research from across the Atlantic and hoped that it would enable more women to be involved. In practice it turned out to be much more valuable than I had expected. Several studies have pointed to the benefits of group interviews/discussions (Lees 1986; Frazer 1988). One of the simplest is that the women give *each other* their account, as well as the interviewer. Only an elaborate and colossal conspiracy could ensure these being organized and planned to coincide and be concealing rather than revealing. Most important, however, was the way in which concepts which focused and highlighted common aspects of their careers were developed and explored in the discussions. This process had already begun in England, but was undoubtedly aided by the group sessions. Like Frazer, I found that these women exhibited what she calls 'communicative competence' (1988: 357), and were also able to handle ambiguity. Thus while on the whole accepting the role of the police in society, they at the same time often questioned it, especially as it affected them.

What emerged from the interviews, and was confirmed and developed as I read, reread, and analysed the transcripts, was a set of soft, pliable concepts which could helpfully be used to focus on aspects of these women's life histories. While these are firstly and basically organizing ideas, designed to clarify and simplify situations, they can be used, I believe, analytically to help to explore certain key questions. For instance, whether gender or occupational culture is the most important factor influencing how effective women are in policing. In deriving these concepts, I have compared what my informants told me with other research findings and also with the 'real crime' or properly 'real police' accounts which also quote extensively from police officers' own versions of their careers (Siegel 1980; Baker 1987; Graef 1990).

As well as the interviews with female police officers, I also carried out several interviews in Britain with women who were or had been security guards or officers. These interviews were conducted under similar conditions to those with the police. One woman had worked for a commercial organization, one for a private social club, and the third in a large public-sector body. (Fuller details are given in the Appendix.) Where comparisons are appropriate, I have used this material. It proved impossible to construct a similar sample of women in the USA, although one of my informants there was at the time of interview no longer working as a sworn officer but as a civilian traffic officer, while another had also left the police and was running her own private detective agency. These women had, however, many years of police service between them, unlike the British security agents, who had none.

Not all the key points which map out the careers of women officers have equal primacy in Britain and the USA. All are listed here, but I shall first present the material separately before comparing the experiences of the two groups.

Concepts in a Career

A sense of mission
Pioneers
Partners
Transformation scenes
Professionalism
Soft cops
Female cop culture
Top cops

As I hope to show, many aspects of policewomen's lives can be seen as focusing round these points. Yet there are, of course, many variations: everyone is not the same and these women had considerably varied views, values, and backgrounds. They ranged from junior officers with three years' service to one with thirty; some were, or had been married and had children. In the USA, but not in Britain, black women were well represented. We have moved with considerable rapidity in studying women from a situation where that was thought to be a meaningful category to one where *difference*, between women from distinct social class backgrounds, racial or sexual preference groups is heavily emphasized and possible conflict highlighted. It is one purpose of the present exercise to find out how far it is possible to speak of women police being a discrete group with common, shared views and experiences, rather than only a subsection of the wider, pervasive culture, and, moreover, a group which transcends local and national boundaries. It is important to note that they themselves believe in this identity. There are local and national associations, conferences, magazines, and newsletters, albeit rather better developed in the USA than Britain, although they are expanding in Europe, too. Questions have also to be raised about how unique to one sex certain behaviour and/or experience is, and how common it is. It is important to know, too, how far biological features of sex differences are rated as crucial and how far the learning of gender roles are critical. It is a prosaic truism that females can be masculine and men feminine and hence it may not be the sex of an official in public life which matters but whether he/she plays one or other kind of varied gender roles.

Careers in Britain: Life Histories in Waiting

Hidden Histories

As the earlier discussion showed, the position of policewomen in Britain before the 1970s was rather better than in the USA. While they served in their own departments and concentrated on specialist work, as was the case in the USA, they did have a promotional structure, some women served in the CID, and they were already 'on patrol' before integration, if not in the fullest sense. Several women had careers pre-1975 and it is interesting to note how their histories demonstrate their adaptability, first, in developing away from their prescribed roles and later, at integration.

It never occurred to me that I should maintain this profile of children, young persons, care and protection. I never saw why I wasn't capable of dealing with all these other areas as well. (Senior Officer, entered in 1960s)

She became interested in CID work, initially dealing with sex offences: 'but there was also a lot of scope outside of that, depending on where you were stationed, and that's what appealed to me, was the facility of doing comparable work to male colleagues.' Her experience was not unique:

in the station I was at . . . we also had to walk the beat. We happened to have a woman inspector there who was a very good street police officer, and she made sure that all her women officers walked the streets, arrested criminals, found lost and stolen motor vehicles . . . and so the women in that particular unit were as good a street beat force as the men, because we only specialized when we were required to. (Senior Officer, describing inner-city station in 1960s)

As this officer observed, officially women were only meant to specialize; reality, however, was quite different:

The whole spectrum we were working, but from the training school, the atmosphere had been that you were second-class police because you were really just going to sit around fiddling with children and young people. So when I actually got to —— and that was not the case, that was a big myth involved. And that may have been happening in other stations, but that myth went on for years.

Another officer, whose work was rather more conventional, also found 'you were patrolling the majority of the time': 'we dealt mainly with the aliens, missing persons, truants, child abuse, neglect', and, as there was a red-light district in her area, prostitutes. The exception to this was when she had to prepare women prisoners detained overnight for court. Such 'matron duty' was detested, while beat work was preferred. 'Matron duty was literally looking after prisoners, most people disliked it intensely. Otherwise you were allowed to patrol streets.' This had hazards perhaps not encountered now:

This was prior to personal radios. So you had to keep in touch, so you often would patrol with a vehicle with a male driver, so that you could get out and watch whether the boxes were flashing because they would flash the old police boxes to call you. There were quite a few of them around but you could go some considerable distance walking and not see a police box or a police post. (Senior Officer, describing urban station in mid-1960s)

(The 'old police boxes' were the type made famous as Dr Who's spaceship *Tardis* in the eponymous television series. They were blue and contained a telephone, and a light on top of them flashed when there was a message.)

I have quoted from these memories of past policing in order to highlight several points to which we shall return. First, well before integration, women police did not work solely within their separate sphere; not only could they move on to specialized work in CID, Special Branch, etc., but they also took on routine uniform 'real police' tasks. Indeed, it may be more helpful to see them as having unique and innovatory roles in which their male colleagues did not share, while they did participate in ordinary work. Secondly, these women, while they all assert their own and their female colleagues' capacity to undertake all policing work, are influenced by the overall values of policing in their views of what was real work and valid experience. These points are important in themselves and also as a testimony to the worth of histories; official versions of the period usually portray the received wisdom version.

It should be stressed, of course, that these officers were the successful survivors of integration and it is possible that their earlier attitudes and behaviour were useful forms of anticipatory socialization. Certainly some of them believed this to be so. The last officer cited recalled the period of integration:

I was a sergeant . . . I'd always performed station duty, I'd always relieve my male colleagues . . . when charges came in, I'd take them. So I had that experience . . . so, I didn't feel challenged by the station officer's duties when it came to integration to do the research and do the charges.

Another found that 'the fact that I was trained as a street copper stood me in very, very good stead when I became integrated.'

When integration took place in Britain some women resigned or retired. Scotland's forces appear to have been especially badly depleted in this way. Several studies have recorded the regret that some female, and some male, officers felt at the passing of the specialized role and the expertise which they thought had been built up there (S. Jones 1986; Bryant et al. 1985). While these respondents, recruited and trained under the old system, had done well after 1975, they too valued their training and the work they had then done and expressed a concern that not just policewomen, but also the police in general had been adversely affected by this often very abrupt change:

Women police could communicate well . . . what was a body blow to the police was . . . that what we had been doing was of such little importance that they could just do that (claps) overnight and it wouldn't have any really drastic effects . . . It was all about at the time 'what are we going to do when you move?' not 'what is going to happen with those areas that the women have been working in?' It seemed as if they'd never actually realized what the women police had been doing.

Another woman valued her training, which had been the same as a man's plus some extra courses: 'We were carefully monitored . . . [and] prepared . . . we had the feeling of being a small, specialist team. We did aspire to perfection.' She even felt superior to her male colleagues. 'I always felt that their professionalism was at a lower level than ours . . . they weren't so particular, they didn't attend to detail in the same way.' A particular regret is that, by the 1980s, the police were having to reinvent procedures and practices, discarded at integration, to deal with the new agenda of policing: domestic violence, child abuse, rape, etc. 'We really had an expertise which involved a multi-agency approach to problem-solving, dealing with people's problems. Now I'm using 1980s terms for what were 1960 realities.' A fellow officer deplored recent developments in social work, especially with children, and considered that she and her colleagues had provided a better child-protection service: 'You tell me another structure in society that actually gives a measure of prevention of abuse of children—the police were the only thing, mainly because of their close contact.' In her own career she

walked into numerous cases and saw women who were going under and, I didn't dream of taking the children away, but really needing help, and you'd sit down and have a cup of tea and say 'come on love, what's going on, what are your problems here, who is supporting you?' And . . . we were that close that we could get in there before that child got battered to death.

It was not uncommon to hear that policewomen were better community social workers than the professionals and that rates of juvenile crime and child abuse had all increased since the loss of specialization.

From an officer who had herself enthusiastically taken up the challenge of integration and succeeded very well, there was a *cri de cœur* which sums up many feelings:

I felt that there had been a devaluation of women . . . people didn't understand how really complex and contentious that job was . . . either they overestimated the demands of their own job [and] they underestimated the demands on the women; because, really, all this mythology about women not being able to do it . . . because being a duty officer was much easier . . . than being a woman inspector being called out at two o'clock in the morning, having to come out and walk into absolute filth with children, who were absolutely filthy undernourished, almost traumatized with neglect, and dealing with that and trying to pick up the threads and trying to establish what was best for the children . . . so I always felt, and have always been a little bit resentful that people didn't actually realize, not only the value, but the quality of that work.

Integration

I have already stressed that all the women whom I saw had survived integration well. Obviously, policewomen who had not would have long since left the force. Nevertheless, these women had found it a fairly traumatic experience. None had received any training, nor had their male colleagues. One woman looked back:

My particular career was developed by my commander calling me to his office, I suppose the Friday before the Equal Opportunities initiative was taken over by the service and telling me, 'Are you going to go for promotion?' I said 'Yes.' He said, 'Well in that case you must go on relief and do Section normal, ordinary sergeant's duties', duties that male officers had been doing.

Even for a woman who had already broken the mould and had worked in CID there was an abrupt entry into a new, integrated group;

talk about a male-predominated world, I mean I can remember my first walking into that room, deathly silence from the male colleagues that were to be, and being told in no uncertain terms, 'we didn't ask for women police officers, we're being made to have one.'

Someone who considered herself well trained in craft skills nevertheless felt herself lacking in management skills:

Nobody gave me an item of advice on how to handle this situation. Neither did they give the relief that acquired me any advice . . . I had never attempted a proper parade of male officers.

Integration could also provide a challenge for some female officers. 'I felt I was a good officer . . . and I wasn't going to let people think women police officers couldn't handle it. Someone had thrown down the gauntlet and by God, I was going to pick it up.' But it still produced its share of sorrow, anxiety, and stress. As one senior officer says boldly, 'it was a traumatic time, nothing has ever been so traumatic since nor will there ever be anything as traumatic.' For all of them personally the changes were ultimately beneficial, even though they had regrets about the process of integration and the loss of knowledge and skills which accompanied this.

The rest of the British women had joined since integration, so that they had not experienced the old system, nor the transition to the new, although they were aware of it. What is striking, however, is the way in which the points of focus and common themes can be found both in the accounts of those who were recruited well before official integration and those who have joined since. Reasons for this have already been touched on: successful 'graduates' from the old system may have been better adapted and better adaptors than those who left and may not be very typical. However, the nature of their training, deployment, and command structure meant that a degree of socialization and subculture existed which would have made them have more, not less in common. Descriptions by former officers (Wyles 1951; Lock 1979) illustrate this. Another factor may be that there was scope for innovation and boundary-breaking before integration and some took advantage of it. As one told me:

A.   I became aware that I was very much more interested in a broader field of work then than being confined to uniform women police work as it was in those days.

Q.   Was it easy to redefine your role like that?

A.   Yes I did meet resistance from sergeants, from senior sergeants. Certainly I was made well aware of the fact that I was a uniformed woman police officer, and I was not a CID officer and there was certainly conflict there. But you know, I seemed to get over that all right.

Many women left the police because of the lack of such opportunities. Joan Lock gives this as one of her reasons and Bryant *et al.* cite it as an important factor. One of the themes which will emerge in the following discussion is how women officers resolve a series of ambiguities and conflicts which they face: they are police officers, but not police*men*, they are part of a law-enforcement agency which, in the way it has treated them, may have risked breaking the law and one where, in order to uphold a particular view about the proper role for women in society, behaviour towards female colleagues has been neither chivalrous nor fraternal.

A Sense of Mission

Police officers' concept of themselves is distinctive. 'A central feature of cop culture is a sense of *mission*. This is the feeling that policing is not just a job but a way of life with a worthwhile purpose, at least in principle' (Reiner 1985: 88). I have already described the missionary zeal of the pioneer British policewomen; this particular form of commitment and action does not seem to have been assimilated into the general police moral mandate. On the contrary, as described above, the specialist work which they promoted was more or less discarded on integration. As Reiner and others describe the police mission, it is about preserving order and protecting the weak, it is victim-centred. This in turn justifies the machismo syndrome of 'the chase, the fight, the capture . . . In a policeman's own eyes he is one of the "good guys" and it is this which gives him the licence for action' (1985: 89). Of course, many commentators are sceptical about both the possibility and reality of such a purpose, because most police work is not good guys versus bad guys anyway, and, increasingly, because police have not achieved certain targets, e.g. crime rates continue to rise, or because their reputation is publicly tarnished by cases in which they have not been the guardians of order. Police officers themselves recognize this and thus, Reiner suggests, 'the core of the police outlook is this subtle and complex intermingling of the themes of mission, hedonistic love of action and pessimistic cynicism' (1985: 91).

That the women officers all reported a strong, and often continuing, sense of mission suggests that they were mainly influenced by the occupational culture which gives it such primacy. Examining their views in more detail shows that their perception of mission was somewhat different and that, in practice, they had to adapt it to the conditions of everyday policing, both inside and outside the force. There are five key areas in which this aspect of their role came into play: on entry; inside the police; on women as victims and citizens; on women in the police; on cynicism.

Entry

Perhaps the first feature which stands out in many policewomen's autobiographies is their struggle to enter the service. This is particularly marked among the older women who were recruited under the previous system when there were few positions available. One had tried six county forces all unsuccessfully, although this was not because of lack of ability. She applied to the cadet service: 'I sat the examination. And the most disappointing thing, as you can imagine, for a youngster—I passed the exam but because they always considered local girls first and I was not in.' Eventually, she had to settle for a civilian post with the police and was accepted after several years' work there. Even in more recent times, a young constable reported how, having failed to get into the cadets in her teens because of her lack of an exam qualification, she ultimately fulfilled her aim by losing two stone in weight and training regularly to improve her running speeds.

Such determination was based on moral values which, while their owners' personal and political views varied considerably, showed very clear commitments to principles:

The fundamental reason for joining the police force [had] . . . something to do with fairness—I use the word justice now but I don't suppose that was part of my vocabulary then. And people. A real interest in people, a real concern for people. Fairness for people. (Senior officer, entered in early 1960s)

Another senior officer, who had never worked with the one just quoted, used very similar terms. Proud of her working-class origins, she insisted, 'I am essentially very identified with people I perceive as underprivileged . . . a lot of the way I look on things is about that . . . I never use the word equality but fairness. Fairness.'

While for the younger women entry in the 1970s and 1980s was no longer restricted to the few vacancies for policewomen, a new set of factors were operating, especially the effect of the crisis in policing and the impact of stories of rising crime rates and reports of attacks on police. A middle-ranking officer with ten years' service recalled, 'there were a lot of people saying to me, "you must be absolutely crazy and out of your mind!"' She described herself as 'absolutely dedicated, driven', and persisted in her determination. Her background she saw as basically conservative and her own career choice, though no one else in her family was in the police, fitted her family's commitment to public service.

Inside the Police

Having entered policing with a strong sense of commitment and often after a long period of expectation or waiting, all of these women felt some degree of shock. The 30 year-old just cited said, 'what shocked me was the military overtones at training school.' This was more graphically pictured by a younger officer (five years' service):

We all stood there—a female sergeant—said, 'stand to attention . . . ' She said, 'Stand up, the answer is yes sarge'. She says, 'Who's the best class?' 'We're the best class, sarge.' I didn't want to join this. I turned to —— I was shocked—he was joining in! He was yelling. Now I understand Nazism—euphoria, you could feel it.

From all that we have considered earlier, it is evident that entry into the police is bound to be somewhat traumatic for anyone. It involves rites of passage into a new, separate world and status. Since that world is so determinedly macho, it is hardly surprising that there is a double shock for women. What is significant is that these women retained and, in some cases, developed their sense of mission after recruitment and applied it to the police organization itself, since it manifestly failed to live up to their expectations of it.

Some did this by criticism: one young woman said that she was 'mouthy' and spoke of numerous situations in which she had questioned rules and procedures and challenged superiors. At training school she was regularly in trouble for flouting what she considered petty rules and for then challenging the system. Indeed she described how, being very fit, she was able to go for a training run with a tutor and argue with him about the lack of a 'thinking, questioning atmosphere'. More surprisingly perhaps, the middle-rank officer quoted earlier had also sought to raise serious social issues and was incensed at being reprimanded for an implied criticism of the police.

More mature officers had been able to use their position to raise issues and alter practices. One who questioned many aspects of management was insistent:

there were so few of us, I knew a lot of senior officers, and they knew me and I actually could be quite stubborn and say, 'I'm sorry, you can't justify that stance at all. You've got to explain to me sir with respect, you've really got to do better than that.'

For others, it was a matter of changing policies or practices once they had attained higher rank. What stands out in these accounts is that all these women held, and largely continued to hold, an idealized, platonic notion of policing, to which they felt they had committed themselves. One younger officer put it like this:

It's all about serving the Queen, that means the people, community, society. I was pledged to the community and thought that was a really heavy thing to do. I felt that weighing on my shoulders. May be that's why women find this job heavy: they're aware of the enormous pledge they make.

It is against this ideal, and their own endeavours to attain it, that these officers measured themselves and their colleagues. A young officer said simply, 'I get upset because I'm living it and I'm upset because I'm not changing it,' while a much more senior woman evoked her 'great disappointment' at the revelations of corruption in the 1970s: 'that person was letting down not only his own colleagues but also the public as a whole; you have a great trust . . . Deeply hurt, I became . . . that the public felt . . . police officers were all in that mould.'

These expressions of moral concern and outrage at the failings of the system raise a number of issues. Standards of this kind are not, of course, unique to women. Holdaway's ethnographic account of his period at Hilton police station is often similar in tone (1983) and many of the comments included in Graef's book echo them (1990). What distinguishes the women is the apparent persistence of their commitment and a certain feeling of separateness from the occupational culture which enabled them to criticize it more freely. Although none explicitly made this connection, it did seem to me that there was often a crucial link between the women's sense of mission and their treatment within the police. Even officers with smooth and successful careers had met harassment and stereotyping, yet they knew they were skilled and professional and had a part to play. Their gendered experience *in the police*, then, affected their views of the police. They did not, however, accept that only men could police properly. Indeed I think they saw their own treatment as disqualifying some men as proper police.

Treatment of Women as Victims and Citizens

The area in which female officers first pioneered their role as moral agents was in relation to women and children. Even today, some of the officers saw this as a crucial issue. It did, however, have two antecedents, historic and modern. Older officers, recruited before integration, recalled their specialist role and lamented its passing. I have already quoted one such regret. Younger women were less influenced by the old specialist role than by various versions of modern feminism and victimology which had given them much greater awareness. Handling rape victims is, of course, a possible cause of contention with male colleagues: 'in order to look good in their eyes, their attitude is "well she asked for it didn't she? She was wearing lipstick"' (young officer, five years in). Whereas she herself would have hugged a victim and 'told her she was beautiful' which is what, she said, her mother would have done. Another young officer with only a few years' service criticized the lack of good training and facilities for such cases and felt acutely her own inadequacies for dealing with the traditional agenda for policewomen. A more senior officer had played a part in setting up new procedures for dealing with domestic violence and was very pleased that the changed public attitudes to the issue meant that it was being taken much more seriously and that her young constables were coming to her for advice and with reports, and that this would have been inconceivable five years earlier.

Women in the Police

Being a distinguishable minority creates the potential for conflict or constraint in any situation; being a part of a small minority in such a cohesive group as the police is a further problem, but to be a woman in such an insistently masculinist culture triples the problems. Young has argued that police*men* see no place for women inside the force at all. My informants had more varied and complex experiences. While one had been the subject of innuendo and lurid rumours about her private life, several experienced the whole range of sexism from ritual ostracism by male colleagues (in the CID) to the trivial insults of meetings, where one woman was present, being addressed as 'gentlemen'.

Whatever their experience, however hard they had tried to be just 'one of the boys', all had had to face questions about their role and status, simply because they were women. It does seem to me that we need a concept for a situation where minorities cannot or will not adapt to the wider culture. For policewomen, while numbers of women remain relatively low, complete acceptance is a dream. There is no true permanent static adaptation, rather a series of negotiated strategies. Hence, perhaps, the explanation of the concern these women expressed for their own and the careers of others in the force.

A senior officer recounted her own and others' actions in dealing with integration and after:

these were women in the frontline smashing through and saying, 'Right you wanted this game, we're going to play full-bloodedly—we didn't want the game but we're going to play it by the rules, and we're going to play with commitment.' So we did smash down walls . . . Not mainly for ourselves . . . but mainly for those women coming behind. And that was pride.

Several of these women felt very strongly about equal-opportunities issues and were aware of pressures against them. One, still retaining her youthful idealism, did admit to finding 'male politics' very hard to deal with in the organization and that it was a major barrier to the advancement of young women. None of these women rejected the idea that the enhancement of women was important to them; it was one topic of which, they felt, they had some sense of ownership. That may, of course, be related to the fact that there is little competition from men; for dealing with these problems was a reversion to type of the old school.

Cynicism

Cynicism, Reiner argued in the passage I picked out earlier, is part of the package of modern-day policing. It is the obverse of the 'mission' and is related to realism. Here some comparison with the security guards is instructive. None could really be said to have any sense of mission about her work. Security organizations, unlike the police, generally do not subject candidates for entry to elaborate routines and tests. While their entry was casual in the extreme, they did develop models of policing and order, and techniques and philosophy once in their teams. At a general level they did all have a missionary view: in relation to rights and posts for women, all had some degree of feminist commitment and each had engaged in a local struggle about her role in security. The social-club bouncer had dealt with the members of the rugby team who had become self-appointed minders at the club and provoked a great deal of 'aggro'. As is perhaps characteristic of those who keep order in *private* spaces, all three were concerned about managing their own patch and not about what went on outside it. The sports and social-club bouncer recognized that the club's relationship with the local community was appalling, but this was not her concern. Once drunks or fighters were outside it was up to the police, who, she remarked, 'come round to play the siren on Friday night'. There is, however, in the growth of vigilantism a clear parallel with the sense of mission amongst police officers. The 'Guardian Angels' were among the first and most famous of such groups; they have female members and also founded chapters, and have all-female patrols in London (Sliwa 1986; 'Guardian Angels', *Guardian*, 19 Mar. 1991).

What all the security agents did report was the impact on their view of human nature which their work had had. A woman in her twenties, with five years' security experience at public events and in clubs, said that she had come 'to hate punters'. She described various audience and membership groups with considerable contempt, very much like a police officer describing 'rubbish work' (Smith and Gray 1983). She was particularly scornful about young women in clubs, their proneness to fight, scrawl graffiti in lavatories, and, above all, to try to get in without paying. 'In clubs . . . you're the first person the punters meet, so you reflect the atmosphere of the club. You take the money. The biggest thing with women is money. They'll try everything. My pride is involved—you're not getting past me.'

The sports and social-club bouncer, who was in her early twenties and had worked in security for two years, had had training in self-defence methods and also ran self-defence classes, both for women only and mixed groups, nevertheless found these skills of no use in her work. 'I learnt a thousand throws but couldn't use them. I got frustrated—I saw so much violence in the club— aggression not techniques were vital.' This was because of the amount of drinking in the club which, she said, made members wild and reckless. Footballers especially, were 'animals'. She found that the work had made her callous; 'I find myself acting very hard sometimes.'

All these women came into contact with the police in the course of their work, but none saw herself as a police officer and certainly for the two younger ones it was a transient employment. The policewomen did not exhibit the degree of cynicism which one might have expected, given the insights they had gained into the nature and capacities of the police organization. That is not to say that they never reported depression, frustration, or anger about their work, rather the process of being inside the police yet not fully of it, of preserving a certain detachment, appeared to serve as a kind of extra immune system against the taint of cynicism. This is well caught in the following dialogue with a mid-career officer:

Q.   You joined with high ideals. Did you find them confirmed?

A.   I felt at a very early stage that I'd made the right decision, because, some of the messages and some of the examples we were given were very harsh and sometimes melodramatic, but at the same time there was always a subtlety of approach to anything we were given and that was very appealing. And I've found that ever since. And I look at it now and I think that was my introduction to politics—with a small 'p'—male politics particularly.

Q.   What do you mean by that?

A.   Well, I think, how facts are interpreted and how a predominantly male organization approaches things is quite different to what most women would approach. So many ways, I think women tend to be a lot more pedantic about what's right and what's wrong and will stick out to the nth degree to establish what's right and wrong.

Q.   Is it a moral or a practical sense?

A.   Possibly both, I think both. Whereas men will tend to blur that in a sort of—so that they can deal with it in a practical way. Very difficult to explain this actually.

Q.   What's an example?

A.   Well, it happens all the time. I suppose, when I went to my first beat in — within the second week I went to a flat which was in appalling condition, had two children who were obviously not being treated properly, filthy conditions, I can remember saying to the senior officer, the more experienced officer, 'Well, shouldn't you take those two children away from this flat?' They were sharing a bed with this old man, and it was absolutely horrendous, you know, and, it was quite a shock to me, this PC was obviously quite experienced, he said, 'No, you'll see that in a hundred homes in this area and there's no way we can tackle that head on. All we can do is ensure we've done our bit by letting social services know, but at the end of the day there's not much that's on offer to help these people anyway.' Now, I mean people were prepared to accept that and that was a prudent way of dealing with that, whereas I think most women would say, 'We've got to do something about this', and take it to its nth degree, 'If nobody wants to help, we've got to scream and shout—it can't be right, you can't let this go on.'

Q.   Was that his priority? Because it was a domestic matter?

A.   No, I think he was just as appalled as I was but he was probably more realistic in terms of what was on offer to help those people and had resigned himself to accepting that and you get that all the time—men will take things up to a point. They see the system operating and they're not prepared to push to get things changed. At times that's very frustrating, I think women are a lot more prepared to take things head on and say 'This is not right, let's do something about it'. It can be negative, and it also can be positive. At times I've learnt that some of my black-and-white views are also misplaced, so you learn also from men, you realize a lot of people have deliberately put themselves in that position, things are not as clear as . . . you can't trust everyone at face value. I think that's the other thing you learn very quickly in this job; on the surface you see things which are pretty horrific and you can very easily feel very sympathetic, but you soon get caught out, because people are prepared to lie and what people do is extraordinary.

Q.   It makes you cynical about human nature?

A.   Yes I think that's fair. Although I say 'cynical' quite reservedly, because I can see tender films and I can still feel very depressed about things I've seen, so cynical in so far as I can get on with the job without being affected but certainly not cynical enough to be able to forget it.

I have quoted from this interview verbatim because I think that it shows how this officer, while being a thoroughly trained and socialized policewoman, was still seeking to keep her values intact and in doing so, invoked an external gender identity. Note that, while apparently agreeing with my point about cynicism, she goes on to deny it.

It may be that I am making these policewomen sound like a group of Pollyannas. This is far from my aim. What I want to suggest is that they had, for the most part, preserved a notion of the moral possibilities of policing, and of women's role within that, notwithstanding what they had learnt about the *realpolitik* of everyday policing. The reasons for this are complex and differ for each woman. Common processes involve commitment to specific aims, especially to do with the community, to the causes of women and children and ethnic minorities, in other words, to groups outside the police and often with low ranking in the police status hierarchy. Yet it was their knowledge of police and policing which they called on regularly as evidence of the value of their work. A senior officer recalled a past case of successful community policing:

When I was an inspector they had a lot of problems with one particular case, there were children dying there, one child died there because of marital disputes, violence, and, oh dreadful! We may as well have had a tramline built between the station and that case because there were five or six calls a day. I actually put a policewoman in and her total responsibility was just that one case. She became known as Aunty to the kids, all the women knew of her. She must have had a very big bladder because she was always going round for cups of tea, but they talked to her, told her their problems, she could see what was coming up, if a man was battering his wife then she got told—aunty. They worshipped her. And within six months that block had no problems at all. She got the support of the community, because they were important enough to her. No children ever got killed while she was there, because aunty was in there, talking. They knew. A man could have done it too. It had to be someone who could handle that problem.

Several of my respondents described disillusioned female colleagues who might certainly not have fitted into the missionary mould. Often they mentioned mitigating factors—harassment, discrimination, etc.—but they could also be judgemental over what seemed unprofessional behaviour. It may well be that my group were untypical. Fielding, for example, describes a group of WPCs apparently fully adapted into the police culture (1988).

Pioneers

It is a very long time since the first policewomen walked beats. Some of my informants were even fairly vague about when exactly integration had taken place as it was well before their current service. Nevertheless, the concept of pioneering, of venturing afresh into unknown territories, recurred as a motif in the lives of these women more than seven decades after their predecessors first took to the streets. There were three ways in which this theme was played: on true 'firsts'; preparation for a 'man's world'; punishment and protection for pioneering.

True Firsts

While there have now been many generations of female officers in the police, it is still possible to find women who are first in their own field, either for all British forces, for their own, or in achieving a particular rank. Female dog handlers are, for example, a rare breed. Lock, surveying this field in 1987, could only find twenty-one in the whole of the British Isles (eight of these were in the RUC). Until April 1988 the Force policy on firearms in the Metropolitan Police 'precluded women officers from becoming authorized firearms officers (AFOs)'; by December 1989 twenty-two women had been trained as AFOs (Metropolitan Police/Equal Opportunities Commission 1990: 23). It is therefore not surprising that some of this group had achieved such 'firsts' in various ways. For obvious reasons, I cannot give details of these, but it is possible to record some of their own perceptions of such records.

Ambition could often play a part in the determination to do something which was new but necessary to a career. An added edge came to several of the women's aims because of the constant challenge which the culture and their colleagues' attitudes offered to their abilities:

I wouldn't allow anybody to tell me I couldn't do anything . . . I would never allow that. And I saw things and I thought, 'Well if a man can do that, I'm going to do it.' And I would say, 'I'm going to do it,' and they might say, 'Oh, a woman doing that . . . ' and I would say, 'I don't care, I'm going to do it now.' So in a way, that's how I acquired so many firsts, because I was absolutely determined that I was going to do it. Not because I wanted to get up in the records, but it was important that women coming behind should have those rules broken down. (Senior officer)

Pioneering police cannot, however, just make records; they must, as these women found, have plans and strategies to manage in the new terrain. Some did it by trying to merge as 'one of the boys' but they recognized that this was never entirely satisfactory and carried risks: 'I was able to get involved . . . on a very much closer level than ever they had been. I was much less conspicuous and I got away with murder really (laughs).' Others employed some of the strategies described below under transformations and professionalism. Yet another way was to exploit such situations for the educative potential they offered to women who did not have access to the old-boy network or to freemasonry:

I learned so much from watching powerful men take important decisions . . . I learned in leaps and bounds every day. I learned the way powerful people operate, how they show their authority. I watched the pecking order. (Senior officer)

'True firsts' are basically only a variant of an essential aspect of a policewoman's role that she must manage: that she may still be a relative novelty in a male world and yet must, in order to survive in this world, become safe and familiar. Yet each true first will inevitably lack role models, rules, and guidance, although some officers had male mentors and under the old system senior women might act in this way.

Preparation for a 'Man's World'

A relatively junior officer (and thus trained in the 1980s) assured me that her whole cohort of recruits were regularly reminded while in training school that they were there 'so we can make men of you'. It hardly needs to be said that such exhortations are not the same as preparing female recruits for dealing with the macho world of police, nor indeed is it the same as providing them with specific skills which might equip them for their role, e.g. body-building exercises or self-defence training.

Younger officers, whose training was more recent and post-integration, all agreed that they had received no preparation for what was for each of them individually a pioneering act of entering a male world. Asked if she had been given any advice about operating in a man's world one said, 'No, nothing at all . . . So there was absolutely no sympathy at all for the fact that you were a woman.' Indeed the only sex-specific advice she had was an admonition not to fraternize with the men in their dormitories. Another young officer, asked a similar question, replied, 'No, you are not really prepared . . . It is very much, you know, boys only club and in upper offices, I would think, it's got to be a very strong masonic friendship or relationship to be in the force.' Their older colleagues did not generally speak much about this gap in training, although they believed that they faced a fairly hostile world in the police.

Lacking a proper course at training school which would have trained them to an acceptable level, female officers had to improvise. They all found discrete and separate ways of adapting to the strange culture in which they found themselves, chiefly by the use of forms of professionalism as described below, and by persistent use of it. A senior woman described how she had first convinced male colleagues in the CID of her value by 'sheer involvement'. So successful was she, in fact, that she was promoted and posted elsewhere and met what I would describe as the 'perpetual pioneer' pattern. She, like so many of this group, had to prove herself all over again at each new posting. This woman's solution on this occasion was to remain around persistently.

> I was aware that they would go out on jobs and just not take me with them and this was very hurtful to somebody like me, who was used to being thoroughly involved.

Q. What did you do about that?

A. I actually made myself available. I would not go home, I just stayed there till they came back and made them feel very bad about it, because they actually said, 'We thought you would have gone home,' and I said, 'No, I was wanting to know what happened. I was interested. I was actually quite hurt about you going off without me.' And I think that happened within the first few days two or three times, and I think they realized that I wasn't to be got rid of (laughs). If you stick in there, you know, they thought, 'see if we can get rid of her by taking her with us.' [Later in her career, when she had once more been promoted and posted to a new job she faced the same situation all over again.]

Q. Did you have to convince people, again, that you could do the job, as a woman?

A. It started all over again, because my reaction from [her boss] was, 'well, I didn't ask for a woman here and I didn't want you,' (laughs) so I said, 'the feeling is mutual, so while we're here shall we try and make it work?'

Q. How did you make it work?

A. Again by availability. By just doing, getting on, and doing [there was a major crime shortly after she arrived]. And I actually thought it couldn't . . . have been better positioned for me to immediately go along and say, 'Let's get on with it.' So yes, involvement, immediate involvement in that particular case.

All police officers have to prove themselves, learn their streetcraft, and show professional skills. Policing literature, whether academic or autobiographical, is replete with accounts of this. The difference for women is that they appear only to achieve conditional acceptance, a provisional licence to police which they have to earn afresh each time. Other women, apart from the one quoted above, described similar patterns, using terms such as 'challenge', 'proving', 'I was a strange commodity', 'they were wary'. And, given the structure within which they worked, which had no alternative channels, they had options only of learning or confrontation. In one senior officer's recollection, 'I wasn't going to allow that sort of arrogant bigotry to stand. So yes I picked up the gauntlet. I certainly did. I thought, "By god I'll show you."'

Punishment and Protection for Pioneering

In an earlier section, I discussed the resistance of male officers to the entry of females and various explanations for this. My discussion made clear, I trust, that I do not find that any of the standard theories, which rely on either *external* social factors, or *internal* features of police culture, adequately meet necessary and sufficient conditions of explanation. They will not do, and this is a topic to which I shall come back. In this section I want to turn to the ways in which these women were sometimes treated when they ventured into these hostile territories. Older officers who had been in post before integration had found their role on the whole accepted then, as long as they stayed within the strict limits of specialism:

We certainly had a role that was valued, by Inspectors and some elders, certainly by male colleagues because, let's face it, they would dump the prisoners upon you and they wouldn't have to deal with all the searches and interviews and paperwork which were very time-consuming.

On the other hand, there was a cost to this, as another officer said: 'from the training school, the atmosphere had been that you were second-class police because you were really just going to sit around fiddling with children and young people.' Yet, as we have already discovered, specialism was not as rigidly practised even before integration as is sometimes supposed, and thus even then there were experiences of exclusion and hostility towards women such as those I have already quoted.

Nevertheless, there can be little doubt that integration is the rationale given if not the true reason for some of the abuse and harassment reported by these women. One young officer mentioned a series of 'debates' about height and physique in which her own ability to cope with drunks and fights was questioned alongside the integrated recruitment policy. Reference, she said, was always made to extremes, to one woman having to subdue 'two fifteen-stone drunks'. M. Young (1991) has vividly depicted the stereotyped abuse which male officers may offer women, and Graef quotes many examples. S. Jones (1986) found that younger, new male recruits were not necessarily less hostile. The women in my group were well aware of such things and some gave examples; paradoxically, of course, since they were not male they did not share in the fullest flow of locker-room talk. What they reported instead was an insidious process which was at once semi-hidden and yet blatantly offensive. The young officer just referred to described the force as being a 'boys only club' with masonic links at the top. Another woman had not appreciated how effectively this had operated before her first posting: 'apparently at —— they knew I was coming for about three months and apparently every-one said "there's a girl coming . . . " so I was obviously some novelty to them.'

There was considerable variation in the degree of reported abuse and hostility. One of my younger informants reported encountering more than others did, but they all were aware that these existed and it was clear that they acted, together with the rumours and gossip about them, as forms of social control. Such a pattern is not confined to policewomen. I have shown elsewhere (Heidensohn 1985) how men's giving and taking of repute to and from women is an important mechanism of discipline. The main differences in the police are that (a) women are only a small minority and a relatively junior one too; and (b) that the police are meant to be a righteous, law-upholding body within which the spreading of malicious rumour and innuendo might seem especially deplorable. But these women had had to learn to live with this situation even if they had not accepted it. One senior woman, referring particularly to the Smith and Gray depiction (1983) of the macho booze and sexism subculture of the Metropolitan Police, felt that it was too easy to be over-sensitive to such matters. The younger officer who had found herself 'a novelty' was also fairly philosophical.

Q. Every woman officer I've spoken to has talked about the gossip, how noticeable you are.

A. Oh yes, you're either a butch queer, or you're laying everybody in sight (laughs). There's no in-between road.

Q. Does that still go on?

A. Unfortunately yes, I think a lot of men are too ready to stereotype.

She also mentioned, without any prompting, that she disliked the canteen culture, 'the general canteen-chat was pretty drab', and did not participate in it. A more senior woman made the same point and noted its consequences:

in the police force there was always that quite different outlook that kept us separate. I mean I didn't want to sit down at the canteen and talk about sex. When I first went on relief I didn't have any other woman, so I worked in total isolation from my own sex.

A younger woman, who had therefore more female colleagues, nevertheless expressed a similar view and suggested the impact that gossip had on women:

Whatever you are they'll neatly categorize you from one extreme to the other to defuse and deny what you're doing. There are two stereotypes for women: the hooker and the dyke. There is no good stereotype for women and both are sexual. Lots of women get fed up with this—they leave . . . it means you don't have many women in the police.

The opposite extreme from verbal hectoring and sexual propositioning is over-protectiveness. Some accounts—e.g. Graef (1990), Lock (1979)—do describe male officers being over-zealous in protecting female colleagues. This can be irritating if well intentioned and as limiting to the career as the more abrasive treatment considered earlier. My informants reported very little protectiveness, although one did recount an event in which a policeman crashed his police car in rushing to back up a woman colleague. There were rather more accounts of encouragement from senior colleagues, although these were balanced by adverse descriptions. Those who had positive help from mentors stressed their 'luck' in this regard. Whether luck or their own ability played the main part was not always easy to discern. One young officer had two (male) bosses, one of whom was 'brilliant' the other 'indescribable'. These factors could equally well apply to young male recruits.

Although there have been women police deployed in Britain in every decade of the twentieth century except the first, as the century closes women are still, to a degree, pioneers in policing. This has considerable impact on their lives and careers, making them self-conscious and aware to a remarkable degree and often forcing them to produce individual adaptations in order to survive within the organization. The responses they meet and the wider expressions of views about women act as a form of 'policing' of women within the police. Ironically, this makes some women try harder to be more professional, more circumspect in their private lives: a disciplined and proper reaction to improper suggestion and indisciplined behaviour.

Partners

The key concept of partners is one almost solely derived from my American material. British policing is different in that officers are not usually assigned permanent partners. Of course, there are occasions when officers patrol together, observe together, or otherwise work in partnership. One of the very few British legal cases involving policewomen did in fact relate to a WPC who had not been able to be assigned to a patrol car with a married, male colleague. However, this was not an issue in Britain in the same way as it was in the USA and I shall therefore return to it in the next section.

Transformation Scenes

One of the issues I was particularly interested in exploring in this project was how female officers managed those situations they are alleged to be least competent in: violence and disorder. A view sometimes advanced (see, for example, Graef 1990) is that what women may lack in physical strength they make up for in verbal skills and many use these to diffuse violent and threatening situations. I asked all my informants if they had dealt with such incidents (they all had) and secondly how they had done so. Their range of replies was at least as varied as those of any group of men would be, probably more so, since one said she would show her hair on intervening in a mêlée so that she would be seen to be a woman and have a calming effect. She, in common with colleagues, pointed out that encountering violence in full flow is fairly uncommon. This was found to be true of downtown New York in the research cited earlier, so it is hardly a surprising feature in

England. Male officers were, as depicted by their female colleagues, not always anxious to intervene in fights. One was described as driving to a brawl in a local restaurant 'by the scenic route', another as 'scarred and scared' by a previous encounter, staying in a police car with locked doors while the WPC dealt with the disorder. What emerged in fact were not a set of war stories about how these women subdued massive drunks (although there were some of these); rather they described events in which they proved themselves in some way, thereby earning the respect of their colleagues. Sometimes this respect was only given grudgingly, almost always it was not a 'class action' which altered the status of *all* policewomen, but only a statement of exceptionalism. What these episodes did effect was a twofold process: the women themselves felt their confidence strengthened and their male colleagues granted them admission, of a kind, to the fraternity of real police. I have called these 'transformation scenes' because they remind me of the final stages of English pantomines and plays in which the poor, shy heroine is transformed into a beautiful and well-dressed princess.

The officer above, who slept in her armchair in order to be included by her male colleagues, found that

it wasn't a very easy time, but it certainly was very effective as far as becoming involved . . . because I actually think they recognized that I did want to become very much involved in the work . . . and I think it snowballed from one extreme to the other. Rather than always being left out of everything, I was always included in everything, you know the phone would ring at two o'clock in the morning, but I loved it. I clearly thrived on it.

Sometimes 'transformation scenes' may be relatively undramatic, involving good, usually street-policing skills, as in this example.

I must have been [lucky] because I was very effective very early on in terms of making arrests and of course I got 'Oh she can do it. She's up to it.' And as long as you can prove it . . . that is the biggest stumbling-block for any woman. A lot of men will say, 'Oh she's just . . . she can type and she can deal with kids,' but you've got to prove the point that you can nick people on your own. And once you've got over the hurdle, it's downhill in many ways, as far as being a PC is concerned. Obviously, if you take promotion there are other challenges you're faced with.

On other occasions confidence and acceptance come from a little drama which reinforces police culture values, perhaps in distancing them from civilians. A fairly recently recruited rookie described the actual transformation she had undergone in her first few months. She had got into an altercation with a motorist which she knew she had handled badly. Some time later, she saw the same man driving without a seat belt, stopped him, and successfully, this time, asserted her authority and 'booked him'. 'I was totally in control of the situation . . . so between the two situations . . . it was the way I acted in uniform and I acted (now) as though the uniform fitted me instead of it being brand new.' Then her sergeant, who knew the history, appeared:

He said, 'I saw X—you could have nicked him—he was driving like a bat out of hell. Shame you didn't.' 'But I already did.' Everybody—it was like being welcomed to a club when I got back to the nick because they'd already heard about him . . . When I got back, they all said, 'So you stitched up X'—'it's police harassment'—'you lot, you're all the same . . . you all change the minute you join us,' and that was it. I was accepted to a certain extent then. What a criterion!

Transformation scenes seem to play an important part in some policewomen's careers. It is usually necessary to go through one in order to gain basic acceptance by male colleagues. Of course, male officers have to go through rites of passage too, to 'prove' their ability and sometimes their 'bottle' or their manhood. The problem for women is that they are initially defined as not belonging, not one of us, *and* as less than adequate officers. So they have both more to prove and are unable in essentials to prove themselves as 'men' because that is what they are precisely not. Transformation scenes are one way of dealing with the pioneer angle, and, often, allied with professionalism, it is the way in which order is kept, both inside the police and in the world outside. One of the sadder ironies is that while in conversation with me this important phenomenon was observed and revealed, it is not generally a topic for debate, let alone for curriculum guidance in police training. Most women, while they recognize that some things have changed, insisted that they had never had any training to prepare them for these encounters, let alone advice on handling specific issues. One officer described how she (and the relief, with whom she then worked) confronted each other, alone, on integration. She eventually won their trust: 'without any introduction I was thrown in at the deep end to swim for the shore.' It does seem that it is possible to script, perhaps even engineer (?), transformation scenes, so perhaps it would be helpful if such knowledge were available and accessible and that staff were able to help young officers to achieve this difference in approach. It seems to be such an important matter because without help, Cinderella can often not get an invitation to come to the secret Policeman's ball.

Professionalism

What constitutes a profession and how occupations become professions and what their impact is on society are all widely and vigorously debated issues (Johnson 1972; Friedson 1973; Wilding 1982). They are beyond the scope of this book. Of great relevance, however, is professionalism in policing and how women define and use it in their own careers and are defined by the standards of the organization. 'Professionalism' in policing has come to the fore only in fairly recent times, but is frequently claimed as an objective and also a justification. The Metropolitan Police, for example, published a handbook in 1985 with the title, *The Principles of Policing and Guidance for Professional Behaviour*, while the Chief Inspector of Constabulary, in his Report for 1989, insists on 'the need for a theoretical, intellectual, ethical and *completely professional base* upon which the practical policing strategy of the future can be developed' (1990, emphasis added). While there can be no quarrel with such aims, there are real doubts about what constitutes professional policing.

For a start, policing is not a profession in the way other occupations are, such as medicine and the law. One comparative study of public services concluded briskly, 'the police have been ranked low on professionalization since, on a strict construction of the term, they lack any of the distinguishing characteristics of a profession' (Day and Klein 1987: 67). The same study goes on to explore the paradox that police officers evoke professionalism in order to justify conduct, and claim, for example, certain resources (1987: 114). As these authors point out, there is a fundamental contradiction between the traditional role of the constable whose powers derive from the law and from the community, and who thus is deemed to have considerable discretion, and the nature of the hierarchical police organization. Yet, in practice, a mass of research (see Chapter 3) has shown that, at street level, police are not necessarily very well controlled and can use their powers in a variety of ways. Day and Klein are inclined to see talk of police professionalism as 'only rhetoric' (1987: 114). Other writers have argued that there is much misunderstanding of what Reiner calls the 'core mandate of policing'. In Reiner's view, that is 'historically and in terms of concrete demands placed upon the police, is the more diffuse one of order maintenance' (1985: 172). Police claims about the 'core belief of the "professional" police' are also questioned by Fielding as 'ahistorical' and over-simplified (1991: 1). These views are not confined to academics. Police authority members, interviewed for a study of public accountability, were very sceptical of the notion of professionalism in policing and frequently sought (though not always successfully) to question decisions (Day and Klein 1987).

In short, even the idea of professionalism in policing has been contested. Thus attempts and claims by any group of officers to police in a particularly professional way take place in a confusing context. Policing is an activity bounded by the rule of law (McBarnet 1979) yet at the same time, police officers have regularly to use their own judgement about when *not* to invoke full legal powers and procedures (Fielding (1988*b*) gives a very good account of an officer in just such a situation and his own explanation of his action). Various attempts have been made, especially in the 1980s and 1990s, to codify rules for police behaviour (Pike 1985) or to set measurable performance standards in policing (Audit Commission 1990). The Police and Criminal Evidence Act (PACE) 1984 was the major legislative contribution to this process, laying down, as it does, procedural rules via statutory provision and codes of practice for the treatment of suspects.

The British policewomen whom I studied, whatever their rank or seniority, spoke frequently about professionalism and often mentioned PACE. For the most part, 'professionalism' was crucial to them because it was a way in which they could demonstrate their skills and do their jobs really well and to their own satisfaction. When they used the term they did so in one of four ways: going by the book, doing things properly, treating the public, including offenders, well, and working extremely hard. It will be apparent that not only are these definitions overlapping, some are potentially contradictory and that others, if followed, may lead the conscientious officer away from what police culture might deem professional behaviour. Indeed in pursuing professional standards the women officers discussed both their own actions and those of their colleagues.

Going by the Book

As pioneers in strange territory, policewomen often and understandably search for guidebooks and maps. Martin, in her Washington, DC, study, emphasized that those whom she described as '*police-women frequently referred to "professionalism" as an important component of their job*' (1980: 187). She listed different dimensions to professionalism, e.g. loyalty to the department and achieving high production norms (ibid.) but the principle is the same. Policewomen believe that the gender neutral concept of professionalism will act both as ladder and shield for them in their careers.

For these women in Britain, a primary concern therefore was to establish what precisely the rules were and to learn how to apply them. Older officers praised their training, especially the additional, specialized part for women only, and the careful supervision of their former command structure. 'We knew exactly what we were doing. And people that then advanced into promotion again reinforced that level of process by supervising the young women officers.' This was, of course, the period when, officially, policewomen played a confined and well-defined role for which 'rule books' were easier to devise. Later recruits often felt the need for such sure guidance and were critical both of their limited training and for poor performance by those supposedly well trained. A younger officer still felt uncertain about certain areas after three years' service. She was also particularly critical of the handling of rape victims which she had observed: 'certainly I don't think I would have reported it if it happened to me because I know what you go through.' She was especially censorious of a woman detective who had dealt with one case. 'And I just generally think that we are not professional by a long chalk.'

Another young officer exemplified the paradoxical situation caused by adhering strictly to rules. She was criticized for being too zealous in following PACE and other rules.

They say I'm sitting . . . in the station office doing my paperwork, but I'm doing the paperwork you're *supposed* to do. They don't, they're too lazy to put up a process file. The difference is I'm doing what you're supposed to do: (*a*) because I'll be jumped on if I don't and (*b*) because I'm not experienced enough not to.

Relatively more female than male officers are junior in rank and less experienced and women make up, despite their low overall numbers, quite a high proportion of operational officers because of this. They are therefore likely to face these situations (which all new recruits may confront) more often. Such bible-based solutions may run counter to the culture which has, notoriously, one key piece of 'legislation', the 'Ways and Means Act', at its core.

Doing Things Properly

Strict adherence to codes is not always condemned; it may lead to advancement if the officer's merit is recognized. It is not always possible because systems may not exist, because problems are new, or have not been seen as important. Some of these officers interpreted professionalism as 'doing things properly' by which they meant not just keeping to rules but giving the fullest commitment to the job and sometimes creating new ways of doing things. The senior officer who regretted the devaluation of specialist work had later, after integration, developed some innovative work in a new field: 'I felt it was . . . very professional. And I had great hopes for that, and I suppose I'm just a wee bit proud of it.'

At other times, the proper way of doing things may mean a very precise self-monitoring of actions, in arrest or confrontational situations. The young officer who achieved a transformation scene (above) when dealing with a recalcitrant motorist described her private pondering by the roadside on the merits of what she was doing and her anxiety that she had managed well both her presentation of self and the correct procedures. Such self-reflective portraits were common and associated with the common view that females did not command automatic respect as peace officers, even when in uniform: 'I actually found . . . that I did not feel that because I had rank on my shoulders I was entitled to automatic respect . . . When it comes to deeper level of respect, that's something you have to earn.' Policewomen then develop a range of value-adding strategies to improve and professionalize their impact. These can range from learning about body language, developing counselling skills, and studying minority languages. None of these approaches would be exclusive to women; what was distinctive was the part they could play in the women's perception of themselves as professionals and their need to remedy deficiencies.

Treating the Public Well

I suggested earlier that these officers were rather less cynical about civilians than a review of other studies might suggest. Of course, they might not have wished to reveal all their feelings on this matter, but some *were* expressed. One young officer was exasperated by the cavalier attitude to crime control taken by an organization on her patch and was pleased to be able to go and talk to them later when offences were committed on their premises, but this made her rather more determined than cynical. In fact, attitudes towards the public were not only fairly positive, but it was often stressed that only good treatment of the public would maintain order and help to solve crime. One remarked approvingly about the inner-city area of her initial policing days that it was 'very rough . . . very rewarding area . . . all wonderful people to work with, superb people. Very moral.'

I have already noted that there was considerable concern about treatment of women and children and some women described threading a delicate path between conforming to stereotyped views of women held by the police ('she's a slag') and genuinely trying to help distressed victims. They were well aware that they might be labelled as a 'women's libber' but they also knew that bad treatment of vulnerable groups has undesirable repercussions for the police. A young officer described a tense situation she was called to in which an apparently drunken woman had made accusations against a group of local youths. Her male colleague was sceptical so she 'read his mind':

I said, 'Oh it's pretty obvious. She's gone to the pub, got drunk on the housekeeping. She's going to get beaten up by her husband if she tells him that, so she says she got mugged. Right?' So I sort of had this approving look from him so I thought, 'Oh God I'm safe, I'm safe but my brain is free to think what I like.'

She was able to establish that the woman was ill, not drunk, and to make arrangements for her care. This officer insisted that such cases were fairly common and cited suspects with severe learning difficulties who were not 'spotted' by the sergeant at her station.

I do not wish to suggest that only women officers have finer feelings and show a proper respect for the public. On the contrary, many of the women referred to good male colleagues who responded sympathetically and without stereotypes. They themselves did not stereotype police*men*, distinguishing between differ-ent characters and often between rank-and-file and senior officers, several of whom were described as 'brilliant'. The main difference lies in the greater need some of the women feel for the added value of professionalism in their career. In this area there also came through a sense of the changing agenda of policing, from law enforcement to social control and the role women could play in the latter in community liaison.

Extremely Hard Work

In an earlier section I quoted the story of a woman who had slept in the office in an armchair in order not to miss a call. Her devo-tion to duty was formidable and, it seemed, total. Perhaps her case was an extreme one, although it was not unparalleled. When I asked another officer if she had achieved promotion by working hard she replied,

Yes I think we women do . . . I can remember sitting up all night with another friend of mine who joined at the same time . . . she was very effective too, she was good. And we used to sit up all night and talk about the job and what we'd learnt, and, I think you do get that amongst men as well, but the nature of the conversation is totally different.

Working very long hours, doing difficult tasks under awful con-ditions are endemic to policing, one of the very few services to be open twenty-four hours a day. Most police officers work hard because that is the nature of the job, some *women* officers do so because they are women and see that as one way they can show professionalism and live up to an ideal standard as well as being possibly rewarded with praise, promotion, or even acceptance.

Throughout discussion of this topic I have tried to show that the pursuit of professionalism is not always a fulfilling one. Some women, including some of those to whom I talked, had succeeded, and professionalism played no small part in their success. Others also seemed likely to do well. However, double standards, based on a single stereotype, persist that a proper police officer is a man, whatever his standards and conduct may be. One young officer summed this up with a description of the scene as she went on her training run each day (she was anxious about fitness and strength and had trained in self-defence as well):

So I'd come out of the house, run across the police yard and there'd be a traffic car pull in—and this great slob of a policeman's stomach would appear before him, he'd sort of fall out of the vehicle and, you know, lunge his eighteen stone into the police station.

Soft Cops

One of the significant features of western countries in the late twentieth century, including Britain, is a shift in the nature of social control and the agencies involved in it. There are several grounds for arguing this and some of them were discussed in Chapter 1. The most salient aspect of such changes for our current purposes is the blurring of boundaries between caring and controlling and between the welfare and policing agencies which manage these areas and keep their frontiers. There are three key areas in which crucial shifts have occurred: community care; the new agenda of policing; changes in social composition.

Community Care

Since the late 1950s, Britain, in common with other western societies, has promoted a policy of 'community care' in most welfare services. These policies have met with varying degrees of success (Bulmer 1986) and there has been considerable debate about their aims and effects. However it is certainly the case that institutional asylum provision for the mentally ill and the mentally handicapped has been reduced. More people who might once have been 'put away' may now live in ordinary communities.

The New Agenda

In the 1970s and 1980s new items were put on the 'police' agenda, and given some priority. In particular, a series of issues connected with domestic settings were highlighted, as well as the cause of victims generally. Domestic violence, child battering, child sexual abuse, rape, and sexual harassment were all much debated (Stanko 1984, 1990; Edwards 1986) and there have been changes in police policies and practices over such matters.

Changing Social Composition

A number of changes have at the same time affected the composition of British society. It has become more plural, with more citizens whose backgrounds differ from those of the white majority. Family patterns have altered, so that more people live in single-parent families. More people live in poverty, large numbers are unemployed, and homelessness is prevalent, especially in inner cities.

As a consequence of all these changes, the expectations faced by police officers have been affected. This can best be summed up as a shift towards a more 'caring' and social-work type of role. At the same time, traditional notions of policing have been under considerable threat. Crime rates have been rising more or less steadily, the image of the police has been damaged by corruption scandals, poor relations with ethnic minorities, and a series of reverses in the criminal-justice system. The loss of credibility in old-style law enforcement makes it harder for the police to reject the new agenda, even though, as one informant put it, to call a police officer a 'bleeding heart social worker' was the worst possible insult. (There has been something of the same process in reverse, a topic for which I have no scope here.) Various strategies have been devised to organize this situation such as the multi-agency approach, in which police, social services, etc., handle a problem or problem area together.

The relevance of all this for the group which I studied is that as women they are likely to be expected to play a part in 'soft cop' policing. Indeed the old specialist departments covered some of the agenda. However, it is not merely a matter of agenda items; also involved are proposed or actual changes in styles of policing, police training, and relations with the public. Many solutions have been proposed to current crises and dilemmas in policing, among them improved management, more technology (Mainwaring-White 1983), and more resources. Another range of solutions could be labelled as more 'feminine' in character: greater community involvement, better communication skills, more home-beat officers, and greater attention paid to minor incivilities. Such issues had considerable salience for these officers. For some, the pre-integration days had focused on these areas; they had also been relevant to recent careers and they also seemed to be on the horizon again.

While all those recruited before integration had joined as female specialists, by no means all of them had relished that role. One

had been surprised at how segregated the police were and had preferred a more general role even then. One officer who most firmly
defended and praised the specialist role had herself enjoyed a wider
scope and had embraced integration with enthusiasm when it
came. While there was some regret at the impact of integration it
was, as I have already suggested, mainly because an important task
had been discarded and no provision made for its continuance; one
of these officers argued that it was essential to return to older
styles and values, otherwise

you actually breed police officers who don't know what social agency is
about . . . you're presenting a job for individuals which is all about
enforcement . . . it doesn't demand from them being compassionate, caring, understanding.

For others of her generation, however, it was a future of integrated
policing which they hoped for.

Younger officers were often faced with dilemmas over being the
'softer' side of the police. Some, as we have seen, were really committed to serving women and children, often from a feminist or
moralist perspective. Yet in a variety of ways they felt ill-equipped
for this task. None had children. One pointed out how lost she
had felt when carrying out school liaison work with very small
children. Graef quotes a WPC who hated children and yet was
always given them to mind in the station. Another recalled being
protected from an embarrassing incident in a brothel by an irate
madame who said, 'You must not call the girls [to arrest a recalcitrant client], it is not nice.' Most female officers are young and
fewer of them are married or have children than their male colleagues. In short, their life histories so far may be typical of their
generation, but they do not represent the full range of female experience. Several said that there were 'gentle' men in the force whom
they favoured for some of these roles. While some had seen signs
of, and welcomed, changes in the nature of policing, others were
still very conscious of the dominance of traditional policing values
with the pursuit of villainy still the prime aim. If the soft cops are
coming, they may steal up unawares as we are facing the consequences of another change.

A Female Cop Culture and Top Cops

These are both slightly curious concepts. The former has much more relevance to the US *political situation* and *structure*; there does not appear, in Britain at any rate, a network or subculture comparable to the traditional male one. In the pre-integration days, while numbers of women were small, there was sometimes a concentration of them for training purposes. Joan Lock (1979) and Jenny Hilton both describe such a situation in the Metropolitan Police. However, while the women with longer service had worked in women's departments and had been supervised by female officers, they did not indicate that an alternative network had existed and indeed one specially denied that it had done so. Several of these women had, as their accounts above make clear, spent periods of their careers as the sole female in a station or on a squad although there is a Metropolitan Policewomen's Association, a voluntary society, which provides a focus mainly for retired officers. Indeed it is a great historical irony that women's role in British policing, which began with such strong support from groups of women who had organized and campaigned to that end, should approach the end of the twentieth century without such an underpinning. Of course, in practice, the various groups became competitive, and the price which they had to pay in the end for inclusion in the police was the loss of much of what they had aimed for. It is doubly ironic, too, in that the macho canteen culture traditionally associated with policing was generated inside the force.

Some signs suggested that embryo networks existed. Several younger officers spoke of sharing problems with other women, although they also stressed that they were still very much outnumbered. One was in a small cohort of women in training school; when they were put into smaller groups for teaching purposes, there was a token woman in each group. Another, who did get support from two female colleagues, nevertheless stressed, 'men is what I work with.' She also indicated that it would be dangerous for women to be seen as too overtly supportive of other women: 'they'd say you're a bunch of libbers.' She had been very discretely helped by a woman sergeant who warned her not to mention the matter.

Nothing is for ever, even in a traditional, hierarchical organization like the police, and there were indications of changes while I was conducting my research and afterwards. Senior women were beginning to meet regularly. The Metropolitan Police began to run Parent Support Groups (mainly organized by women) (1990).

A notable aspect of these women's views of themselves and their careers was that they did not have role models. One or two had had (male) relatives in the police whom they admired but in whose footsteps they could not follow precisely. This relates both to the questions of subculture and top cops. It was very apparent that these women, especially the most senior ones, had to find and create their own solutions to all the problems they had faced. Their answers to questions on how they had coped with integration, with isolation and hostility, always came back to drawing on their own resources: their training, their personal dedication. Some did refer to support from male colleagues—'it was team work'—but, as I suggested earlier, they could never rely on being permanently selected for the team; they had to earn their colours afresh every time. Despite this, the police organization could and did claim them enthusiastically as their own and offer the kind of loyalty and support only such a tightly-bonded body can. One officer had had 'wonderful consideration' during an illness. The deaths of policewomen on duty have also evoked a strong response from colleagues (Lucas 1986).

No woman has yet been appointed as a Chief Constable in Britain, although at least one woman has reached every other rank available. The careers of senior police officers are not well researched and it is therefore not easy to compare with my benchmark what those to whom I spoke said about the rank they had attained. None had found it easy to achieve her present status, but they suggested that the demands on senior men were also formidable. Stress was seen as a major factor in modern policing, especially at senior levels.

Conclusions for Comparison

In this chapter I have tried to highlight the major points in the career histories of a group of women officers interviewed in Britain in the late 1980s. The presentation and selection of material is mine; the words are their own. I have, I trust, been faithful to the meaning of what they said and felt. Several common themes have emerged in considering the concepts in these careers. To use Martin's terminology, these officers were *police*women and police-*women* at once. They all wished to be part of the police, often had a sense of mission, accepted occupational values, practised streetcraft, and defended and were loyal to their colleagues. They retained, for the most part, faith in policing as an agency, even if their own ideal force would have been unrecognizably reconstructed. At the same time, while they had wanted and tried to be one of the boys, they were debarred from entry or gained only conditional acceptance. Gender was made important to them, rather than by them, at the insistence of some male colleagues. Moreover, it was not just the office of constable which was regularly defined as a male prerogative, the processes of law enforcement and social control were also seen as 'owned' by males. As a consequence, when women *did* act successfully in 'transformation scenes' or by the use of exemplary professional skills, they had to depend on men for the granting of legitimacy to their actions. Even when, as with professionalism, they might consider themselves wholly right, this had no salience until confirmed by male authority.

In the next chapter we shall go on to look at and compare experiences in the USA. Even without such comparisons, however, I hope that this chapter has provided some material for debate. It may be that this material and my interpretation of it is open to challenge. If so, I hope that challengers will come forward because there are items here of significance to everyone. It matters a great deal who controls social control in our society and how they do so. I have tried to provide a framework to discuss how some sworn officers do so, but within certain constraints. The question mark in the title of this book has to remain for the moment. We are, I hope, a little nearer to understanding why it must.

5

Policewomen in the USA

In the introduction to the last chapter I outlined some of the aspects of the research which I undertook in the USA. The main difference there was that it was possible to have both group interviews/discussion and individual ones. As some of the dialogue I quote later shows, the women were often particularly effective in interviewing each other. Sometimes they disagreed. More importantly, they both developed ideas and themes and, especially, encouraged each other.

I have published a report on my survey of Equal Opportunities in the USA which highlighted a key feature of US as compared with British policing: optimism. Almost everywhere I went, there was a great deal of confidence about women's role in policing (Heidensohn 1989b). This was true even where figures of recruitment were fairly modest, as in New York City Police Department where the proportion of female sworn personnel is similar to that in London, but with fewer in senior positions. Nevertheless, there was great confidence amongst the most senior staff that they had reached a 'tip-over' point for female recruitment, that it was rising, and would continue to do so. This view was also held by rank-and-file officers even where, perhaps most of all where, they had encountered great difficulties in 'breaking and entering'. A woman who had over twelve years' service, had been a pioneer throughout, and had endured various forms of harassment and hostility, said, 'so it's getting a lot better as, you know, as time comes along.'

Integration

Integration was in some senses more traumatic in the USA than in Britain. Until the 1970s Britain was seen (Sherman 1977) as having the edge in policy terms. Women in the USA formed an even smaller percentage of sworn personnel; they worked almost exclusively in women's bureaux, but these often did not allow for any promotion: in New York City Police Department women had to sue the City in the courts before being allowed to take sergeants' exams. The deployment of women in the bureaux also meant that they were moved about to provide matron services and thus could have very little career development (Feinman 1986). I did not interview any pre-integration recruits in the USA, but some of the veteran officers I spoke to mentioned that there had been a few women in Vice and the CID as plain-clothes officers in the 1940s whom they recalled. There did not appear to have been the easing of the role observed in Britain and thus integration, which was almost wholly symbolized by women going on patrol for the first time, was a very traumatic matter. It will be recalled that in Britain integration also meant women sergeants and inspectors commanding men.

Several differentiating factors are important here. While police organizations in both countries are hierarchical and bureaucratic, with discipline as a key feature, all these are probably more marked in Britain. We have already seen that, by the 1970s, Britain was policed by only forty-three forces, having unitary control over their territories, while in the USA legions of departments, large and small, keep order sometimes in overlapping areas. US police departments, other than Federal Agencies such as the FBI, usually come under local political control, with police chiefs and senior officers appointed by local politicians. There was thus quite a different context for integration there; sometimes it was introduced more swiftly, and sometimes in a fairly turbulent fashion. Remmington's (1981) account of the Atlanta experience illustrates these features very well. Another obvious factor is that for women to go on to the streets to patrol in the USA has quite a different connotation from Britain: crime rates, especially for violent crime, are much higher in the USA than in the UK; as a matter of routine, all officers are armed in the USA; very few are in mainland Britain and women were not trained to use arms in Britain until the end of the 1980s. Thus for a woman to go on the beat in Britain would mean walking or driving it in a uniform which is, to this day, different from men's. In the USA it meant going out, well armed, also wearing a bullet-proof vest, in the same uniform that men wore. In the city of Boston, for example, uniform for women was only introduced with integration.

Local variation in the USA can be very considerable. Size is one simple but key factor: I interviewed women who worked or had worked in tiny departments where there were only six or eight sworn officers, as well as some from cities. Size not only had an effect on specialism, promotion, etc.—one woman found herself Chief of Police in a small township shortly after joining (see below)—but was also determinant of whether civil-service rules are applied at selection. These give, as one would expect, guidance on the selection of recruits and forms of testing. The federal funds mentioned earlier would not usually be available to departments not keeping to civil-service standards. This was not of such great significance in some smaller rural departments which seemed to apply somewhat idiosyncratic procedures. An effect of this, in some places, was to enable women to enter more easily, where, for instance, there was no upper age limit. Another important feature is the plurality of US policing: most of my informants were officers with city or township police, but some worked in sheriffs' departments and one had previously worked for state police.

Politics

Politics play a much more overt role in US policing than in Britain, mainly because most police come under direct local-government control, or are strongly influenced by local political considerations. Since US political parties are broad interest groupings, local politics often involve providing for local interests. Thus residence requirements for employees are quite common and have an impact on recruitment. Boston and New York had such requirements in 1988, as did Washington, DC, although this was being challenged in the latter case by the unions. Senior appointments in the police will usually be political, rather than simply bureaucratic. At these levels promotion may only be temporary, as one informant in an eastern city put it: 'there are Lieutenants being commanded by a patrolman . . . Do you know what that does do for morale?'

However, there is much diversity in such matters and in Dallas, for example, the city had had a policy of actively recruiting elsewhere and thus employed officers not only from other parts of Texas, but also from out of the state. Another important difference involved the resources available to pay for public services such as policing. New York had undergone fiscal crises and this had led to the sacking of some police officers. On a 'last in, first out' basis this had particularly hit women. There had also been a long gap since sergeants' exams could be taken with a consequent effect on promotion. Again, this had had a disproportionate effect on women who made up a higher proportion of lower grades. Until the oil boom burst in the mid-1980s, Dallas had been relatively prosperous and thus able to fund its public services well. In Washington, DC, there were also particular local features because more resources had been pumped into the city to clean up its image as a crime capital.

One area in which US police differ markedly from their British counterparts has been in their ability to recruit from ethnic minority groups. The Metropolitan Police Department in the capital city employs a majority of black officers and over 80 per cent of the female officers were black at the time of my visit. There was enormous variation, however, in such recruitment patterns. Under 20 per cent of officers in Boston were black and the city was operating its recruitment policy under court orders, called consent decrees, which obliged it to redress past discrimination by taking half its recruits from ethnic minorities. In consequence, more than half the females were black and Hispanic because they had been recruited in the 1980s, under the terms of the decree. Only minorities were the subject of this decree, not women.

Many informants specifically mentioned local politics as an aspect of the policing situation. Further, it had clearly been a factor in their own careers. One had previously worked in a small town in the Deep South and had confronted hostility as a woman, a stranger, and a Yankee. Crude Klan symbols had been left in her locker. In Dallas there had been much tension as a result of the deaths of three police officers, and a dispute between the City Council and the Police Association. As a result, many of the women officers had been closely bonded into the general body of the police, although there were signs of some divisions along racial lines. This is perhaps the most important difference between British and US policing and it had some bearing on other aspects. However, in this chapter I want to look at the accounts given by American women in policing within the same framework that I applied to the British. It must be borne in mind that these women are or were sworn, trained police officers. Their years of service ranged from three to seventeen. They came from a variety of regional and ethnic back-grounds and were, or had been, serving in uniform or detective work with a few specialists, such as a dog handler. Unlike the British group, no one had pre-integration experience and none was in a senior capacity. While they therefore do not match the British group, they are relatively representative of modern American women police who have overwhelmingly been recruited since inte-gration, have in some cases benefited from affirmative action plans in terms of recruitment, although in terms of promotion and spe-cialization these plans were relatively slow to mature.

A Sense of Mission

One of the things that will become clear in this analysis is that sharing a career concept does not always involve giving it the same meaning or interpretation. Rather, it becomes a key word, or a symbol, which can trigger or encapsulate a variety of behaviour or experiences. These may not all be the same, but they will bear a likeness to one another and often the speakers will appear to be describing the same thing, even though there are discernible differ-ences. A sense of mission is a very good case to demonstrate this, and I shall start with the point of entry.

Entry

Many but not all the US women had tried extremely hard to enter the police, as had the British. However, this meant in practice quite different things. Moving around the country was not usually an option, because of residence requirements, although several of the women in Dallas had gone there because of its open recruitment: one had moved down especially from the Midwest. Another took advantage of her husband's transfer to a southern state to apply.

The most striking difference was that some women had had recourse to law, using various equal-rights provisions, to enter the police. Only then were they recruited. Another feature of the fight for entry was education. In order to fulfil the minimum require-ments of two years at college one determined woman adopted a drastic solution:

so I took leave of absence for thirty days and I had twenty-one hours of college that I needed to complete. So I went to three different colleges in thirty days and got twenty-one hours. I was going day and night and everything to get my hours. And I had a baby and I had a home. So I didn't have time and my mom, my parents were right there together and I said, 'Hold on to my kid, I'll be back in thirty days.'

An older woman had paid for her own training in the police academy, with no certainty of being hired at the end. She had, she said, a scrap-book of her applications—and rejections—but she had eventually made it.

Sometimes the motivation for such determination was, as with British women, a moral one. A woman who had grown up in poverty and had seen many of her peers become juvenile delinquents became determined, as a result, 'that I never wanted to be on that side' of the law and to join the police and prevent others from following them. 'I think that I made a little bit of a difference . . . that's why public service has always meant so much to me and continues to.' In other cases there were moral motives to do with improving the police from the inside, especially from several black women. One of these described her motives with an interesting gloss of hindsight after ten years' service

Being a civilian back then you saw a lot of things on TV about police brutality. Then one night I was driving home and of course not being a police officer and not having any prior knowledge I didn't know why these bad police officers had this guy round the back of the neck and were slamming his head against the hood of the car. And I looked and said 'God, they're killing him.' and you know, now I know better. First thing I thought was, 'It would just kill me if they did that to one of my kids! So . . . I guess the main reason I joined was for my kids.

Another black officer had consistently taken on challenges throughout her career to be the first black female in each successive position and to 'push progress' ahead.

There was another aspect to this which did not appear, or was perhaps not voiced in Britain, and that was a frequently expressed desire to join the police not only because it was a moral agency, nor to (re-)moralize it but also because its structure and its culture were seen as cohesive, even familial, and thus giving support to the tasks of officers and a special quality to their work. Now, some of this was partly due to family links in recruitment. Police families are not uncommon and S. Jones observed this in her British study (1986). One of the earliest women recruits had a father and brothers in the same department and one of the most persistent applicants was the daughter of a police officer. A further group had, however, observed the police from inside as civilians, generally as radio dispatchers, and they had sought to join the group whose role and cohesiveness had impressed them:

I worked in the actual dispatch office . . . you could always tell with a group of officers . . . you could tell on their faces that something major had just happened, something really important, and it was like they would all really pull together as one big unit and they would stay right with each other until whatever had happened was over with and all the officers were fine. There's where I really saw the unity and saw the family part and I wanted to be part of that.

Another young officer, who had originally been in a different public service post used very similar terms: 'I noticed that I'm real family oriented and I noticed that police officers seem to have the cameraderie of the family . . . I just watched S and his friends . . . and I just thought it was neat and I wanted some of that.'

Some British officers had sought variety and a different kind of career with challenges. As an expressed aim a search for excitement was quite common as a motive for US officers. One youthful officer had joined the police cadets in her city:

and my first assignment was with —— and his detective . . . and I became addicted . . . you know it was fascinating . . . it was always exciting . . . they have great stories . . . you know once you're a cadet you're just destined to be a police officer.

New York City Police Department had recently found this to be the case and had increased their intake of women and of college graduates by taking on female cadets still at college who then were recruited into the Department (Heidensohn 1989b). On the other side of the country, a woman in her mid-thirties, already married and with a family, was attracted in a very similar way. As a temporary dispatcher, 'well, lo and behold the guys kept coming in, "Well we've got a murder out here", "We found a dead body", or whatever. And the old bug started in the back . . . "Well, what happened? I want to know more."'

In Britain, as I showed in the last chapter, women had often had to struggle to enter the police, both before integration and even afterwards when unofficial and illegal quotas appear to have operated. Several officers met hostility or exclusion on entering the

police. What goaded a number of US women, and these were usually from small departments, into developing fierce commitment to
this career can best be described as counter-productive provocation. Women who expressed a desire, or just showed an application form, to join the police to the local chief were sometimes met
with such a hostile response that they became determined to persist.

We had a male chauvinist pig, with capital letters as a chief. Capital letters! Women were fine as dispatchers, but not as police officers, well the
academy was opening up . . . and I said, 'I want to go' as a jest, and
strictly at this point, as a jest. And he says, 'You couldn't make it' and
you know what that is to women . . . so here I went.

The determination of one to become a sheriff was increased by the
attitude of the men:

I had a certain faction of the men—there are still a few to this day—saying to me, 'I still don't think women should be doing this kind of work.
This isn't woman's work.' These are the ones who want to keep you pregnant in summer and barefoot in winter.

Another realized only gradually the resistance she was meeting: 'I
guess I should have known at the very beginning . . . when I first
went down and got the application and everything.' She was not
hired, though men were. Her response was to file suit and she was
eventually taken on.

The attraction of police 'war stories' and excitement described
above is far from gender specific. Indeed it is a love of adventure
which is supposed to draw young men into some of the most traditional masculine occupations such as the military. What might be
called the reverse Groucho-effect is, however, much more gender-
specific, since it is almost certainly only women who are told that
certain roles or jobs are not for them. Several British officers
described hostility among their families and friends. None, however, seemed quite as spurred on by this patriarchal proprietorship
as were the Americans.

Inside the Police

Once inside their police departments, the US women had some
similar experiences to the British as far as shock, hostility, and so
on went, but there were a number of differences and, more important, their responses and their context were different. Earlier in this

volume I discussed the concept of cop culture and how valid it still was. Walker (1985), as I noted, had observed that cop culture studies had been undertaken rather a long time ago and in all-white, male-staffed departments. None of these departments conformed to that pattern. Boston was closest to it, but had begun to change, and in some of the other cities rapid change had occurred. It was thus improbable that the traditional culture had survived completely intact, although that seemed less true of the small, rural departments.

It was not only ethnic and sexual diversity which had altered the composition of the police. Several women remarked that abolishing the former minimum height standards 'has let in all the short guys'. Others remarked on the increased educational requirements at entry for many departments and the effect that this had on the police. Thus the context in which these officers worked when they first joined differs from the original macho culture somewhat and also from the British situation which is, as yet, far less plural and diverse.

Significant distinctions can also be discerned in what might be termed the personal-political cultures of the two societies in general and, especially, in relation to policing. There is an almost tangible climate in the USA which aims at equality and rewards for all. Often, as was the case with these officers, there is also a commitment to feminism. It was often hard to judge which was the philosophical justification being used to criticize unfair or discriminatory treatment. Sometimes criticism of behaviour by fellow or senior officers was countered by, 'it's just as bad for the guys'. Certainly many of the women who sympathized with strong criticism of chauvinist colleagues and chiefs would not otherwise fit notions of feminism. Some held quite right-wing views on other matters, went hunting, and were opposed to extending certain citizens' rights. I think what one can say about women in modern America is that either in it feminism is so pervasive an aspect that it is almost taken for granted as designed into the system now, *or* that the culture of equality, whether or not it is based on myths about the American Dream, informs aspirations of women and empowers their assertion. These conditions do not make for enormous differences in *outcomes*, but they do influence the atmosphere of confidence.

This is an interesting example of a major difference in culture and ideology between the two countries and one which has resulted in distinct divergence in attitudes and even behaviour. Its effects have been observed in other aspects of the criminal-justice system. Paul Rock, for instance, in comparing the development of provisions for victims of crime in Canada, the USA, and Britain, has suggested that in the two former countries, feminists did have an impact on the form that support for victims took. In Canada he found three key factors which influenced patterns and policies: the existence of a government minister charged with monitoring all legislation with regard to its impact on women, the presence within the public bureaucracies at province and national level of significant numbers of female policy analysts who took part in the policy process, and, finally, a dialogue between the feminist movement and government which enabled the former to influence the latter. The position in the USA was not quite the same, but certainly both the *legitimacy* of the approach and the possibilities of dialogue were. The consequence was, Rock concludes, that there was 'a pronounced feminization of the victim in North America— that is, the raped and assaulted woman was the archetypal victim who secured funding, assistance and publicity' (1991). In contrast, he argues, in the UK there was a much greater gulf between the women's movement and government and there was a 'gender neutral victim' as the archetype of campaigns. While I find that Rock underestimates the different legal and political cultures which were responsive to feminism in North America, but not in Britain, his main point, that feminism and feminists significantly affected North American victim support is important (Rock 1991).

Inside the Police and Women Inside the Police

Having said that the US officers were perhaps more confident than some of their British counterparts, because of political and cultural differences for the most part, it has to be acknowledged that some of them had had to face formidable battles once inside the organization. While many of these were to do with overcoming critical hostility from male colleagues (and, very occasionally, from their wives) there were also a number which had to do with training and supervision and some over the use of disciplinary proceedings. In the latter cases these women felt that they were persecuted because they were successful, female officers (and, in one instance, black), who posed a threat.

Facing Down the Culture

As Martin (1980: 151 ff.) makes only too clear in her extensive observational account of policing in Washington, DC, the forms of harassment and hostility which can face female police officers are common to both sides of the Atlantic. The significant differences lay in the relatively well-accepted uniformed women in their specialized roles before integration in Britain, and, perhaps, the degree of vehemence with which hostility was expressed.

A black officer, recalling the first years of integration, described her male colleagues as suffering from 'female fever'. She diagnosed this as a disorder brought on by seeing women in uniform and on patrol for the first time. They were often, she mused, outraged and incoherent, but they had learnt to cope with it. For a white woman in a small town, it took longer and eventually she moved on to another department:

basically, it was an uphill battle all the time. A lot of the guys took a while . . . to adjust . . . when I moved . . . I told one of the officers there, 'I am tempted to walk in and explain, make an announcement, I'm not after your bodies, I'm not after your jobs, I have to make a living, this is the way I have to support myself and if you have a problem with that I'm sorry but I just want to do my job,' and they said, 'No, no don't do that, that'll be coming on too strong.' And I can't tell you how many incidences since I've been there . . . It's not too bad now, it's taken me eight years to finally feel I can be comfortable with where I'm working and what I'm doing.

Such resentment was not universal. An integration 'veteran' in another department said that while a married woman found hostility for taking on extra paid work, 'I was by myself and had two children; they thought that was alright.' For others, especially the more recent recruits, only a minority of male colleagues had been troublesome; nevertheless, there were occasions of disillusionment: 'I was very disappointed to find out that it's not just the dirt bags that are dirt bags, its also some of the good people.' A white officer found:

My feeling is that the black men are less threatened and less intimidated and less uncomfortable working with women because they're used to having women in authority roles. And because of that I got along with them very well.

While all raw recruits to any all-embracing institution undergo rites of passage which may scare or humiliate them, the position of women entering the police is special in several ways. The institution is already established and, in the case of the police, with an occupational culture whose traditional 'marks of affinity' they cannot match. Their numbers are still small and their relative power within the organization limited. This is not just a matter of numbers, it also has to do with relative positions in the hierarchy, which can affect patronage and networks and even protection. Several women clearly felt that they had been bullied (my term, not theirs) and that male officers were both protected from such attacks and from the consequences of making them. One reported a conversation with a male colleague recruited with her:

there were two of us got hired at the same time and we had a lot of talks over the course of the years I was there and he said to me, 'I can honestly say, if they put me through what they've been putting you through since you've been here, I'd have quit a long time ago.'

While for another, protection of a kind had been exercised by a male relative who was an officer in the same department: 'finally he said to me one day, "I'm sick of sticking up for you and the girls" (laughter). I said, "Forget it . . . that's OK."'

A further factor which hampers policewomen in their attempt to assert themselves properly in their role against the cultural resistance they meet is that they initially lack the inside knowledge, the trade secrets which can be helpful weapons. As we shall see, and as the British accounts showed, US women often called on professionalism and transformations to validate their roles. There were however, signs of their additionally using their own, growing streetcraft and/or police procedures to resist. This was another aspect of what I have earlier called counter-productive provocation working. A woman had met persistent scorn and abuse from a male colleague who doubted her capacity to manage on the street. When he insisted on taking over in a situation that she felt she was coping with 'he said, "we're causing a big scene. I'm the senior officer. We're causing a big scene, let him up." And I let him up (the suspect) and he spit right between his eyes.'

On another occasion a short male officer who prided himself on his muscular superiority to females took over an arrest from two women whom he told to 'leave it to me'. 'The guy starts giving him trouble and is going to choke the guy—then the guy stands up and starts carrying . . . because his feet were this much off the ground.' (An added irony in this situation is that short men often owe their recruitment to women who campaigned and petitioned to have minimum height limits lifted.) A black rookie successfully complained of harassment after prolonged mistreatment:

they were going to fire him . . . and when I heard that, I went to the sergeant. I said, 'Sergeant, I don't want him fired, because I want him to get fired on his own. I don't want it said that I'm the one that caused him to get fired. Because it's coming unless he changes his ways.

A detective who had experienced hostility from a male colleague was similarly prepared to bide her time and let the system catch up with him: 'someday I'll get even with him. I haven't gotten even but someday I will. And it won't be any of my doing. He'll do it all for himself.'

These examples illustrate two slightly contradictory points. On the one hand, the feminist mission of some women is somewhat blunted as they accept the code and procedures of the police organization as legitimate ways to fight back: they are resisting through traditional rituals. On the other hand, they have perceived ways, and sometimes used them adroitly, which achieve their own ends without the expense of enormous amounts of energy on being questioning and outspoken or, as many admitted they had done, on grief and tears. Occupational socialization may exclude women from the mysteries of policing and in its very display, show them the levers to pull in the trapdoor to spring some traditional, but unexpected surprises.

Having given these examples of somewhat innovatory strategies, it is important to stress that US policewomen, like their British counterparts, most often use voice as a mode of protest or criticism, even though they constantly recognize that, as women, they may be penalized for this as the following dialogue from a group interview illustrates.

A. I think what she's talking about there's a good example of being a female. I know when I was on training you're scared to say anything but once you've become outspoken then these people, the men, you know like you're supposed to be meek and mild, and I went through this in dispatch, boy when I wanted to get out of there—once they find out you're outspoken you've automatically . . .

B.   That's funny you said that because in that interview I went through with a selection panel they asked me what my favourable characteristics are and then I told them, I said, 'I'm very outspoken—I said I will say exactly what I think,' and they said, 'Oh, do you feel that's an admirable quality?' and I said, 'I do in my case . . . '

C.   Sure that is in a man but that's not acceptable for . . .

D.   They want a woman to be just meek and mild, not saying anything.

E.   If a man is aggressive, then he's you know, but if a woman is then she's a bitch . . . some really feel that way.

By far the most interesting feature of this particular discussion is that it then led the group to consider the role played by one of their number who had become the voice, or the speaker for *all* their colleagues, male and female, because of her skill and determination. As one put it

And there's officers that have more experience around and excuse the term but when the shit hits the fan, who do they call? They don't call these other guys, they don't call Supervisor, they call Y. 'Y help me write my letter to the Chief', 'Y do this', and they just know that Y is going to be fair and honest.

This was not the only example of women becoming the voice of the police which I came across in the USA.

Taking on Training

From the examples in the previous section it is clear that rank-and-file male officers in the USA were not prepared for the arrival of women on patrol, a point made also by Martin. This reflects British experience, too, with the added factor there that a few women were suddenly put in charge of men on integration. One of the British officers did say that preparation would have been pointless: 'the men would never have been ready.' Nowadays at least one minimal form of training occurs for male recruits: it is quite clear that they will be joining an integrated service. Training is obviously a key area for all police recruits, both in the police academy and in the apprenticeship period served afterwards under the supervision of an experienced officer. It is particularly crucial for women because they have to learn both professional skills and how to adjust to an occupation whose supposedly defining characteristics they lack. It became clear that many women had had to take

on their training and trainers in order to ensure that they were
well prepared.

Those who had been recruited and trained in the 1970s found
their academy training was often uncompromisingly macho, even
brutal.

But doing the academy, it was really something, because . . . being women
we had to prove ourselves and everything . . . we worked, they didn't give
us anything . . . we did the boxing . . . it was four women and we were
out there boxing, and the thing about it was, I think this guy was out for
blood. But T is a lot smaller than me, short, and she wouldn't . . . so I hit
her in her lip and she was bleeding, I could see blood and blood all in her
mouth, so, I stopped hitting her and he got hold of me and said, 'why did
you do this, why did you stop?' and I said, 'She's hurt. Why should I fight
somebody that's hurt?' So, right away we weren't on good terms.

This group of women then banded together to train and give each
other support because of the physical demands of the course, particularly from a trainer whom they called Bruce Lee, 'every time he
saw blood his eyes glazed over.' The woman whose mouth bled in
the above account was thus able to come through her training
intact and with humour.

[We] just stuck together quite a bit and like I said . . . I was weakest
physically, so that's why I earned the name of 'Oh my God' . . . because
every time I hurt or I didn't do something right I said 'Oh my God' . . .
and it stuck since then, and I even got a little charm that the burglars took
away that used to have 'Oh my God' on it.

Physical standards were stressed in other academies although not
always so fiercely. An older recruit was only required to improve
her performance, not meet a single target. Several questioned the
relevance and purpose of the physical standards as, first of all,
irrelevant to policing. Doing a body drag was a commonly
required performance, yet most insisted that they had never needed
to use this, nor had they seen it used. Others pointed out that
upper-body strength, particularly forearm strength, is where the
sexes differ most markedly in terms of physical powers, yet men
who develop their powers in this way may almost disable themselves:

G couldn't do anything that had to do with flexibility, cos he lifted
weights. Touching your toes, bending down, he couldn't do them and the
instructor, if you weren't far enough down, he would push. He went over

towards G and someone said, 'Hey, how come you never push him?' And he said, 'It would rip muscles with him because he's so muscle bound that the resistance would tear.' I wish I could use that excuse.

As well as the group noted earlier who all undertook extra physical training in the academy, many others mentioned taking extra courses, working out, or running, so determined were they to make it. One

went to the academy. Studied like crazy still with my baby at home. It was hard, cos I did a lot of it by myself. And ran . . . I hate to run . . . but I ran three miles a day and cried every day. But I thought, if the lord really wanted me to do this job I was going to make it round that track . . . and I did.

By the 1980s it was, however, possible to discern some changes in the Academy which the advent of women had brought about

that allowed all the small men to come in too . . . because once the women got in all the five foot one guys got in too. And I'll tell you, all the men that I worked with in the . . . Police Department, we had a lot of small guys, a lot of small guys. So they needed defensive tactics too.

Later recruits had obviously benefited from their academy courses:

I think I did real good in the academy, I did real good in training and, I woke up, I was able to say, 'Even though I am a female, there are things that I want to do, I have my own ideas.' I decided I liked myself after going through the academy.

Colleagues of another woman told me that she had achieved the highest score when graduating from the academy. So well adapted had the courses apparently become that a woman who had herself trained while she was pregnant and 'didn't miss a thing' (the baby was born a month after she graduated) reported, 'we have had numerous [pregnant] officers in the 80s going through the academy.'

Trainers themselves could be crucial to the career of a rookie. Some male officers simply refused to take on women as trainees:

The first training officer that was assigned to train me refused to train me. He said he would quit before he would train me. They just didn't want me there . . . it was just that simple. They wouldn't talk to me, they wouldn't help me. It was very difficult.

The welcome received by others was hardly more positive:

I'll never forget my first trainer. He had never trained a female and we got in the car and he said, 'Now I want you to understand something. There's three rules in my car. One is, don't ask me to take you anywhere to go to the bathroom, because I'm not going to. Secondly, we will not eat on duty. And thirdly, make sure that no one wants to speak to you while you work with me.' So for three months I never went to the bathroom on duty and none of the other officers were allowed to talk to me . . . I did what he wanted me to do . . . I figured this is what I was going to have to go through, it was my training. I was going to prove to them that there was nothing that could deter me.

For a fellow officer the situation was even worse: 'there were no female trainers, we had all-male trainers and it was pure hell.' But from this situation for her and for others there came the determination both to resist and to change. This officer and another female rookie decided they wished to patrol together after so much bad experience with men.

And when we approached the sergeant about having our own beat it was a big gasp 'Ah two females' and then they came back and said, 'Well we thought about this real hard . . . and we don't want anything to happen to you,' and we said, 'we're friends, like a lot of these guys here are friends, and we can do the job.

They got their way, although they were still subject to considerable protective patrolling: 'we had squads following us . . . I got so upset, I said "Get the hell out of here."'

Other women also had, to use a slightly dated term, their consciousness raised in training. For one, the lack of any female role models throughout her training proved a major gap. There were none in the academy, no trainers on the streets, not even any female figures in the films used for in-service training. This made her determined to become a trainer herself to offer a constructive exemplar not only to female trainees, but to the males who would see her as a senior and authoritative figure. In another example, a woman officer deliberately chose to stay on patrol and as a field trainer because of her sense of mission to train the most professional officers in general and also especially to develop her female trainees' skills and confidence:

I really feel good about myself in a patrol position, I feel . . . it's necessary for women to stay in patrol . . . and field training . . . the female recruits I've tried to show them by how I act and how I respond to people, that yes you're going to have to be professional . . . and they learn that they can do that and still be a woman . . . you can still do all those things and be yourself. That's what is good about having a female trainer. That's what some of the women would like—they never had.

Some had, however, and did find that it made a great difference.

Z was my second trainer—I had two males and her—and she taught me a lot . . . I always hoped I could get a female officer when I came out, so I could understand. The guys were great when they were training me, as far as confronting people and that sort of thing . . . but having a female officer there, you learn from the female standpoint how to handle yourself.

Female trainers were, of course, a rarity, especially as most of the women had trained some years before. Not all male trainers were obstreperous and difficult. The officer quoted earlier, whom the male trainers had refused to take on, was eventually trained by a very capable and professional officer to whom she presented a challenge. He became determined to make her his best trainee. Some of the integration veterans recognized that there had been too little preparation, both for rank-and-file officers and in training and supervision:

My big point has always been . . . on preparing the men for the women . . . Because that is where they made a big mistake. I don't think things would have been significantly different for the women—the women would still have had to prove themselves against the men and all that, but I think it would have been a smoother transition for the supervisors. They were simply not prepared for all that.

She thought that this stage was now past and everyone had some knowledge and experience of women officers who were no longer a novelty. In training, then, as elsewhere, women had made some responses of their own to what they perceived as the defects of the system. Their most dramatic reactions occurred when they faced and had to contend with the appropriate police procedures for suspension and/or dismissal.

Police Procedures

I have already mentioned that some women had taken out legal cases against various police departments for failing to hire them. Much more dramatically, some were themselves the subject of disciplinary proceedings. They were all convinced that they were pursued for being women, being 'different', and, particularly, all characterized themselves as outspoken, forthright, and direct. The cases differed in a number of respects. In case one, the woman was suspended over an alleged citizen's complaint at exactly the same time that she had done extremely well in promotional exams. She was sacked, but then went to court and succeeded in getting full reinstatement and back pay. She had suffered a great deal during this case, both financially as a result of being unemployed, but most of all emotionally because of her sense of injustice and the loss of a job she loved. Despite this experience, she was still dedicated to a career in policing, still committed to equality for women, and a staunch believer in the cause of women in policing:

I think that women and law enforcement here in the United States have come a long way since they started in entering in great numbers, and the equality issue came to the fore. But I also believe that you have continually to pound on doors and pound desks to make sure that we continue to be brought in and continue to rise through the ranks because there isn't a man alive who is going to do it unless he is forced to do it.

In case two, another outspoken woman, also the sole female in her squad, had faced possible disciplinary proceedings over what seemed to her trivial infractions. The case had eventually been withdrawn and she had been advised by lawyers to sue, but 'my feeling is that I don't want to make my reputation that way. I have to work here and if I start suing just to get my job . . . it's not going to make it any easier for me. I just want to do the job.' While this case had not been resolved in court, there were parallels with the first. Both women were the sole females in their particular sections, there had been known and overt hostility to their recruitment. Both were forthright and unafraid, both had good professional records and had done well in assessments. Understandably both felt that one part of the cause of their treatment was that they were women and notably strong, controlling women, precisely the sort who might make very good police officers. Neither was disillusioned by her experiences and both wanted to continue to promote the cause of women in policing.

The third case was rather different. The woman concerned had a long and outstanding record—she had more than fifty commendations—in a specialist area and had always got on well with her bosses, but she then came up against one with whom she disagreed and who appeared to have tried to use disciplinary proceedings against her. In the end she received a mild sanction which she was trying to have lifted at the time of the interview. Her confidence had been affected by this clash, which seemed to be partly due to gender: 'So they take your desire, I guess you could call it, to really get on with the job when you've been treated like that. So for right now that is the end of this long sad story.'

Victimization of 'whistle-blowers' or 'trouble-makers' is nothing new, nor confined to women, in the police. At the time this research was being carried out in the USA John Stalker's book on his own case had been published in Britain and had become the number one best seller. In it, Stalker (1988) outlines the story of how, as an exemplary and highly successful senior officer he was appointed to conduct an inquiry into the alleged 'shoot to kill' policy in the Royal Ulster Constabulary. He was then suspended while an inquiry into various allegations against him was carried out. Ultimately he was reinstated but he left the police a few months later. Stalker was a Deputy Chief Constable and his case had enormous political ramifications and consequences. It is interesting that, in the way he describes his sense of loss and betrayal, he sounds, at a much more exalted level, something like the rank-and-file female officers whose cases I have cited.

That is not to say, of course, that they did not have proceedings brought against them as women. It seems very likely that this was one, extreme way in which the trouble of troublesome women might be dealt with when other strategies, such as harassment, had not worked. Hierarchical law-enforcement agencies may find it very hard to accommodate virtuous deviants who stick to the rules and expect justice. If they are women they may not understand the hidden rules, such as 'don't rock the boat', or they may read them all too clearly and reject them as unjust or corrupt. It is not possible to tell whether women are involved in more or fewer of such cases. Significantly several women mentioned incidents which, they said, might have escalated into disciplinary incidents or harassment cases, but had not done so. Two kinds of messages for missionaries emerged from such histories. First, that even total, moral, and legal victory could not compensate for the enormous personal and social costs involved. That is really a message about control, about not breaking the silence, or being out of place. The second was that, such was their dedication and determination, most protagonists in these dramas wanted to soldier on. They had not wholly lost their faith.

A major difference between the USA and Britain was that acting as guardians of their own sex *outside* the police was hardly mentioned by these officers. Almost the only time women citizens figured was in a series of 'war stories' about women drivers who asked for their cars to be towed or pushed when they were stuck or failed to start. In some instances, more often it seemed in the south, a male officer was requested, 'a real policeman'; in others, the women themselves pushed. It may be that the lack of continuity with the older bureaux or the different nature of social work were factors in creating a difference here. Also of significance, however, was the regularly expressed preference for exciting and controlling jobs and often for crime-fighting. One mature patrol officer announced, 'I love traffic stops. I have a very controlling personality.' A young black officer described her day's work in a downtown area: 'One shooting, two stabbings. Hauling bums. I love it.' From the examples in this section it will be clear that there was still very considerable enthusiasm for and commitment to policing as a job for women. A woman who had left the department for another job in law enforcement but came back specially for the interview put most eloquently the attraction of the job:

It's something that you'll never forget. When you leave, when you see a squad car, the flashes come back, the memories come back, when you see an officer in uniform, some of the memories come back. Some of the cases and things you worked on . . . that's why I don't watch, I never have, even when I was on the department, I don't like these police stories, I don't watch police stories on TV, because they bring back too many memories. So I don't and I know a lot of it is too make-believe, and its not like that out there. And I know how the adrenalin is when you're out there and you're out there and they tell you you're going on a call and the man's going to shoot the first police officer that gets to the scene. And they out you in the car with a male police officer and you got to show that you are going to be just as calm as he is, and you're breaking out in a cold sweat—and you can't show it! And there are some that'd laughed and grinned in those officers' faces but that's not the way it was, I'm a person—and A and B we wanted to prove that we could do it. And we're not just here because we're females. And we're here and we put that uniform on like you do because we want to be here.

Pioneers

The concept of pioneering, of striking out into unknown territory, to conquer it and find yourself, is a very American one. Certainly there were many examples amongst the women I interviewed of what I called in the chapter on Britain 'true firsts'. I have already considered in the last section the training they had experienced, which was, as in Britain, not so much a direct preparation, but an aspect of an initiation ritual which let them into the mystery of policing. Belatedly perhaps, one department was planning a course on street survival for women only while I was there. None, as far as I know, had planned or even contemplated one on surviving the culture.

'True Firsts'

If anything, true firsts were rather more common in the USA than in Britain because of the later and more rapid expansion there, and there was perhaps a somewhat different emphasis to do with the frontier culture to which I have referred. This was brought out well in the following reminiscence:

There weren't that many women there, but it was getting better. We were having a lot more, they realized they couldn't put us in the shower room any more, so they moved us to the men's locker room, and I used to laugh because I said it was like cowboys and Indians. When the cowboys make the little wagon train wheel around, all the Indians were fighting around them and all the covered wagons were in a little circle. That's the way our dressing room was—all of us were in a circle and all the guys were behind us. I mean all they had to do was stand on a bench, and look over. And they did.

This nicely catches both the *collective* pioneer spirit that was evident in several US departments and the controlling presence of male colleagues, either the US cavalry in chivalrous attendance or a collection of peeping Toms.

A surprising number of these women had been literally the first woman officer hired by her department, something that would be hard to find in Britain now. One had achieved this 'first' twice by moving from one small rural department to another.

Q. Are you the first woman in this county?
A. Yeah,

Q. And the first woman in — too?

A. Yeah, and it was basically . . . there's another woman on this department now who got hired after I did. And she had it a whole lot
easier . . . I took things.

Another was the first sheriff in her department: 'See I was the first
female took the job, they had women deputies in the office but I
was the first to put the uniform on and put on the street and I got
the same thing . . . "This isn't woman's work."' In another area
one woman was encouraged to be an auxiliary officer, attending
the academy in her own time (this is a system similar to special
constables in Britain). 'I found out that this was the only way I
was gonna have a chance. What they wanted to do was have the
honeymoon before the marriage. They wanted the chance to look
me over and see if I fit in.' This may not be simply a treatment
designed for women. Men were reported in another area as having
similar reserve or auxiliary service experience.

Most of these 'firsts' had experienced confusion and lack of
preparation for their arrival. A member of the first uniformed
cohort in her department said

they put a few here and a few there and we were out on walking patrol
mostly. They wanted us to be visible, they wanted the public to see us to
show the public that we were here on the streets, they weren't really sure
of us and we weren't sure of what they wanted us to do . . . but they
found out. Even when we first went to the academy they did not know
how to take us, but like anything else once they get to know you . . .

In quite a different area and some years later, the same problems
confronted a first: 'They obviously didn't know how to handle a
woman then . . . when I came to Sheriff's nobody quite knew what
to do with me. Is she supposed to be special? Is she supposed to be
like everybody else?'

Such are the disparities and distances between US departments
that at least one woman experienced a sensation akin to travelling
back in time. She had worked in a department in the West where
there had been women in senior positions and had found herself
returning to pioneering when she moved. The pressures on true
firsts as torch-bearers was often intense, and recognized by them as
such, as the following dialogue shows:

A. I was working so hard, not to be a goody two-shoes, but because I
    wanted to look good, and because I was the woman and because I
    didn't want to get fired.

B. And especially coming in as the first, you are under so much pressure.

C. Even the guys who liked me . . . if you screw up, its all dumped on
    you.

D. I know one of the first departments I went to, I went to a seminar,
    and the first woman they hired, apparently didn't work out for some
    reason—

A. And everythings based on them . . .

B. 'We can't hire another woman, she was awful,' well, don't they know
    there are some awful men too? And, 'Give another one a shot, they
    might be better.' When we had the second woman hired, we had some
    problems initially because, I'll admit the fact that I resented that it
    was as easy for her to come in as . . . I'd already come in, and I
    looked at it and thought 'God, I had to work my buns off here, and I
    took so much grief, and she can just walk in and . . . ' Fortunately,
    the better part of me.

C. Yeah, everything's based on them. And everything is so dead set
    against them.

I suggested, in considering the British examples of true firsts,
that these women had to develop strategies of their own for managing the new terrain which they had reached and that transformation and professionalism were important in that regard. This was
also true in the USA as we shall see later. What was interesting
and different were the pioneering pre-emptive strikes made by
some of the women. I have already noted the two who, as a result
of the very hard time they had had from men while in training and
because they were very committed to making it on their own
terms, asked for their own beat as two women together: 'We were
out to prove it, which we did. We never called a squad unless we
needed assistance.' Using the police union and its contacts with the
police chief to improve the position of women was another
significant strategy to aid the pioneers. At first the woman who did
this raised very basic, practical issues which involved barriers to
pioneers. As so often, the gender divisions over plumbing were crucial.

I said, 'Chief, we need a bathroom at . . . ' Later on I had another meeting with him because most of the women could only have side zippers . . .

the side zippers were a hassle, you had to take your Sam Brown off and I thought, 'this is baloney' so I went and requested pants with the zippers up front and I was told that this was not for women . . . So I went to the Chief and he said, 'Why? That's the style.' And I said, 'Chief, it's hard to pee with these pants on.' And I thought he was going to die. We got front zippers.

Having involved herself in union politics in this fashion, as a way of improving things for the pioneer generation, this woman went on to become much more involved and to be a key and central figure, not only for women, but for all local officers.

A raised consciousness about pioneering could have an impact even on women who were not strictly 'true firsts' themselves. In Britain, as we saw, enough women were employed before integration and stayed on afterwards for there to be some kind of link between generations. This was far less common (and less likely) in the USA. A veteran of one of the first 'new' cohorts could recall only two or three women in her department before 1970 and they were not in uniform and had originally not been armed. By the late 1980s, however, it was already possible for at least one woman to recognize the pioneer role of some of her post integration colleagues and seek to emulate it by being a field trainer:

I always tell them [the pioneers], 'you know, if it wasn't for what you did, how you came along and did all these things, I wouldn't be where I am now' . . . those women have long since been in investigative positions, they didn't stay on the street very long and I think by staying on the street it's kind of surprising to a lot of men, it's like 'What is she still doing here?' So in a way it is a kind of pioneer type thing.

In the British examples, I noted the phenomenon of perpetual pioneering. Perhaps the case I have just quoted suggests that this need not be a permanent cycle; only if she chooses need a woman be perpetually tested out. There were, however, plenty of examples of this happening in the States, by no means always connected with promotion or specialization. Simply transferring from one patrol assignment to another in the same city caused this woman to reply to my question.

Q. Do women still have to prove themselves?

A. Yes, and I tell them that too. I always tell women they're going to have to prove themselves twice. And I hate to have to say that and I hate that that's the way it is but that is the way it is. What makes it

bad is, like if I've proved myself—like I was at —— Division first and
I proved myself, I had my own beat and I arrested people. I did my
job and I did it just as well as any other person. Then I came to . . .
Division and they want me to prove myself all over again, and why
should I have to do that?

There were much stranger examples than this, however. Joining
a very small rural department, one woman found herself first acting, then substantive Chief of Police:

Before I got through certification school the . . . council decided to fire the
Chief of Police . . . One minute it's fine, the next day he's gone. So I got a
call and was asked if I could try to cover the streets until the department
got a new chief, because half the department went with the chief.

Eventually the council made her chief and after several years she
moved to another larger place as a patrol officer. Despite further
study and considerable experience, she did not achieve promotion:
'One of the supervisors said to me, until I grew balls between my
legs, I wouldn't be a supervisor.'

These instances just cited serve to highlight the fact that there is
enormous variety in the experience of policing in the USA.
Sometimes this can give considerable scope for innovation; on the
other hand, many urban departments are not dramatically different
in many ways from British forces based on major conurbations.
These features partly explain some of the distinctions in patterns in
pioneering, but not wholly. There were interesting differences in
the way some women took up the pioneer role themselves and
turned it into something they wanted to do. In Britain it was more
often a challenge. But these are nuances; it is remarkable how
often parallels can be drawn between these distinctive histories.

Punishment and Protection

This is the title I gave to the final segment of analysis of the British
interviews on pioneering. It is almost as apposite, save that it may
also be appropriate to include barriers in pioneering since, in some
places, these were still in place. 'Punishment' for pioneers in the
USA ranged from the purely petty to the gross. Make-up, perfume,
and hair-styles of the first women in uniform seemed to preoccupy
inordinately some supervisors and even chiefs. These were two
examples from women who were the firsts in their small rural

departments: 'my lieutenant was upset for about four weeks that I
had some eyeshadow and mascara on, and he said to my sergeant,
"I want you to know, I don't like the make-up. You've got to put
your hair up. I don't want a lot of make-up. I don't want gaudy
jewelry . . . "' But an almost identical conversation took place in a
progressive urban department:

I got called into the office the very first day and I was told I couldn't wear
make-up. And I said, 'There's nothing in the regulations that says I can't
wear make-up' He (the lieutenant) said, 'I'm saying you can't.' And I'm
saying, 'You show me the order and I won't wear make-up.'

A whole bundle of issues about women's entry into policy is
encapsulated in these dialogues. First there is the anomalous
strangeness of women who do not fit neatly into pigeon-holes provided by the rules. (One set of regulations about haircuts was so
phrased in one department that no length was specified, only a
taper cut: i.e. that the back should be no longer than the front.
This rule enabled a female officer to wear her hair waist length,
but pinned up.) Not only do they not fit, they protest and resist
attempts to treat them in that way. Further, their supervisors are
confused and bemused as to how to handle them. There is a further theme of licensed disorder or disarray. Women frequently
found themselves pulled up for not wearing their hats, or for having non-regulation sunglasses or wearing ear-rings. Yet, they
argued, their male colleagues were not always smartly attired or
shaven.

Clearly all these episodes were, at a fundamental level, to do
with order and discipline, rather than these trivial topics.
Supervisors had to try to negotiate two sets of problems to do with
order. One concerned how to 'fit' women into a law-enforcement
agency, given that they visibly lacked the characteristics supposedly
required for that purpose. The other was, and this was far deeper,
what happens to an institution which so visibly changes its public
image in this way. It is perhaps not surprising that perplexed
supervisors retaliated sometimes by seizing on petty symbols of
femininity in an attempt to establish boundaries and their own
power. As a result, they sometimes encountered organized feminism: 'Then I got all the other women that were [there] . . . to
start wearing make-up and perfumes and the whole works, just to
anger him.'

More seriously, perhaps, women who sought transfer to specialist posts did not find it easy and some complained of bias in selection for promotion. A young woman who had applied for a
specialist branch was quizzed about her possible plans to have a
baby. For a member of a pioneer cohort, the refusal of a specialist
post was due, she felt, to personality clash. She did not pursue any
redress because there seemed little point, but it was clear that she
might have had central support for this had she done so. In short,
some grievances at least are now regarded as valid.

While some women feel that promotional boards are biased
against them, others actually do well in formal selection procedures
but find that the barriers then consist of the informal agendas and
unspoken assumptions of the occupational culture. Several women
had done outstandingly well on exams and other tests, but suddenly found their paths blocked by the attitudes of an older generation of police.

These included here, rather more than they did in Britain, over-
protective attitudes of paternalist police. The first two-women
patrol already mentioned observed, 'We'd be out on traffic, and go
places and I'd see over there parked, watching us, you know, following us . . . we had squads following us.' As a result, she and
her partner determined never to call for back-up and she found
herself one night in a difficult situation and had to call: 'And I got
about ten squads came.' These women were insistent on trying to
make it without such 'chivalry' but others welcomed it.

I found out they will back you up . . . I think they'll only do it if they like
you . . . they'll make it a point to go by just to make sure you're OK . . .
I appreciate —— I know some of the girls who I came on with resented it,
'I can do this job just as well as you.' And I would do it for them.

Of course, it is important to distinguish over-protective back-up
from sensible support. The hostility towards one woman 'first'
meant that she did lack proper back-up: 'A lot of times I was out
there on my own . . . So many times my back-up was just a
figment of my imagination.'

Pioneering as a concept has different cultural meanings to
Americans and Britons. Britons typically go abroad to pioneer,
while for Americans their own country is the stage for such activity. Yet the notion covers well the initial experiences encountered
by women who enter the police in both countries and how they

learn to deal with those experiences. These thoughts from a trail-blazer could come equally from a British counterpart:

So I was doing a lot of firsts for a while . . . I got on this police department by myself, no special things were done because I was a woman. And I felt like the way I was going by, too, I was helping somebody else come along and say, 'Well hell, she can do it and women are alright.'

By a very considerable margin all these women thought that things had improved very much for women in policing and were definitely on an upward slope.

Partners

If pioneering is a cherished central notion in American culture, then partners is certainly another and associated one. Countless road and buddy movies as well as innumerable television series testify to the centrality of work- or friendship-based couples. Classically such relationships are between people of the same sex and are not overtly sexually based. Working in pairs in US policing owes a great deal to the presence of strong unions in some cities who have been able to insist on this practice. Several of the women whom I interviewed usually patrolled in one-person cars. Many, however, had worked with partners, of both sexes, and had clear views about the value of these relationships.

Martin (1980: 97–8) also stresses the importance, and some of the problems, for women in partnering. A good, reliable partner can be critical in difficult situations. Panicking or freezing can cause problems:

I've men [partners] that have frozen up . . . another was an officer that had been on a while, and he was a body builder, he was extremely strong, and we had a crazy guy crawling around the ground—we had to arrest him and he never lifted a finger, not one finger. And I got my watch ripped off and I got slightly hurt, and I had to make the arrest and he stood there the entire time.

Failure to give proper backing can be fatal, especially in the USA, where firearms are relatively common. Police war stories there often centre on the fatal shot, or the failure to pull the fatal trigger. Since, as in so much of policing, male behaviour, or myths about it, is the norm, women are regarded as unsuitable, unreliable partners who will not stand up in a fight or a shoot-out. Such myths can be especially robust in this area:

Years ago there was a female officer that, her partner got hurt, shot, and she missed the suspect when she shot. She was almost crucified in this department. Two weeks ago we had a male officer that missed the suspect. He shot twice and missed the suspect. And there hasn't been said one thing about it, not one thing. May be the times have changed, but I think that if it happened to a female officer again, they would crucify her. We had, a couple of years ago, we had a female officer, her partner got shot, he has lost total mobility in his shoulder. She did manage to hit the suspect, and you hear the comments, 'Well I'm surprised it was a woman', and they looked at every little detail of that shooting from her standpoint. They were much more meticulous in analysing that shooting than if it had been two male officers.

While such dramatic episodes do occur on patrol in the USA they are rare there: few US officers ever need to use their guns in this way. After nearly a decade in the police in patrol and detective work one woman said, 'I know I qualify for firearms, but I don't enjoy that part of my job. I would hope—I've never had to shoot at anyone as of yet and I pray that I never do.'

In reality, a cool nerve, common sense, and quick thinking will be more valuable assets than marksmanship in a partner. Reliability is also crucial. Many interviewees commented on the need for a partner 'to be there for me'. Not doing so for women could be particularly disastrous: 'If you sit in the cruiser and freeze . . . because that happens . . . some girls do that, those girls will never find anyone to work with them.'

Of course, since policing, as officers endlessly tell researchers, consists of 95 per cent boredom and 5 per cent terror, it is the co-operation and comradeship in the boring parts which can be critical in cementing partnerships. In Washington, DC, Martin found that males said that they did not know what to talk to female partners about because the usual topics of sport, sex, and fixing up cars were inappropriate and so patrolling with women was resented as less friendly. However, Martin cites another viewpoint from a police chief who had found that, in mixed-sex patrol cars, the main topic of conversation was policing itself and that this improved the professional performance of males who had not previously been reflecting on their work while on patrol.

Yet another side to this was, however, suggested by several

women in different areas. Some men, they argued, now preferred
female partners because they could talk more freely to them and
did not have to maintain as macho an image as with 'the guys'.

In the car, I've noticed they talk a lot more than they do with [male]
officers . . . they're always getting advice, you know, what to buy as presents, problems with their girlfriend, problems with their wife: 'What should
I do about this?' And I've noticed—of course I do work with a lot younger
officers—I noticed that they do seem to come to female officers . . . for
advice and I know the things they're telling me, they're not telling their
buddies.

One woman found that all her male colleagues, who had previously been hostile to her, wanted her as a partner: 'the schedule
revolves every three months and I had changed partners and I had
the three guys go in and ask to have me as a partner.' This kind of
shift obviously has a good deal to do with the maturing of a generation of female cops. In Martin's project, all the women were
fairly recent recruits. By the late 1980s women had been deployed
for almost two decades and some were senior enough to be supervising rookies themselves.

One aspect of male–female partnerships in policing often raised
in the media is sexual. Martin cites it as a problem area in her
study. One US chief achieved some notoriety in the 1980s by suggesting that mixed-sex car patrols could only lead to fornication.
Several women commented on this view and said that it was
largely harmful to women because it could be used as an excuse to
keep them off patrol and also demeaned them and their motivation
for joining the police.

One solution to some of the problems women have found in
being partners is for there to be two-women patrols. This was
already happening in many areas by the time of my visit and, as I
pointed out, some women consciously sought this. They were
allowed to do this and at the time of this research there were many
such partnerships, but they had seemed strange at first and had
been mistrusted. They were initially subject to over-protection:

I know the guys meant well—but every time—I felt like the little red lights
we had on the car were really big beams because every time we made . . .
a traffic stop or something we'd see all these cars cruising by . . . but it's
just that they have never experienced having two women—first they
thought we were going to fight—well they were wrong there because we
got along fine.

I interviewed and observed female partners and it was manifest that they did get on well and could cope as well as their colleagues. Martin also advocates more such partnerships, more female trainers to act as role models and also possible partner models. This was a view shared by several women whom I interviewed, although the one canine officer to whom I talked found her dog to be her perfect partner.

Partnering epitomizes an aspect of police culture: the need for loyalty to one's colleagues. While British policing, and British society, do not give partnerships such a central place as they have in the USA, the issues they raise about loyalty are very similar. In traditional police folklore, women are treacherous, they break up buddy relations, bring in sexuality, and lack strength and courage in fights. But most of this is from fairyland. Modern policemen do not patrol some distant frontier in pairs: they are linked by radios to base, their movements checked and recorded by computers. They are rarely likely to unholster weapons (most killings of police are in ambushes) and in such situations it is by no means clear that males will remain staunch.

Again, behind the resistance to women as partners shelter deeper presumptions about whose the partnership is. Objections are raised in terms of their impact on policemen, and possibly on discipline. That all-female partnerships were also, at least at first, also strongly objected to, rather proves this point. Their gradual acceptance demonstrates another one. Hostility towards women in the police from policemen themselves seems to derive from deep-seated fears and feelings. There are, however, almost no acceptable or rational arguments which can be used to support such views. Indeed, this very hostility and scepticism proved their own undoing, by stimulating shoals of performance studies, women's capacity to police was 'proven' and, ultimately, questions began to be raised about men's own capabilities. In both the USA and Britain, problems of police stress, loss of nerve, and post-trauma syndrome are increasingly being recognized. One of the main factors for women was that they were newcomers to policing and therefore not yet tried and trusted. In turning next to transformation scenes we shall see how this was overcome, at least in some cases.

Transformation Scenes

In examining this concept in the British context I observed that there were really three aspects to it. First, such episodes gave women themselves confidence, secondly, they made them more acceptable to their male colleagues, but finally, since it was male colleagues who legitimated such scenes, they had limited value in the long run for women. Men not only were key audiences and critics, they also believed or asserted that they owned the theatre, wrote the scripts, and held the copyright.

Transformation scenes certainly abounded in the US accounts. A sheriff was abused by a male prisoner:

And one of the guys came over and put his arm around me and said, 'No she ain't, she's just one of the guys' . . . And that was it, that day I went home and I felt so good . . . The whole attitude toward me had just changed.

Just as in Britain, women often recognized that they needed to work extremely hard, bring extra skills and attention to their work in order to ensure transformation. More than once women were told not to be rate-busters, working too hard. Sometimes it might involve taking on 'masculine' tasks to prove oneself one of the boys. One of the pioneering veterans outlined her *Bildungsroman* of adventure stories as she clocked up 'a lot of firsts for a while'. Each one culminated in a scene as she proved she could accomplish each task. She then moved on to car theft:

And one of the first deals I had to go and identify a car and me, if I have to change the oil in my car I take it to the service station, and I didn't know any name of tools or nothing like that, I said show me what to do and I'll try. And . . . I . . . found those numbers (secret identifiers) and all that stuff, well we took that car apart and put it back together . . . so we did it and they were saying, 'Well I guess she'll be all right if she doesn't mind this part of auto theft.'

As this example makes clear, a key feature of such scenes often requires women to act in a way which is seen as unfeminine or uncharacteristic in order to break down barriers and to encourage feelings of affinity. After she had failed to get a coveted specialist position at an interview, one officer was confronted with her own stereotype:

And he just simply said I didn't have any experience, thank you for coming to the interview and I walked out. And he said, 'Come here' . . . and he said, 'everybody told me that when I told you you could not be transferred to . . . you were going to start screaming and yelling and getting on top of the table and demanding that I accept you in this position.' and I said, 'That has never been my style.' He said, 'Well, I'm pleasantly surprised.' I still didn't get into —— but I proved him wrong.

Most felt that, while all officers were tested when they start, 'they want to see if you're going to arrest this guy six foot six or whatever,' only women had to keep on proving and re-proving themselves. 'And I don't think men have to go through that. I think they're accepted in the role the way they are.'

There were certain differences between British and US experience in this area. It did seem that while such stories were frequent they were not quite as frequent as in Britain and had a slightly different tone. This perhaps had to do with a rather more self-conscious use of images than could usually be the case in Britain. As we shall see in a later section, some police officers devoted considerable efforts to scripting and running activities which served to transform the public image of the police. Another had used the media extensively to promote her own position. The steps taken by others consciously to avoid the mutual conflict with male officers showed them at their most innovative in pre-empting transformation by writing part of their own scripts.

Professionalism

In the parallel section on Britain I suggested that this had four dimensions there. For the USA, the patterns were not quite the same. Most themes on professionalism dwelt either on hard work, which was often stressed, or on 'going by the book', sticking to rules and procedures which should be followed. I intend to treat these both together as they often turned out to be two sides of one coin.

The pressures to work hard, to take extra training, to be near-perfect police were very evident. When threatened with considerable hostility one response was: 'I became better trained. I forced myself to take things on my own, to read books, to just be the best that I could be, because I knew that when it came right down to it I'd have always to protect myself.' For another it was a question of proving herself: 'The chief called me in and he said, "I am really impressed with you, you are doing a really fantastic job. You are doing more work than all my new officers put together." I just came out ten feet tall.'

One interesting feature of some of the group discussions was the way in which various, sometimes quite distinct notions of professionalism in policing were put forward and compared. In one the unorthodox style of a successful community relations officer was contrasted with a much more 'by the book' approach of one of her colleagues. The community officer was, in fact, in the tradition of preventive policing which we have met many times before:

I see no real advantage in getting out, busting down doors to drug houses as a patrol officer because there's just so much of it out there. But I do see an advantage . . . of work within the community, doing good solid police work because you were helping the hungry and the poor.

The work of another officer was repeatedly stressed as being that of 'a professional officer', a policeman's police officer, and a proper pride was taken in professional skills and crafts. An officer was proud of the fact that she had recognized that a handicapped girl was in a coma, not drunk when she was found by the roadside.

Interestingly, and it is always hard to gauge such omissions, the US women were rather less likely than the British to note procedural imperfections in their colleagues' work and to try to perfect their own. However, they did, perhaps, more often stress pride in their own policing standards and sometimes in their own department. It did seem that a rather similar effect could be created, nevertheless, as in Britain, with the stress on going by the book, that is of causing resentment by being too good. One woman assured her colleagues and everyone else that she was not 'goody two-shoes', despite her phenomenal work rates.

Particular circumstances may have played their part in creating some real differences in this area. PACE was relatively new when this research was carried out in Britain and it may have attracted more attention as a result. ('Mirandizing' and similar processes in the USA have much longer histories (Mckenzie and Gallagher 1989: 128–9).) A further difference lies in the degree of meritocracy operating in each system. While it is true that political decision-making can affect selection at the very top of the British constabulary

(Reiner 1991) this is less true of lower ranks, whereas in the USA there is greater influence on the top tiers of police. Moreover other political considerations have, especially in recent years, altered routine hiring and promotion procedures. In some cities it was fiscal crisis which did this: New York had to sack police officers and held no sergeants' exams during the 1980s. Policies on equal opportunities and, in some places, legally backed affirmative action plans meant that some officers, or some groups of them, faced longer waits for promotion than in previous times. Such a situation was depicted by Remmington in her study of Atlanta (1981). There was no direct reporting of demoralization or unprofessional conduct among my sample. They were, however, very aware of such influences. White women also sometimes expressed concern that they were not being treated as a minority and no longer being 'targeted' for recruitment purposes.

Professionalism in their work was an issue for these women if not quite in the same way as it was in Britain. They believed in their own capacities as professionals but often had to contend with the double bind that pervaded so much of their work. What did emerge in the USA in this area, as in others, was the pace of change. Many of the women who expressed their views here had already had long periods in service: some were veterans of the first recruitment to street patrol. While their numbers were not vast, neither were they insignificant and they were, in various ways, beginning notably to influence and alter definitions of good or appropriate policing. In part this was simply following broad social trends in policing: towards higher educational standards with less emphasis on physical fitness. Not only did they hold their own views about proper policing and its importance, they were, in some places, beginning to put such ideas into debate and even into practice:

things started, you could tell things were changing because I think chief . . . at one time asked . . . they were redesigning the station, they finally realized that the women were there to stay and that we needed more room, and we had more personnel than we had room for. And he came to me and he was asking me about the design of the station, and what we would like to have. Not just from the women's standpoint, but all the officers, as far as what kind of equipment, locker rooms and all that stuff, and I said, 'I know there is more officers that have been here longer than I have, male officers,' and he was asking me, my opinion, and he went to ——

[woman's name] and to —— [ditto] and she's always been outspoken, and to —— [ditto] and we were always doing something or straightening out something or speaking out on something we didn't like . . . We came a long way . . . and it's not bad to think it's getting better.

Soft Cops

While both British and US female policing movements had their roots in protection campaigns directed at women and children, and these determined their initial development, the links became looser in the USA and in some senses, female policing could be said to have been reinvented there in the 1970s. Where there were 'survivors' from before women went on patrol there seemed a much greater gulf between them and more recent recruits than was the case in Britain, as the following dialogue makes clear:

A. Some of those first females, they never even worked the streets and even worked in skirts . . .

B. . . . Because when they were hired on, when they came out of the Academy they were assigned to a bureau and almost all of them went to a youth division, and they're still there. There's a lot of them that are here have never been on the street . . . and that's not their fault but that's the way it was but now that it was opened to women out on patrol they never really volunteered to go out . . . [They discuss a senior female officer of that era.]

C. And then when she made sergeant they put her in . . . for about two days to ride patrol because she was going to be over patrol and had never worked a day in her life in patrol.

D. I know that one, I always call her the highest paid secretary 'cause she's always been up there'.

The distance between these groups of women is the more remarkable in that this was a department with a fairly strong female subculture in evidence and with a good deal of solidarity, which crossed ethnic and age divides. But the crucial dividing-line being stressed here is between 'real' police work, as defined in police culture and the 'soft' activities of prevention and welfare. While the war stories of the first cohort of veterans fascinated more recent recruits, this is how their predecessors were seen: 'the ones that were before us and that never really went to patrol but they were hired on and *I imagine* they got a lot of stories to tell about, you know when they hired on' (emphasis added).

It is thus perhaps not surprising that there was generally little awareness of these past activities and on the whole, little desire to pursue that agenda in policing. Dilemmas were confronted about how *as women* to handle people in fraught situations.

You don't want to show your vulnerabilities, your compassion, because that takes away from your strength and your authority . . . [yet] . . . to the people, the families in the . . . court if they get into a fight or a child is hurt . . . you can console them, and you become entirely different. You are a concerned individual and they just think the world of you.

A few women consciously chose to avoid the conventional areas just because they felt their own feelings would be too strong:

One of the reasons I never got interested in the traditional female law-enforcement type of jobs like child abuse and rape investigation was because very early in my career I realized that because I'm a mother and because I'm a woman, I just couldn't be objective.

For others, such avoidance had more to do with these being traditional and thus 'no go' areas for women. Moreover, most found mainstream policing 'where the action is' more interesting. There were a number, however, who were involved in activities ranging from units specializing in sexual crimes (arguably not a 'soft cop' job at all) to the newer mandate. One officer had, like a British counterpart, set up procedures for domestic violence. (On patrol with a male and a female officer in another city I observed a male rookie very carefully following another set of approved guidance in a situation of domestic violence.) Police officer stress was a major current topic and female officers were involved in the programmes to counter this. (A feature of the US health-insurance system is that it may be possible for it to pay for, for instance, alcohol or drug rehabilitation programmes and this required much liaison work.)

Others were involved in community relations work. All these officers recognized, sometimes ruefully, that such roles might become ghettos, or culs-de-sac for them, and one had resigned herself to this, finding great personal satisfaction in her work: 'I learned a long time ago to not look outside for any satisfaction, to work to please myself and do things that I would be proud of.' Those who were in Community Relations obviously had to respond to conditions in their areas, but it was clear that this was essentially a public relations job: 'my job is a lot of public relations.' In one case this meant that the officer concerned had developed very close ties with local citizens, including some from minority groups, and had spent her time in community work which was closely akin to social work. In another city, 'it's mostly people who are in the community and they just wanna know that somebody in the Police Department is listening what their complaint is.' Given the most prevalent complaint on hot summer days, she said with feeling that their motto should be, 'We don't do plumbing.'

In another city, women officers were particularly involved in police-based charitable and voluntary work. These activities, which were extensive and very time-consuming, were amply justified in their own right. It was also clear as well that, aside from their intrinsic worth, these very public activities gave the local police, whose relations with some of its citizenry had been strained, a much better image. Indeed, what links all these examples of the 'gentle touch' in policing is the positive image which the public presence of women gave to the tarnished picture of traditional policing.

Britain differs from many other nations in the way in which police–social work links are maintained in sensitive areas such as child sex abuse (*Guardian*, 12 July 1991). Such ties are closer in Britain than is commonly found elsewhere. Partly this stems from the historic role of women in British policing. Modern trends have combined to reintroduce such matters into the British police mandate. Such pressures were less common in the USA where social work takes different forms and where modern policewomen are distant from their history and prefer their present.

There is, I think, a profound process at work here. It is probably rash to generalize from such modest numbers, but I offer the observation anyway, wreathed in a protective layer of caution. Policewomen in Britain may choose to express their feminism, or female identification, in terms of their concern for women (other women) as victims. They may see this as one legitimate way of expressing female solidarity in an organization where other versions would be less acceptable. After all, policemen can be just as horrified by child abuse and wife battering as women are. In the different climate of the USA overtly expressed views about women's rights and equality are neither as deviant nor as dangerous. (These conclusions match Rock's observations, cited above.) American culture is more receptive to feminism than British culture. It originated there and it was in the USA that the evaluation studies which 'proved' the value of women on patrol were carried out. American men, women, and children may well need the attentions of 'soft cops' of both sexes as that society addresses many of the problems of the late twentieth century. American policewomen may be less attracted to this side of policing than they are to the hard stuff of crime and the streets. They have observed that silken ropes can bind as closely as hemp despite their apparently gentle hold.

Female Cop Culture and Top cops

Perhaps the most striking difference between the experiences of British and US policewomen was the beginning of a form of female police culture in the latter. This was emphatically *not* a counter-culture with subversive values. It was rather a reflection of the traditional occupational culture, sharing with that the same values and priorities but with certain key shifts of emphasis. Indeed, it may be helpful to think more in terms of the development of networks, rather than cultures.

There were a number of ways in which such development was manifested. Some were very direct and straightforward: as well as a glossy journal (organ of the International Policewomen's Association) *Policewoman* there was also a simpler and more radical publication called *Balancing the Badge* which circulated amongst women officers nation-wide. Both carried listings of courses, meetings, and other publications of interest to policewomen. In some places, most notably New York City, although integration meant that there was no longer a separate association just for policewomen, another body, an 'endowment association', existed to promote their interests and was encouraged to do so.

More significant, however, were the very apparent ways in which networks were demonstrated during these interviews. As I indicated earlier, my US contacts initiated these as the best way, in their view, for me to learn about them. In two cases where women from several departments came, the originator was surprised at the numbers who responded and found that she did not know everyone present well. The existence of networks is very clear in some of the dialogues quoted earlier; they were also, in some instances, being built upon in these discussions. For example, the vexed question of how far women are treated in certain ways because they are women, and how different is males' experience cropped up several times and was discussed and developed: anecdotes and war stories were matched and compared as in the following:

A. I'd hate for her [FMH] to go back to England, you know; with all these horror stories and not see the good . . .

B. Did you feel like you got treated that way by your Sergeant—was it more because you wouldn't do what he wanted or because you were female or was it more a personality deal where he didn't like you?

C. Yeah, I think that—see he had a real large ego, it's about the size of a buffalo . . .

A. A male officer, you're saying that, too, that a male would have got the same thing . . . ?

B. I've seen just as many male officers be ostracized for crossing their supervisor . . .

C. Well you know, I kind of disagree a little bit because the same sergeant had another officer working under him and this officer . . . and he came to me and gave me the story to let me know, you know, there's something wrong with this gentleman, he said, 'You know, I could have been where you are.'

They did not, in the end, come to final conclusions about gender and discipline, but they did state the issues, debate them, and even begin to theorize about explanations.

In other ways, too, networks were apparent. One of the most interesting was in jokes, a classic anthropological source of shared meaning and cultural symbolism. There was a great deal of laughter in the group sessions, often rueful, over cross or abusive remarks from colleagues and the war stories when women said they had won. There was a whole stream as well of craft-related jokes such as are often shared between members of a specialized trade or skill. One series concerned the searching of female suspects, including the most prevalent of all, the 'female' suspect who, in a strip search, turns out to be a male. Other searching stories were about where women had hidden money, weapons, or drugs and what happened when the items were found by the searcher. Another theme was confrontation with citizens who demanded a 'real' cop; here the punch line would turn on what the male officer called out as back-up, or the female herself had said. The points about all these stories were first that they were widespread, and second that they were recognized by other women as shared experiences. Such tale-telling is significant in policing (Holdaway 1983) but these tales are exclusive to women by their nature.

The histories given above show that in a number of cases, women themselves had sought to develop and control their own networks by working together and by giving each other support. This had, in turn, led to this being 'normalized' and to it becoming a routine practice.

It would be wrong to be too sanguine about this. Women in small departments were still relatively isolated. Several said their departments could not possibly have two women on the staff at once. One woman had been a sole female in an office and had belonged to a policewomen's group, but she found very little support from them especially when she had problems and was scornful of the women in consequence.

In this chapter and in reports on this topic I have tried to make clear that there was very considerable optimism and confidence about the role of women in the police and their future. This was often despite long discussions about discrimination, over-protectiveness, and other problems.

There are some important riders to add to this argument. Racial divisions were sometimes apparent. In one department there was clearly a strongly supportive network of black officers who shared jokes, veterans' reminiscences, etc. A white officer here emphasized that she did not fit into this network. In another situation, black officers did join the group of (mainly) white officers, but it was clear that most black women in this department did not readily identify with white female colleagues and faced tough decisions about 'Which side are you on?'

In the chapter on Britain I suggested that policewomen there lack role models. This is also true in the USA. There have been examples of women becoming police chiefs in the USA, but they often quite quickly lost the post because of the infighting in such positions and their highly political nature. Role models were beginning to be formed as younger officers heard about their seniors and used the knowledge successfully. One officer was quite certain that women should train women: 'I think there should be a female training officer for every female recruit.' Yet, as in Britain, true role models were hard to find.

While they might lack role models among women, some men provided these in terms of exemplary policing or acted as mentors to women. Women also, despite the lack of concrete models, planned and talked enthusiastically about utopian futures for female police.

Comparative Conclusions

The framework of concepts and turning-points I have used in this book derived from my British data, which I collected first. Nevertheless, in the broad sense it fits the US data very well. There are important differences, however. Some of the most salient are not very well researched or easy to justify. Thus the general ambience of quiet confidence seems quite widespread. Once one digs a bit beneath the surface of the key concepts it is apparent that they are not identical. We saw for example that both groups had a 'sense of mission' even if on examination it turned out to be very different. US women were more concerned about politics, but rather less about professionalism.

My summary at the end of the last chapter could stand very largely for US as well as for British policewomen. Mission, loyalty, law enforcement, being one of the boys/guys—these were all common to both groups of police. The two major areas of variance were central to cop culture: pioneering and female cop culture. Both the latter flourished in the USA. Part of the reasons for this lay in US attitudes towards change and equality, but there was also something else, what one can only describe as the 'I have a dream' concept. Here is how one officer saw the future of policing in the USA. This vision is not her own, but it contains her hopes for the future within the police.

Have you seen Robocop? Robocop was in the next century, and it was really high tech. It showed men and women showering and changing clothes—they were all police officers—it showed them all in one locker room, and not to say that we want to do that, but they had reached that point where they worked as one and they all worked together and there was no more doing that, no more line between . . .

6

Comparisons and Contrasts in Policing

In the previous two chapters I have set out the perceptions of the women I interviewed in Britain and America. I did so separately but within one framework. Now I want to draw this material and its broader background together and tease out the useful similarities and differences. It is not, however, my aim to repeat the lengthy quotations, but rather to suggest conclusions which may, perhaps, tentatively be based on what has gone before. While women's role in policing has been the focus of these sections, and it is lessons about that on which I wish to speculate, there is also instruction to be gained about more general themes such as the comparative study of policing and of social institutions, social change, and social policies generally.

Comparing Policewomen

There are many pitfalls in the process of making international comparisons. Like should be matched with like, differences not exaggerated, and the innumerable complexities of social and cultural patterns recognized. Nevertheless, the exercise can be worth while and instructive as I trust the last two chapters have shown. In that analysis I grouped what the women themselves said about their careers under a series of headings. Four key themes linked these topics and spanned the Atlantic, although the local meaning was often transformed in mid-ocean into a different conception. These four themes gain resonance from their relation to other topics to do with gender and with women in late twentieth-century Britain and the USA. These themes are: an unsuitable job for a woman; equal opportunities; the gentle touch; a desperate remedy.

An Unsuitable Job for a Woman

Women have been in policing, as I keep stressing, for most of the twentieth century, since, indeed, before they got the vote nationally in either country. Despite this, becoming a police officer is still not wholly accepted as appropriate employment for women. As the examples cited under a 'Sense of Mission', 'Pioneers', 'Professionalism', and indeed elsewhere, show, these women had met resistance at the outset of and often throughout their careers. Each individual's history testified that she had had to make a series of stereotype-challenging steps and decisions in joining the police. The variety, complexity, and thoughtfulness offered in their explanations, as well as the determination they manifested, were equally eloquent witnesses of this. They met objection and resistance outside the organization: from partners, family, friends, the general public, and offenders *and*, most notably, within it, from male officers. Time made some but not much difference to these objections. The most important changes—the 'transformation scenes'—were effected by the women themselves, although they depended on reactions from key colleagues and the public.

What they might achieve through their own efforts was important. Here, unlike much of what I have outlined so far, lay differences. A female network sometimes worked supportively in the USA and provided a base for countering the costs of stereotyping. In Britain individual, immaculate professionalism was more likely to be the way of dealing with prejudice. To draw attention to women as a group was in Britain not seen as a 'helpful' procedure.

Apart from this, the 'unsuitability' theme was played almost in harmony, practically in unison, for both systems. What is most illuminating is to consider the basis of this position and, in particular, what the comparison reveals. At least five strands of the unsuitability argument can be discerned from this study and other material.

First is the *nature of police work*. Police work is deemed to be hard, dangerous, and requiring authority in its execution. At the same time, it brings inevitable involvement with sordid aspects of life, with the dregs and dross of society. Some academic research has supported at least part of this, although there are studies, as we saw, which seriously undermine it. Women are considered unsuitable as police officers on both counts: they cannot cope with danger, do not command authority, and should not be exposed to degradation and counter-contamination. These arguments can be found on both sides of the Atlantic: identical versions of the 'how can women tackle fifteen-stone drunks?' query were cited in each country. Yet the situation in policing and hence the nature of police work differs in numerous ways. Major organizational divergence means that, in the USA, sworn officers' tasks may involve much or little crime, patrol (by car) throughout a shift, or court and other duties.

Other differences are also significant. Since US urban crime rates are much higher than those in Britain, with particularly notable divergence in homicide and serious violent crime, the nature of police work is bound to differ in the two nations. It also does so *inside* their boundaries, especially *within* the USA where there is vast divergence between urban, especially inner-city, situations and rural ones. Paradoxically, it was in some of these small rural departments that the greatest prejudice and barriers were reported.

City police departments also presented obstacles, but it was in these that women felt that they had come furthest. It hardly needs saying that the range of police experience between the toughest US cities and even those parts of Britain with the highest incidence of crime is enormous. The annual toll of homicides in a city such as Washington, DC, or Dallas is at about the same number as in the whole of England and Wales. Drug use, weapon-carrying, levels of organized crime, and other indices of danger are also hugely different. Moreover, while studies show police in both countries *in practice* preoccupied with the trivial pursuit of minor infringements, this tendency is more marked in Britain. In short, while the obstacles and their supporting arguments appear similar, their bases are so different that a degree of rationalization appears to be at work.

The effect on policemen is another thread woven into this particular tissue. The thesis is that if women police are deployed, this will undermine male solidarity, threaten their security (the 'weak link of the weaker vessel' assertion), and their self-image. Beneath this thread lies one of the core issues in this whole area: the implicit but widely-held view that male officers own the agencies of social control which they man (*sic*). Consider only the number of times female officers were told, 'We don't want you here,' as though they were trespassers, or invaders, and the strategies employed to test or deter them described also by Hunt (1984) and

Martin (1980). Yet, here again, comparisons are helpful; by the late 1980s US police were already considerably more diverse in ethnic background, physical attributes, and, to a lesser extent, sex, than they had been in 1970 and very much more so than in Britain (Holdaway 1991*a* and *b*). Moreover, this argument begs the question, as my subjects frequently protested, as to whether men actually do make good police officers, or whether conventional masculine gender-stereotyped behaviour is a sound basis for keeping the peace. Various sources suggest that this is not always so. My informants, while themselves accepting much cop culture and displaying loyalty to it, frequently questioned this. A few research studies explicitly challenge this by pointing out conflicts between, for example, masculinity and 'helping' behaviour in a crisis (Tice and Baumeister 1985). In others, observations of actual police behaviour suggest that hard coppers can be harmful (Smith and Gray 1983; Southgate and Ekblom 1984). Certainly modern training programmes endeavour to alter such stereotypes in the Metropolitan Police in London and elsewhere.

More dramatic testimony to the disastrous effects of machismo comes from the USA, where the Christopher Commission reported on an investigation of the Los Angeles Police Department. This occurred after a black man had been beaten and the beating videotaped and widely shown. Among the Commission's findings were that women officers handle suspects more successfully than men do as they are 'less personally challenged by defiant suspects and feel less need to deal with immediate force or confrontational language' (Morrison 1991). Despite these attributes, the Commission found that women's presence was resented on the force and that they were considered 'unfit even a hinderance in a macho cop culture' and were frequently subject to abuse and harassment (Morrison 1991). In the spring of 1992 riots devastated parts of Los Angeles after the officers were acquitted.

Once again, it does appear that we are in the presence of a myth, or an ideology, which does not derive from the reality of policing but from beliefs, or perhaps wishes about it. Its very persistence in the twin policing cultures is evidence of its strength. It also survives in both climates in spite of some basically different assumptions about appropriate management of encounters. *All* my US informants were armed, although most did not resort to weapons nor did they expect to. Patrols whom I observed carried their own back-up weapons (and wore bullet-proof vests) as well as their regulation guns. Hunt depicts gun culture and marksmanship as central to the core of traditional policing in 'Metro City' (1984). It was cited several times by my US subjects as a key site of conflict with male colleagues.

Yet in Britain few officers are even trained as users for firearms and the disputes about female weakness revolve around physical strength and stamina. Particularly current in Britain in the 1980s were accounts of the miners' strike and of the print pickets which focused on the weaknesses of women in public order situations when they cannot 'hold the line' (A. Brown 1988).

While there is some consistency in negative views expressed about the impact of female officers, this is not wholly true. A few researchers point to improved male performance as a consequence. My informants suggested that they had some effect on their own colleagues and in both countries there were clear examples of informal counselling occurring. Less directly, the recruitment and presence of women had led to other changes which were of benefit to men. Training programmes in particular had been or could be replanned so that less emphasis was placed on physical action— climbing six-feet walls, dragging bodies, or boxing—and more on interpersonal skills in diffusing tension and managing conflict. Men as well as women can gain from such innovations. As one study of stress and masculinity in policing notes, 'Most police officers begin their careers in excellent physical health and end with some job-related disorder' (Reeves and Austin 1985: 5).

Both the quoted research studies and my informants suggested at once a *variety* of responses to female officers and evidence of *some* changes in these reactions. Rank-and-file colleagues appear to be more hostile, although surveys usually only test them, and accounts of favourable responses from senior officers are anecdotal rather than systematic. S. Jones (1986) suggests no great difference in attitudes between older and younger police in a British force. However, the most aggressive criticisms from Britain come from ethnographic and observational studies (M. Young 1991; Smith and Gray 1983) and these may suffer from what Klofas and Toch (1982) have called 'pluralistic ignorance'. They use this term to explain the persistence of a tough, traditional, and anti-treatment image of a whole prison guard force; in fact these views were held only by a minority in the group, but they are what Klofas and

Toch call 'subcultural guardians'. These individuals are highly visible and vocal. Guards with opposing views kept silent about them partly out of fear and isolation, but also because in that particular social-control situation, *any* dissent was held to be divisive and thus a threat to control. A similar process appears to operate in the police, although the social-control situation is one of order maintenance and some crime fighting, not of custodial coercion.

It is instructive briefly to consider the role of females in corrections in the USA—or 'women guarding men'—as the title of one key study puts it (Zimmer 1986). This is an area of policy where US and British experience diverges much more sharply than is the case with policing. As we saw in an earlier chapter, female reformers in the nineteenth century focused on imprisoned offenders as they did on women on the streets as targets of their moral purity movements. Indeed, such projects pre-dated the women police movement. Elizabeth Fry first visited Newgate Prison in London in 1813 and founded there in 1817 the Ladies Association for the Improvement of the Female Prisoners. Eventually, the aims of separate penal establishments for women, staffed by women, were attained (although not for every inmate everywhere). Thus by the mid-twentieth century women's prisons with female governors and discipline staff were well established in both countries. In Britain, some mixing of staff has been intermittently pursued. Women worked on the staff of boys' borstals. Women were appointed as governors of several men's prisons in the 1980s and a few female discipline staff were brought into male establishments at the same time.

In the USA, however, a much more widespread integration of women into correctional posts in men's prisons followed the equal-rights legislation discussed in Chapter 3. There was some resistance to this and one case (*Dothard* v. *Rawlinson*) reached the Supreme Court in 1977. That judgment allowed only 'legally sanctioned "near equality"' (Zimmer 1986: 8) because an exception was allowed for women to be barred from 'contact' jobs in men's prisons. In practice, women have been increasingly recruited into posts as guards in male prisons, including those in the most high-security institutions. While there have been many lawsuits brought by women, as with the entry of women into the police in the USA, there have also quite distinctively been countersuits filed by male prisoners endeavouring to protect their privacy from female guards (Horne 1985; Potts 1981; Jurik 1985; Zimmer 1986).

The situation in the correctional establishments reported in a series of research studies parallels that of the police. Women faced a strong occupational culture profoundly resistant to their entry (Zimmer 1986: 53–5). However, male inmates are much more equivocal, and while some sought to prevent the advent of female guards for reasons of privacy, others were in favour, finding that women were 'fairer' (Etheridge *et al.* 1984) or softer and kinder (Zimmer 1986: 60–3). Administrators did not directly plan to integrate prison staff; this was a position forced upon them by the law and one which they resisted for some time. This is quite different from what happened in policing, where decisions to integrate and to put women on patrol were taken in the early 1970s.

In short, many of the factors alleged to influence the view of policewomen taken by their male colleagues are different in the prison system. The law was used in another way, and later, inmate responses have no counterpart in policing and the approach of management was quite distinct. Yet the outcomes, with a strong, resistant subculture and the consequent development by women of a series of negotiated strategies for coping (Zimmer 1986: 108 ff.) are remarkably similar. This is bound to arouse considerable suspicion that the subcultural resistance to women, and its sometimes gross manifestation, have little to do with functional responses and much more with self-sustaining myths and ideologies. The most telling illustration of this comes in the form of the 'weak link' story which Zimmer found circulating in the prisons where she conducted her research:

In every prison, male guards have stories about female guards who have failed to respond properly during momentary crises. For example: 'We had a fight on the yard last summer and the female guard out there froze.' (1986: 54)

Zimmer comments that she heard the same story in three separate prisons. Such stories are part of police mythology, too, although as the earlier accounts show, women may well develop their own stories about scared men. Several of these surfaced during the interviews which I conducted.

Other Reactions

The reports from my respondents suggest reactions to women in policing in relation to three other areas: from the *public* in relation to *crime* and from *offenders* themselves and in *public order* situations. I have already suggested that the supposed weakness of women in public order disputes is often highlighted by male officers and is a focus of anxiety. In this study, major public events or disturbances were only really mentioned by the British respondents, several of whom had had considerable experience of these. The plural nature of policing in the USA may account for this difference; 'riot' situations may be dealt with by the National Guard, for example. It is also the case that, especially in the 1980s, Britain saw a series of civil disturbances and riots which did not have parallels in the USA. This was quite different from the 1960s when the situation was reversed. Thus, even among British officers who had not taken part in public order events there was a high level of awareness of them and the arguments about women's role in them. One remarked ironically that there were few riots in her patch, an attractive suburban area.

It is important here to retain some caution about comparisons. Situations which may seem like riots or unrest in one culture may be either exuberance or crime in another. Events such as the Notting Hill Carnival in London are just such an example of a contested episode (A. Cohen 1992). It seems that in some US jurisdictions at least, very high levels of disorder are tolerated, albeit differentially by race, class, and area (Davis 1989). In short, US officers *perceived* themselves as handling crime and crime fighting, gang warfare even and, while a few had handled visits by politicians or attended disasters, none seemed really to see herself or her force as having to engage in the policing of civil or political strife. Indeed reference was made a number of times to terrorism in Britain and Europe, to the search of buildings for bombs and other devices, and the management of crowds in such crises. All these were instanced as examples of activities *not* confronted in the present-day USA. No one suggested, however, that she or her colleagues would dislike such work, or feel unable to do it. Indeed, the opportunity to work for example, in the mounted branch which might well involve some such experience was eagerly sought by several.

Public order policing had been a significant issue during the careers of most of my British informants. All had been at work during the urban riots of the 1980s. (One point they often made about these occasions was that, when only men had been deployed to police them, stations had been 'manned' wholly or largely by women, who thus dealt with all the 'real' crime for the time.) One officer had insisted on participating at a highly-charged event and pointed out that she had experience of many such events. Others had had to deploy other officers to deal with fraught or threatening situations and were well versed in (and sometimes critical about) the strategies adopted.

The public's reported attitudes to women officers varied across a considerable range and did not appear to do so on any national lines. From both countries and from all types of agency came versions of a female police folk-tale about citizens who demanded 'a real policeman' when a woman appeared. Some of these involved disputes or fights, but the most common concerned traffic or plumbing or other trivial incidents. Some drivers, for example, wanted 'a real man' to move a car, change a wheel, or tow them home. Many reported that male colleagues would back them on these occasions, since no officer actually liked being called out to do these tasks, whether male or female.

The persistence of the 'feminine' work-load on the shoulders of some British officers did lead to differences in reported reaction to them in situations where the gender agenda was being pursued. There were a number of accounts of close rapport between women policed by policewomen over child care, domestic violence, and even prostitution. Such recollections could be sentimentalized, of course, although some US evidence cited above suggested public preference for women officers in certain situations as did some British work.

There was some desire on the part of British officers to have the worth of the traditional mandate of female policing acknowledged. However, in *both* systems there was a strongly and widely-expressed view that female officers should not be narrowly stereotyped into taking only certain kinds of conventional postings. Many expressed specific preferences for counter-conventional tasks: for serious crime work, helicopter patrols, traffic patrols, drug squads, and dog handling, for example. One tentative assumption I had made at an early stage in the research was that women might prefer police work which was 'order maintaining', rather than 'crime fighting'. Such a choice would imply a preference for the traditional (and British) role of the office of constable, as opposed to the American model of the police detective. What in fact emerged was that maintaining order was given slightly higher prominence by the British group in their conceptions of policing and rather wider views taken of society and the role of police in it as well as a sense of history. As one described a period in her career: 'we brought the full majesty of the law and a system that had worked since 1829.'

It was possible to find in the descriptions from officers in both nations expressions for *personal* preferences which covered the full range of police work alongside clear, and different, views about the role of women in general in the police. The American officer quoted above is a typical example, who, while she described herself as very maternal, consciously avoided police work with children. Her story is paralleled by the British officer who had determinedly moved out of conventional work with women into much more serious CID activities.

In the two countries in which a distinctive form of policing by women was pioneered, female police are still exceptional and their exploits remarkable. They may still face assertions that they are in an occupation which is inappropriate for their sex. Such views come overwhelmingly from some sections of their male fellow officers. Where there is evidence of job suitability it tends to show that women do as well as men on male-based performance norms. Much wider questions arise and so far have not been fully addressed as to whether there are clear aims, and ways of measuring them, for policing, and secondly, whether men, or particular categories of them, are especially good at achieving them.

While these large questions still remain, and become more insistent as both societies face considerable crises over law and order issues, I trust that this small study has made certain aspects of this topic clearer. First, all the officers whom I talked to believed that theirs *was* a suitable job for a woman. Sometimes they mentioned appropriate characteristics they felt women had, such as patience and compassion. Their examples were not always 'feminine' traits; a British officer emphasized that police officers needed to be decisive and that she found that women were much more decisive than men and that this should be stressed and acknowledged more. On the other hand, most subjects, whether American or British, accepted a fairly orthodox view of policing but rejected the notion that it was necessary to be a male to fulfil the role properly. In careful, sometimes complex, accounts they made two kinds of points: they themselves had proved the validity of this assertion in their own careers: they could also cite their colleagues as examples.

There were tiny shifts of emphasis over this between the USA and Britain. In the former, networks, women partners, and trainers gave support and substance to such views. In Britain this was less likely, yet the belief was as strong, even if confidence was lower. There was generally a recognition that this issue could be a battleground with fellow officers, but that the battle would be worth fighting.

Equal Opportunities

As I argued in Chapter 2, the history of women's entry into polic- ing makes it very distinct from that of their breaking into several other occupations. Part of the thrust of first-wave feminism in Britain and America alike was economic; women sought to over- come traditional limitations on their lives, such as the lack of polit- ical power, or of access to higher education, in order to secure more resources for themselves in the labour market. Alongside this ran many other currents, notably those bubbling with the notion of the remoralization of society. Sometimes these flowed in well-syn- chronized streams. Florence Nightingale, for example, provided both occupational advancement for women and an example of the imposition of order, organization, and bureaucracy in nineteenth- century hospitals. Nightingale would not, of course, have regarded herself as a pro-suffrage feminist.

Many of those who sought to bring women into policing had been vehement supporters of the enfranchisement of women. This was especially true of the first pioneers of the movement in Britain. Others, such as the group who finally 'succeeded' in being accepted as female officers were not as radical. What united them, and joined them too to their American sisters was their moral sense, their righteousness, in its proper sense, about the state and situa- tion of some women and the links they saw between these and the state of their own societies. There were also associated aims of improving chances for women, but it does seem that in policing this was less marked than in other occupations whose barriers women breached at about the same time.

This, I think, explains in part why there was such a long latency period between the two world wars in both countries. If there had been an emphasis on equality or rights in the pioneering days, it had to do with double standards of morality as applied to men and women and the need to 'protect' women (and a few men) from evil and vice. In short, it was fair treatment for female citizens rather than for female cops which was pursued.

Such a model could not easily thrive, especially situated as it was within the police systems of both countries. In fact it flourished more successfully in Britain than in the USA. While there may have been financial and other reasons for its lack of robustness in the USA it seems likely that moral crusades for purity fell out of fashion after the problems of Prohibition. It is also probable that such a concept of policing fitted especially ill with the more crime-oriented US police.

Even before the integration phase of the 1970s, both countries saw considerable expansion, from a low base, of female recruitment. Changes in the labour market, demography, and family life all played some part in this trend, although, as S. Jones points out (1986), a key factor in increased female recruitment in Britain was undoubtedly the fall in recruitment and retention of *men* when pay was considered poor.

In the USA it does appear that other factors were at work, in particular the climate and legal framework, for the implementation of equal-employment opportunities for women. Those legal changes were, of course, also related to economic developments, but in addition had a crucial and distinctive US basis in the Civil Rights movement. It was the US model of equal-rights legislation which was, with some modifications, adopted in Britain in 1975 and was a key factor in the integration of British policing.

The history of both systems in terms of 'equality' in its various meanings is complex. Women first came into policing to improve the lives of *other* women and the state of society. It was, after all, the image of the virtuous, maladroitly handled Irene Savidge which swung public opinion in favour of women police in Britain. The equality legislation enacted in the USA in the 1960s turned out to be a relatively powerful weapon. Not only the police but other key masculine occupations such as the correctional system and the armed services (Zimmer 1986; Enloe 1988; Stiehm 1989) had to take women and use them in different ways. It is often said that the USA is a much more legally-based system. That is true of policing in general (McKenzie and Gallagher 1989) and also of the wider society.

As a result, equal opportunities has a far more robust legal framework in the USA and contains some legal doctrines not found or even permitted in Britain, notably that of affirmative action. It would be foolish to be complacent about the US system. There is much criticism of it from both right and left and the Equal Rights Amendment to the Constitution was not ratified. Nevertheless, there are real differences, as I showed in Chapter 2. What do the results of this study reveal about equal opportunities for women in policing in both countries?

Initially I must stress that it was not a primary aim of this part of the project to focus directly on this aspect of policy. I did so for the USA in another report (1989b). Nevertheless, while I carried out the research it was clear that this was or had been a major issue in the USA and was becoming one in Britain. It will be helpful to consider the comparative experience in terms of policy, practice, and outcomes, and of confidence.

As I have already suggested, American political and policy approaches to these matters have been far more radical and far-reaching than the British. Two key differences are important here. First, the legal basis and framework for equality: 'the notion of legal rights, which forms the foundation of the United States constitution, has provided a justification for and impetus to this type of action' (Holdaway 1991b). Secondly riots in the ghettos of US cities provided a seismic shock which led to major political and policy developments (Leimen 1984). An 'equal rights' or 'weak' version of equality was superceded by the positive action model which introduced employment and promotion quotas. There seems fairly widespread research-based support for the view that such policies were very effective in increasing ethnic minority representation in US police departments (Cowley 1982; Hochstedler 1984). 'The key feature of development in the USA was the introduction of formal employment quotas within a legal framework of individual rights and positive discrimination' (Holdaway 1991b).

This 'hard' positive discrimination policy (J. Edwards 1987) has had a mixture of effects for women. Undoubtedly it has been generally successful. In consequence, minority women are relatively well represented in US departments (Martin 1989) although not as well as are men. There does appear to be an observable link between legally enforced policies and those which are only aspirational. Few US departments recruit or promote women under consent decrees; where they do, as in Detroit, where promotion is the subject of decree, for example, the proportion of women is above average (Adler 1990).

However, what is also striking is that many other factors have some impact, ranging from the fiscal viability of the local government involved to the availability of female role models and leaders in that government (Warner *et al*. 1989; Heidensohn 1989*b*). Most significant of all, of course, is the stimulus to minority recruitment given by urban unrest and violence. Although women are not a minority but, in fact, form the majority of the population, they are unlikely to riot or cause a collective disturbance of the kind that might galvanize a government. That some did so in Britain in the struggle for suffrage in the early twentieth century is perhaps the striking exception which proves the rule.

It was obvious during my discussions with senior officials in US police departments that they felt that considerable progress had been made in the recruitment of women. In New York City the situation was described as the 'tip-over' stage, when they could move on to another level of policy-making. In other departments, recruitment targets for women were no longer being set, or other groups, such as Hispanics, were being targeted.

Such confidence was fairly remarkable, as the recruitment levels achieved thus far were still fairly low and promotion rates were modest. It was this confidence in both administration and, to a large extent, among women themselves which was striking in the USA. This seemed to owe something to the framework of equality—many women acknowledged that they had benefited from these policies and some from using the legislation themselves—and a good deal to the mutual support they offered to each other and the elusive American concept of 'opportunity'.

In some ways, the British situation is a mirror image of the American. While about 5 per cent of Britons are black or Asian, under 1 per cent of police come from these groups. Whereas women are less well represented in the USA, they are relatively better represented in Britain than are ethnic minorities. While this study was being conducted there were indications of some 'American'-style moves in British policing. Urban unrest in Britain has had some impact on thinking about policy for ethnic minority recruitment (Scarman 1981; Holdaway 1991*a* and 1991*b*). As far as women are concerned, various policy developments have focused on them (Metropolitan Police/Equal Opportunities Commission 1990; Brown and Campbell 1991) and publicity has been given to some key cases.

The overall *outcome* levels in both the USA and Britain, despite the substantial divergences in policies, are not dramatically different. National averages of about 10 per cent of police being female conceal large local variations. There seems to be optimism in the USA (Martin 1989; Adler 1990) that their model is successful and improving the situation, even though the climate and the legal setting for equal-rights cases has grown cooler.

The voices of women themselves were usually against policies of positive discrimination. Several US officers declared that the right goals had been achieved already and they preferred not to have 'unfair' help. Others were more concerned that recruitment targets for women had been dropped. One or two were uneasy at the situation for race relations in departments where both women and black people had hopes for a system of positive discrimination.

Those who were against the use of quotas or who felt that they had served their turn in the USA and were no longer needed were obviously accepting the viewpoint of a male cop culture. As I pointed out in Chapter 2, strong anti-discriminatory measures were enacted and widely used in the USA in the 1970s and 1980s, although something of a backlash against them occurred from the late 1980s on. Yet positive discrimination in *favour* of males was and continued to be practised in both systems for most of their history.

Women were able to take up only a certain limited number of posts in both countries, were paid less, and their duties restricted. In the USA their promotion chances were extremely limited. While formal integration took place from the 1970s onwards, many male colleagues of my research group had been recruited before then and had thus benefited from the old patterns. A striking feature of these was that women were usually expected to achieve higher educational standards than men: two years of college education as against a high-school diploma. Some veterans' and Vietnam veterans' preference schemes also still operated which were in practice discriminatory in favour of males. In Britain, while official quotas for women recruits were meant to be abolished in the 1970s, they in fact survived for much longer. Male entrants still had poorer educational records on entry than women in 1989 and 1990 (HMSO 1989). These are examples of positive discrimination which favoured male entrants. I have deliberately not included here height requirements, role stereotypes, etc., which may well indirectly favour males, because I want to stress the point that women officers in both countries saw equal opportunities in terms of 'special' (or 'fair') chances for women, not as a *reduction* of positive advantages for males. They usually accepted here, as in many areas, the conventional police-culture wisdom about such provision. Most, in short, believed that women should have access to jobs in policing fairly or equally, that is, on the same terms as men. What was obscured to them were the conditions on which men had been and sometimes continued to be recruited and promoted. Sometimes they did see this very clearly as unfair, although they rarely described such events as positive discrimination: in a subtle way they were transformed into the norm, rather like the weather and as unchangeable.

In this part of the discussion, I have primarily focused on US experience where positive discrimination had gained footholds and where senior officials still blessed it in some places. In Britain, where such practices would be illegal, officers generally rejected them and insisted that they preferred to rise on their own merits. They too sometimes perceived that positive advantage had accrued to males in policing and that such practices might still persist. Notably, it was the British officers who raised questions about aspects of welfare provision or job organization which might affect the recruitment and retention of women. These points were less likely to be mentioned in the USA, although New York City Police Department were examining child care and job sharing. This bears out Hewitt's contention (1985) that equal-opportunities concerns in the USA are focused on jobs whereas in Britain wider welfare benefits are seen as just as crucial.

American policewomen were often organizing networks and support groups. In New York City, at least, this had official sanction and funding. The situation in Britain was different and while some respondents liked the idea of the US pattern, others actively disliked it and said that it would be 'too much women's lib'. In short, a majority in both countries were reluctant to be given positive advantages (or to gain further ones, some must have benefited under certain policies and decrees). In practice, what they understood by 'equal opportunities' was very varied and was largely conceived of in relation to themselves.

In all the debates on this issue there seem to be two quite distinct strands which are often twisted and looped together. It is worth trying to untangle them. Equal opportunities in policing can refer to equal access to a reasonably well-paid secure job with pension rights. Laws in both countries made such access possible in the 1970s. So far, success has been fairly modest in increasing female recruitment and their retention rates, and improving their promotion prospects. These rates vary widely, however, and this in itself suggests that if, for example, Detroit or West Midlands can achieve the totals that they do, others could do at least as well. More strikingly, recruitment from ethnic minorities in the USA has been substantially increased and, to a lesser degree, from women from those groups. Evidence suggests that strong enforcement policies, positive role models, and very precise and explicit affirmative action plans are keys to achieving these results. Solvency is also important, better still a boom. If this is so, the US model will run further and faster than the British, which lacks most of those characteristics. In many ways British policing is becoming more Americanized and this may be one area which develops in this way.

There is another aspect to the debate about equality which really refers to matters outside the scope of the law. By this I mean the question I have already talked about: equal access to control of social control. Earlier I suggested that it was deep-seated unease about this that lay behind objections to women police. Some of these objections may be routine resentment at 'extra' competition for jobs. There does, however, seem to be a deeper concern about who has a right to manage law and order. In this debate, and 'debate' is perhaps the wrong word, because it is not a serious, rational discussion, equal claims to control are not legitimate since this is perceived as a male preserve, or one where males should be in charge, assisted at most by female subordinates. This, the view that men 'own' order and have sole rights to preserve it, seems to be at the core of much of the equality debates.

Consider, for example, the references made by almost all the women to topics such as *territory* (especially within police stations and precincts) to *weapons* and/or *physique* and *strength*. Most telling are, I believe, the repeated allusions mentioned in the earlier section of this chapter. By far the majority of arguments about the suitability of women, or otherwise, for policing focus on the effect on their male colleagues. This could be described as the 'porcelain policeman' argument: that policemen are so fragile and delicate that they will feel threatened and undermined, their solidarity shattered, and their loyalty over-stretched by the presence of women. If the issue is seen as one of possession and ownership of something as crucial to society as its control, then such reactions can perhaps be understood better. I am not suggesting that every male officer, probably not even the majority, holds such opinions, or does so strongly. The 'subcultural guardians' do so, however, and can be very vocal in expressing versions of them.

There may, of course, be very different ideas about control behind the conflicts which I have discussed. Members of the public certainly have varied views about what are problems which they want dealt with (Shapland and Vagg 1988) and it is also clear from research that public and police priorities differ (Wilson and Kelling 1982; Kinsey *et al.* 1986). For instance it is possible that dominance, rather than control, is the object of certain kinds of police and certain styles of policing. Certainly some of the rhetoric used by and about police, 'the war against crime', 'the battle against drug pushers', can sound more like that of a military campaign than the sustaining of order. Research on multi-agency co-operation (Sampson *et al.* 1988) suggests that the police may find co-operative strategies difficult and wish to be in command. In urging caution about the modern fashion for inter-agency co-operation, Sampson and her colleagues say:

two things need to be confronted. First, the power of the police. The police are often enthusiastic proponents of the multi-agency approach, but they tend to prefer to set the agendas and to dominate forum meetings and then to ignore the multi-agency approach which is capable of balancing power differentials and checking the practices of the more powerful agencies. (1988: 491; emphasis added)

It is most interesting to find Sampson *et al.* in another part of their paper acknowledging that they do not

address one of the most fundamental and yet neglected areas of potential and actual conflict between state agencies, which is that of the gender composition of these agencies, an issue which is particularly important in the relations between police officers and social workers. (1988: 479)

In a footnote they point out that the considerable literature in this field tends to ignore gender relations.

There may be differently gendered concepts being used as well with police officers being socialized into 'patriarchal dominance' models of control, or at least such models being seen as the norm for policing. Hence, for example, the repetition of the fear about subduing the fifteen-stone drunk which so bedevils debates about women police. As my informants tirelessly pointed out, no single male can actually subdue such a character on his own either, it will always need two or more officers. There is an alternative folk heroine for policewomen, the small demure female officer who finds an aggressive drunk who has knocked out her male colleagues. She puts her hand in his, says sweetly, 'I'm lost, can you please take me to the police station?' and he meekly complies.

Further discussion of this point belongs in the next chapter. In terms of the mixing and matching of the two systems under comparison it would seem that, in one sense, the British version of policing is more 'feminine' since it is traditionally based more on informal control, community, on symbolic presence, and on the positive image of the office of constable. The US version with its weaponry, heavier technology, and above all its formal, legal base could be said to be more masculine. These are suggestive comparisons, but organizations are not gendered. Rather, policing in both countries appears until recently, at least, to have been based on huge but implicit assumptions about who should police and how they should do so. At the core of these lie notions about gender and, probably, gender-specific notions about dominance and subordination, control and order. It is only when one separates out these strands that one can start to understand the fairly modest progress made by women in policing in the twentieth century, even in the USA where conditions were most favourable. Questions about equal rights, about testing, and interviews, promotion panels, and female mentors belong to the first agenda and are common to most occupations. Police officers have a unique role, and who owns the rights to that role and how they perform in it are the key questions on the second agenda. Stability and order matter to everyone in society; the policewomen in this study wished to play a part in achieving these and thought that more women should do so too. They were unimpressed by claims to a male freehold.

Changing Police and Policing Change

The two subtitles I chose earlier for this section were *The Gentle Touch* and a *Desperate Remedy*. By these I wanted to convey two aspects of change which have come increasingly to affect the police of both countries and are likely to continue to do so. I have already suggested much earlier in this book that policing is in something of a crisis in Britain and the USA. Among the many factors that can be cited in support of this view are some common to the two nations and others which are unique.

Official crime rates have 'soared' (to use tabloid terms) in the late twentieth century. Britain had its highest ever levels in 1990 and 1991 (Home Office 1991). The USA achieved record homicide levels in the same year. A number of specific problems were associated with this. A range of 'hard' crime problems became common to both systems: serious drug abuse, organized crime, sophisticated white-collar crime. Fear of crime also advanced steeply. Relations with certain ethnic groups and the police were well known to be very poor.

Britain saw a dramatic decline in support and respect for the police from mid-century on. Among stimulating factors were the series of disasters in the criminal-justice system, which led to numerous people being imprisoned and then discharged on appeal often after a long period in prison. Britain also saw several urban riots in the 1980s and 1990s as well as major industrial disputes. Much of this marks the special case of British policing which obviously endured a rapid and spectacular fall from grace. Illusions about the police in Britain were dramatically swept away by a number of scandals. Few such illusions ever comforted or deluded Americans.

There are many factors which can be linked to the state of policing in the twentieth century. Many are to do with social changes, such as the greater diversity in both societies, decline in community, authority, and a dozen other sociological commonplaces. These are not of the police's making. Very much of the police's making are, however, the claims they have made, and have been unable to fulfil, not only to solve these problems but, through the unique ownership of order which they claim to have and the main and key solutions to them.

A specific set of social changes have had considerable impact on the agenda of modern policing. The traditional mandate focused on 'real' crime. This is tellingly caught in the title to Bittner's key paper 'Florence Nightingale in pursuit of Willie Sutton' (1990*b*) and in the vignette provided by Smith and Gray of the Metropolitan officers arresting and escorting with great respect a 'serious' villain (1983). Since the 1960s there has, however, been the growth of a new agenda in policing in both countries. Among the causative factors have been the series of crime surveys begun in the USA and widely copied. These revealed the extent of crime victimization and laid the foundation for the social construction of the victim and of patterns of victimization.

From these and later studies emerged also the image of the fear of crime; a phenomenon in itself, it is arguably discrete from actual criminal victimization. In addition, the feminist movement played an important part in setting the new agenda. Feminists contributed to two key 'discoveries': the gendered nature of much personal crime in which men harm each other or damage women and children by violence, rape, sexual assault, or sexual abuse. The second is the size of the hidden part of the iceberg of personal crime and its seriousness (see Heidensohn 1989*a* for a summary). Much of this has been seized upon by politicians and some police officers. Some changes in procedures and policies have taken place. Domestic violence and rape are now handled differently both in the USA and in Britain (S. Edwards 1990). These are still highly contentious areas and both nations have seen major public debates about the extent and policing of child abuse, and the existence of so-called 'date rape'. Nevertheless, it is clear that there have been attempts at least to change policing priorities. Three reasons can be suggested for this. One is that the police are responding to social conditions and the ways in which they have changed. The other is that in the climate of disenchantment with the police, this new agenda is seen as one way of gaining public support. Another factor is that the fear of crime is a phenomenon in itself and appears to have critical influences on crime control and on peoples' behaviour. Fear of crime is strongly related to gender and in order to reduce it, it is necessary to regain women's confidence in policing.

Additional recruitment of women to the police and a greater role for them in the sections which handle such work have thus become an issue once again for policewomen. In both countries some women had been in posts of this kind and several had been involved in setting them up. For many these activities held irony. They felt that senior management commitment was not sincere, or that sufficient resources were not available. The older officers in Britain who had been recruited to undertake all this varied in their reactions. They saw it as vital work, but did not always want to carry it out themselves.

This was less of an issue in the USA where the impetus to increase female recruitment has come much more from legal pressures for access to jobs and promotion. Concern about policies towards citizens and clients was much less apparent. Aside from the varied modes of policing discussed above, which clearly affect this kind of agenda, there is also the question of the plurality of US police agencies. There are so many of them, with so many overlapping jurisdictions that no one can claim a single territory for their own. This seems also to make a difference to the degree of command and authority assumed over a particular patch. Also affected by this situation were small-sized departments which could not, for example, provide specialists. In a group discussion in a rural area much of the focus was on the patchy provision of specialist officers. A further problem lay in the complex mix of political and fiscal factors: in the more democratic system it is harder to change priorities than in the more hierarchical one, even though it was in the USA that many of the new approaches were pioneered, such as experiments with responses to domestic violence and to rape.

Most of the women whom I saw did not believe that policing priorities had altered very much. Highest values still attached to those who caught serious villains in both systems and 'domestics' were seen as rubbish work. Whether such work attracts the highest status in the police hierarchy it is now added on to the existing police agenda. Through this we can begin to question, albeit very tentatively, how the kinds of person conventionally recruited into policing might alter, and how profound that alteration might be.

Even without the new emphases in the content of policing there were fresh winds blowing through it. New kinds of training, new skills were being stressed. A considerable exercise in replanning probationer training was going on during the course of my study in Britain. This project was consciously based on visits to a series of US establishments. Essentially, this training had two characteristics. First, it was not gender-specific: the model officer on whom it

was based was neuter. Secondly, the skills and strategies it advocated were not based on traditional norms but on what was
required for success in specified situations.

There has been a considerable debate about what constitutes
appropriate policing, police skills, and tactics during the late twentieth century in both countries. In Britain, public attitudes to the
police strategies in dealing with disturbances or with ethnic minorities have all come under scrutiny and have given rise to reports,
research, and recommendations. There have been similar crises in
the US.

These developments have significance for the theme of this book
and of this chapter in particular. Law and order have been political
issues before and policing has often been contentious, although
arguably less so or less often in Britain. Present disquiet is more
threatening to some of the central assumptions about policing
which have long supported the Anglo-American model. If police
officers need interpersonal skills, rather than tough physiques, if
their job increasingly involves crime control of petty offending and
dealing with abuse and violence within the home, then not only is
the macho crime fighter obsolete as a model, he may actually prove
to be a liability. I am by no means suggesting that all female
officers are automatically qualified by their sex for such tasks,
while males are not. Such skills are found or, more important, can
be developed, in both men and women. Many of my younger
respondents felt uneasy at dealing with small children because of
their lack of knowledge. Others insisted that rape victims needed
very special care and handling for which training was required.
Male officers who were good at such tasks were cited in every
place I visited.

There are two conclusions to draw from considering this aspect
of modern policing. Specifically 'masculine' traits are no longer
particularly functional for much modern police work. They may
never have really been so. Mythology and culture have long underpinned such a view. This shift is, in part, at least already acknowledged although the expansion in female recruitment was certainly
not launched with any feminization of policing as its purpose. If
such an idea is now being tentatively toyed with, it has probably
something to do with what I have called desperate remedies.

In some of the interviews I undertook, women seemed to be suggesting that their presence was sometimes exploited in order to

improve the public image of the police. This was very clear in one US city where local police–citizen relations had been very strained. Press coverage of various events had been hostile. Women officers, and some men, began a series of projects which conveyed a very positive picture of the police and in which women officers featured prominently. These women were not cynical about this, although not entirely naïve. Their commitment was overwhelmingly to the police organization. They knew that their activities neutralized some of the adverse effects. No such conscious strategy had occurred in Britain, but some women felt that their presence was used as a smoke-screen to disguise the failure to recruit members of ethnic minorities.

This is only a speculative point. It derives in part from an observation by Reiner who, in reviewing the fictional presentation of the police, suggested links between their public support and their portrayal in novels, films, and TV series. The crop of female cop shows from the 1970s onwards (*Policewoman*, *The Gentle Touch*, *Juliet Bravo*, *Cagney and Lacey*) and their presence in most police teams in TV fictions were perhaps due not so much to their greater numbers in policing, more to their greater acceptability. After corruption stories, accidental killings, and rising crime rates, it became credible to produce stories about heroic cops only if the hero was a heroine.

Conclusions

Comparing policewomen's histories from two cultures reveals numerous insights. The most profound is that there do seem to be common experiences which link them and can be distinguished from those of men. They present a challenge, and are challenged at most points in their careers. Nevertheless, they can be committed and capable. There are common patterns in the origins of both systems and they curiously achieve like outcomes despite largely different legal, organizational, and especially cultural climates. This again suggests that we are talking about something fairly profound and robust. Much of what needs to be explored, after this exercise in surveying the land and mapping it, turns out to be outside the strict territory of my major themes. The story of women in Anglo-American policing is part of a wider tale of their role in social control and that, like the last but one in a set of Chinese boxes, is contained within still larger ones. Neither women's role and position in these, nor their importance to them can be understood without acknowledging the gendered nature of control, of the controlling agencies, and the series of contradictions and conflicts that pattern these boxes like flaws in lacquer or marble.

Comparative Criminology

Comparative studies in criminology have begun to flourish in the late twentieth century. I have suggested in Chapter 3 some of the purposes and types of comparative research, and in the Appendix alluded to some of the problems. Strictly speaking, this is not, of course, a *criminological* project; rather it lies within the fields of deviance and control. Deviance, because of course most of the women studied here, both those in the empirical sections and the historical were deviant in seeking a role in law enforcement and during their police service. Control is their chosen area of work.

Criminological work which involves making comparisons across national boundaries requires, as I have suggested in writing about Europe,

three conditions . . . to be met. There must be sources of material and data with which to make comparisons: crime statistics, victim surveys, research studies. Second, translatable concepts have to be available to make possible the collecting, ordering and analysis of such data. Finally, some kind of framework, part universe of discourse, part set of common concerns, must exist. (Heidensohn 1991a: 10).

Much the same can be said about studies such as this one. It will be apparent that these terms were only partially met. Even basic data on numbers of women in policing, their deployment, and promotion is not readily accessible. Cultural and political contrasts are very apparent. In the USA the complexity and diffusion of policing bodies means that only surveys can establish figures (Martin 1990), while in Britain caution about the publication of official data limits the scope of research (S. Jones 1986).

As I have outlined, the stock of existing concepts proved to have limitations, too, and it was necessary to invent some of my own to make sense of the findings from the study. What was an important aid both to framing the research and to creating a public climate in which to carry it out was the existence and acknowledgement of feminism. Everyone whom I contacted or interviewed shared an awareness of the salience of issues to do with women and their role in law enforcement. This was by no means an identical awareness, but there were enough common characteristics to contribute in a significant way to the comparative study (see the Appendix and Heidensohn 1992). It is possible to conclude then that my conditions do, ideally, need to be met to achieve reasonable standards in comparative work, but that it is feasible even when there are restrictions on them.

Another, more vital result of this study from the comparative perspective will, I trust, be the revision of two frameworks already widely-used in the field. In the first and final chapters of this book I have shown that the dispersal of discipline thesis cannot explain what one might call 'gender resistance'. Historical examples of the refusal by governments and police agencies to incorporate women into law enforcement are legion; Chapter 7 includes an analysis of this in Britain and indicates parallels in US experience. The second framework which should be sent for a refit is that of the notion of Anglo-American policing. All the studies of which I am aware ignore the entry of women into both systems, their struggles for acceptance, and the modern developments. At most, an aside refers to these phenomena (Reiner 1985).

There is, notwithstanding the observed differences between women's experiences in the two nations, enough similarity between them to suggest that they have more in common with each other than with their male colleagues. This can be attributed to two key factors. First are the distinctive origins of women's role in policing. These were shared by the USA and Britain as aspects of first-wave feminism and the moral purity movement. The second is the resistance mounted by policemen in both nations to the recruitment presence and promotion of women which remains a major feature shaping female officers' lives.

Comparative study can illuminate analysis and improve policy-making. As to the second, I have tried to look at both British and North American experiences as containing lessons. Some comparative research seeks examples of good practice elsewhere to improve performance at home. There is much which is admirable in the USA but confidence there is perhaps higher than recorded achievements warrant. It may well be that, as Martin suggests (1990: 162), some of the best departments for women to work in there may not necessarily be those which record the highest participation rates. Britain, too, provides lessons for the USA. The lack of weapons, both for female and male officers is only one example. A further one is provided by the capacity of the British system to develop towards greater equality *without* a strong legal framework. This may become more important as key legal decisions in the USA reverse trends which have helped to sustain affirmative action programmes (Martin 1991). In sum, comparative research presents problems, but its benefits in increased understanding and available policy options far outweigh these.

7

Conclusions: Are Women in Control?

THE title of this book is a question. It was with this question and related ones in mind that I first began this project. Were women now more involved in social control? If they were did this make a difference either to them or to the agencies which employed them? It would be easy to say that the answers to these queries seem respectively to be 'yes' and 'no, not very much'. In fact it has turned out to be a much more complicated enterprise to pursue than such straightforward enquiries might suggest. Nevertheless, while there are many caveats and qualifications to be made, there is now enough material available to respond to such questions, even if it is necessary first of all to summarize some of the difficulties I encountered in trying to answer them.

Reconceptualizing Control

The first problem was and remains with the concept of social control. It is a vague idea, yet highly contentious, the focus of considerable academic debate. Much of this can be rather arbitrarily divided up along continua from 'nice' to 'nasty' or from 'hard' to 'soft' versions. Janowitz, for instance, presented a nice and soft notion, arguing that social control was about self-control and avoiding awkward issues such as coercion. On the other hand lie the range of scholars loosely grouped under the 'dispersal of discipline' theorists (after Foucault). Both approaches proved to be limited. A full appreciation of the maintenance of stability and order in any society needs to include the informal as well as the formal structures which sustain it. Public and private spaces also have to be included.

These might be said to be key sociological additions, the latter tinged with feminism. From historians' criticisms, and their own work in recovering and presenting careful case-studies, come further important qualifications. Social control should not be perceived as something between a flat-iron and a tank: no social institution simply pushes on, flattening all in its path. Even if some enormously oppressive agencies have existed and operated in some societies—the Final Solution in the Third Reich, the trials and camps of Stalinism, the Pol Pot regime in Cambodia—they have proved unsustainable. It is important to add to the concept that members of society are capable of interaction with its institutions, they can negotiate and challenge.

Feminist approaches to social control have also been somewhat restricted. While there have been important contributions which have pointed out the gendered nature of much social control, the main thrust, especially of the most recent work, has been on women as *victims*. Their victimization is seen as multiple: they may suffer once as victims of abuse and violence and again through unsympathetic police response and yet again because the judiciary is harsh. Women, it is argued (and I have urged this myself and still do so), face distinctive and additional forms of social control.

On the whole there has been much more emphasis on social control as oppressive to women—the double jeopardy argument (Heidensohn 1985; Carlen 1983) and much less on what might be termed the assertion of 'success'. Although they may pay too high a price for it, women are generally the more successful graduates of social-control systems as their delinquency and deviance are so much less marked. The portrayal of women in much feminist writing is therefore in danger of reinforcing certain stereotypes: that males are always dominant (and the dominant are always male) and females are victims. There are many problems with seeing social control purely as male oppression. It creates difficulties of analysis: it is not possible to reduce control, especially when the additional aspects I have already noted are included, simply to gender oppression. Class, race, and change have all to be added at the least. Empirically too there are limitations: women participate, and have done so for many years in most agencies of control from police and probation to psychiatric nursing. Feminism has proved helpful in highlighting the masculine nature, and the male dominance, of almost all forms of authority (still) in modern society.

What feminism had focused on much less, and some feminists were far less happy with, was women sharing such roles (Cain 1991; Enloe 1988).

This project started then with certain limitations in its equipment. Concepts had to be remodelled on a trial basis. There were plenty to choose from but, like a motley collection of tools, they do not fit easily together nor are they appropriate for its aims. It was necessary to rely on 'grounded concepts' derived from the research study itself. In seeking to explore questions about women's relationship to social control I chose to focus on their role in Anglo-American policing. This example proved to be both at once extreme and central: extreme because policing is not a traditional area for women and their entry into it was highly contested; central because police officers play a unique and very distinctive part in order maintenance in modern societies and one which has been increasingly the subject of scholarly and popular debate. Prison guards and the military are both instances of highly unconventional careers for women, which they do now enter, but neither has the same core role in official control as policing does.

I chose to compare British and American experiences first for all the reasons which usually justify international comparisons in social research. Comparison provides a kind of experiment: it is possible to suggest what is invariable and what is flexible in situations. There are, in policy areas, insights to be gained from mutual observation and exchanges. There were some particular grounds as well. The 'new police' are thought to have been invented by the British in 1829 in London and the model copied by many US cities. It is commonplace to describe subsequent developments as Anglo-American policing and to contrast this phenomenon with French or Continental versions (Mawby 1990). The history of women's entry into this system, while again there was some transatlantic twinning, had not been assimilated into the main model.

When I endeavoured to achieve this by reviewing the respective histories, some significant elements emerged. Women had participated in policing for almost the whole of the twentieth century in both countries. There were broadly two stages: the first from the 1900s to the 1970s was a phase of specialism and protective activities, in the second women became integrated into ordinary police work. The striking thing was how much certain groups of women themselves had wanted this, how determinedly they had pursued this goal and what support they had had from other women and from some men. From this analysis it became clear that, while women had joined the conventional police agencies and sought police powers, there developed, certainly initially, a very distinctive phenomenon that one might call, were it not so clumsy a term 'policewomaning'.

The transatlantic comparison was at its most helpful here in showing that, with large historical and political differences between the countries, there were nevertheless very many similarities in this area. Woman police volunteered themselves, they sought work with women and children and in the fields of moral protection. They were often allied to feminism, even though they faced conflicts of principle about dual standards of morality. They were often popular with the public and, in times of tension, governments, sometimes with senior officers. From their male colleagues they faced hostility and rejection. It was these latter above all who recognized women police as other, different, and a threat. These points can be made about both the USA and Britain with very little distinction.

This movement for women to share in social control, despite its relatively modest aims, stagnated and almost foundered between the two world wars. When women finally and fully joined mainstream policing in the 1970s there was a restart. The old version was largely jettisoned and old and new recruits alike had either to keep to the new ways or leave. Since there had been at least this one historic episode of women seeking, and thus challenging, roles within control agencies, I then set out to explore how officers in the modern systems of both countries saw their own histories and experiences in the light of this past. Using historical accounts, police research on police (men, usually) and on policewomen as well as the comparative study of two small groups of female officers, it is possible to present a set of 'findings'. These can help to fill out *descriptions* of women's part in social control and perhaps further its *analysis* too.

Some Conclusions in Confidence

When social control is defined, as I have argued it properly should be, to embrace informal and formal agencies, home and family as well as school and work, the private areas as well as the public, it is obvious that women have always taken part in this activity.

Even in societies, perhaps especially in such societies, where women were segregated or kept in purdah, they exercised important roles within certain narrow confines. With certain rare exceptions—ancient priestesses, medieval abbesses, a few monarchs— women's roles in such activities in most pre-modern societies have four characteristics. They were confined to *private* and/or to *informal* spheres (Dobash and Dobash 1981) they were always *subordinate* to an ultimate male authority and they were invariably *disarmed*, they did not have direct access to judicial powers nor to arms, nor the command of supporters who might carry them.

During the course of the nineteenth century changes took place in the modernizing societies, most notably Britain and the USA, which began to alter the first two aspects of this pattern. Large numbers of middle-class women became increasingly involved in public life. They could not vote, nor could they enter professions. Nevertheless, they significantly shaped their own societies, notably by their contributions to conceiving, creating, and sustaining key institutions. Social Welfare was probably their major preoccupation and, as Thane has pointed out, their voluntary efforts were certainly crucial to the development of welfare in Britain (1982). Material welfare was a central aim of many projects from the reorganization of nursing and improvement of housing to practical advice on baby care for mothers, but with it almost invariably went moral ambitions. Most of these women were inspired by Christian or similar moral codes and sought to rescue the poor, the weak, and the oppressed from squalor and infamy. Hence the campaigns for temperance, against prostitution and gambling.

Many of these projects were highly successful and we can still recognize their influences in the shape of contemporary institutions. Their descendants include social work in both the USA and Britain. From their attempts to alter social lives and social provision in both nations, many of these women came to see enfranchisement as the key to extending their activities. This was given an added edge in the USA by the participation of women in anti-slavery campaigns. The suffrage came to be partly an end in itself, but also as the means to other ends, especially those of equity and justice, which could not be achieved, as I have suggested, by those who were always subordinate to men and lacked weapons to resist them with.

Enfranchisement and social morality are then two of the godmothers at the cradle of the infant policewomen movement in both countries. While there were, especially later, those who saw policing as an occupation which should be opened to women as others were, this was clearly much less important than the moral project which was the primary aim. Since it was initially women who were the objects of this concern, this has seemed an uncomfortable campaign for modern feminists to assimilate. While it is true that some of the pioneers had worked in the courts and observed double standards in morality and punishment for men and women which they wished to expose and alter, many, and this became the dominant thrust, sought to intervene to protect women from men and from their own 'worse' instincts. The support given to double standards by policing prostitutes or by enforcing curfews for women in wartime England may seem profoundly inappropriate today. Yet these early pioneers were often committed feminists. In fact their position and their dilemma reflected another protectionist debate which divided American feminism in the 1920s. In 1923 the National Women's Party came into conflict with the League of Women Voters (daughter of American Women's Suffrage Association) over-protective legislation for women in industry. The dispute was about whether interventionist laws ('for her own good') helped or hindered women (Fuchs Epstein 1988: 129).

Although few of the pioneer policewomen directly appreciated such dilemmas for what they were, they represented key issues for women in modern societies as they decided whether or not to join or co-operate with state institutions. If they do so, they may end up reinforcing their own, or other women's oppression. 'The disputes on these issues among feminists today indicate that the debate is still very much alive' (Fuchs Epstein 1988: 129). For women who sought to widen their participation in social control the dilemma was particularly acute and complex. Even where their target was to alter the behaviour of men, as in domestic violence or child abuse, they were restricted by the subordinate, disarmed status I have described. Yet at the heart of formal control in ordered societies are *authority* and *legitimacy*. Without these it is not possible to impose sanctions, nor to achieve redress for wrongs.

(It is of course, possible to turn to the alternatives of vigilantism or violence. There is evidence that women had been involved in community punishment in pre-modern societies (see Heidensohn 1985 for a résumé) but they had lost this role as informal justice systems were increasingly displaced by formal ones (Dobash and Dobash 1981). The use of violence is of course as much governed by rules in most groups as are conventional punishments (Corrigan 1979). Often these circumscribe women's taking part in fights, though by no means invariably prohibiting them (Campbell 1984). Recourse by women to organized violence against, for example, abusers and molesters does not appear to be well documented. It is interesting to speculate on the reasons for this.)

Since the only access to authority and legitimacy was through conventional organizations, women only had the choices of 'exit or loyalty', of being incorporated or leaving. It must be said as well that some undoubtedly enjoyed the authority they exercised and missed it sorely when they were stood down after the War in Britain (M. Allen 1925). At about the same period the success of the policewomen's division of the Detroit Police Department was attributed by its director, in part to a 'loyal staff of policewomen who have pursued their work with zeal and devotion' (Hutzel 1933: 8).

Policewomen's bureaux and departments were set up with specific, rather narrow, and mainly preventive purposes: for women to police their own sex and children. They achieved their entry largely because of their narrow aims, which became irresistible. Paradoxically, these then served to restrict their activities within the police organization. They were within, yet not entirely of it. Hutzel's handbook from which the above quotation comes is optimistic and practical in its adjurations. Yet there are also constant references, after over twenty years of female policing in America, to 'the element of novelty which seems to characterize the work in many places', 'an unwarranted invasion of the uniformed man's field of work', 'policewomen's work . . . is regarded by the "old timers" as a fad and an unjustified police excursion into social work' (Hutzel 1933: 2–3). The remit may well have been a worthwhile one. Some of its latter-day inheritors in Britain certainly regretted its abandonment. It is arguable, however, that it was inappropriate to carry out social work from within an organization associated with crime and delinquency.

Much the greatest problem, however, in both systems lay in setting up policewomen's departments or bureaux within the framework of mainstream police agencies. This proved generally to be both the only solution and no solution at all. It was the only solution because there really was no other available way for women to enter and contribute to this formal type of control. Nor was there, and this is not necessarily the same thing, an obvious alternative form for such rescue work to take without some kind of link to courts or agencies with certain powers. (This for example is still very much a dilemma for child care and child-protection agencies in the 1990s as they face conflicts and criticisms about their interventions (Blom Cooper 1985).)

At the same time, it proved not to be a long-term solution, only a cul-de-sac, because women had to accept such narrow and restrictive terms for their activities. In saying this, I am not of course denying that this is what they had in general asked for. However, they aimed for specialist work, but they also sought full police powers and in both systems there were early and strong pressures towards women becoming real police. In Britain, this was the issue during the 1920s, as indeed was their survival. In the USA the tensions thus created are encapsulated in advice on the ideal recruit: 'She should be the type of person who can become a real policewoman without in any sense ceasing to be a real social worker' (Hutzel 1933: 8). There was then a task which had been identified as police work. Much of it involved women and children. It did not therefore have to follow that only women should carry out this task nor that this should be their only role in the police. In practice, that is what happened for several decades.

In Britain the account of women's role in policing during the Second World War sounds exactly and agonizingly like a reprise of the same theme thirty years earlier, save that there was strong support from central government for increasing female recruitment because of manpower shortages. The Home Secretary, Herbert Morrison, announced in 1944: 'it is my policy to encourage the appointment of Police women in any area where they seem likely to be useful.' Once again there was strong lobbying and support from women for the move: 500 women from 70 organizations 'gathered in London to demand the employment of more women police and the Archbishop of Canterbury, Dr. Temple, gave as his opinion the view that "the main obstacle has been sheer downright, stark prejudice"' (Smithies 1982: 192).

Some opponents of the movement showed all too well that they were in a repeat performance. The Chief Constable of Salford announced that 'his views did not differ from those he had expressed to the Watch Committee as far back as 1927. He was of the opinion that the less decent women saw of the steamy and sordid side of a policeman's life the better it would be for them, the community at large, and future generations.'

Another authority member 'protested against those who "want to put women in uniform to go swanking as police"' (Smithies 1982: 192).

Smithies, in his history of crime during the War, notes that others were more subtle, favouring the *principle* of women police 'but going on to point out either that there was nothing for them to do or that the type of work was unsuitable for women'. He records a version of an objection which we have seen many, many times before from the Chairman of Salford Watch Committee, who 'said that "patrols like those in the dock areas establishments are problems enough for hardened men, let alone for women." Yet was patrol work the only kind of work that was available to police women?' (1982: 193). He notes the dishonesty and prejudice involved in the objections and his view of those is clinched by pointing out that

this was the stormiest controversy affecting the police in 1944—the fuss was about a total increase in strength in England and Wales from 282 in 1940 to 418 in 1945 . . . In 1945, after all the debate and discussion, there were precisely thirty-three more women police in England than there had been in 1944. (1982: 194)

While he does not explicitly make this link, Smithies, in the same historical account of crime in wartime Britain, records first the enormous increase in prostitution during the War, due to the various obvious factors of mobility, mobilization, tension, and changing sexual mores (1982: 139–42). He suggests that there was a major morality campaign in 1944 especially against brothels and brothel-keepers. There was a crack-down and an increase in prosecutions and fines. Ironically, not only was this work in which policewomen might have been involved in both 'rescue' and observations, but the manpower required to support successful prosecutions was considerable. In short, Smithies' description suggests that many of the police, including senior officers, were as opposed to policewomen in 1944 as they had been in 1914. Almost nothing had changed and law officers were prepared to defy the spirit, if not the black letter, of lawful orders in favour of prejudice. The battles for full entry were to be left until the 1970s.

This example illustrates well the limitations of the 'dispersal of discipline' thesis for this topic because of their consistent failure to include gender in their models (Donzelot 1985). Garland has discussed (1990) the ways in which the state became more and more involved with voluntary bodies in the late nineteenth century and early twentieth century, thus making them part of what Donzelot calls 'the new sector of the social' and committed to informal social control (1985: 122). Stan Cohen has developed this argument to point to a tendency to greater and greater incorporation of such agencies and increasing 'net widening' of their aims (1985). Yet here we have once again examples of the exclusion of significant groups who sought to be involved in the control process. It can be argued, of course, that either *all* women were perceived as being already sufficiently incorporated into the system, or that the specific groups who sought a greater share in control for women had been so included. Yet the latter clearly did not feel that this was so and their incorporation was often avoided or resisted when the logic of the 'discipline' model would predict the opposite.

That is not to say that such theories have no explanatory power at all. They can help in understanding, for example, the inclusion and, indeed, transformation of radical feminist protectionist projects during the early part of the twentieth century. What they fail to clarify is why, when so many other initiatives were accepted, this one was not. The omission of gender is not the only flaw; as Ryan and Ward point out in another context, this perspective is 'altogether too pessimistic' and too all-embracing, and that, most of all, it misses the crucial point that it is possible to make a control agency a site for resistance from within (1989: 90). I am not suggesting that all women entering control agencies have been bent on subversion, rather that some were so and some became so, even if their goals were to reform and strengthen their agencies as 'virtuous deviants'. A complex and interactive model is needed to clarify this.

While both systems saw the integration of female officers during the 1970s and a continuance of the rise in their recruitment which had already begun, they did so from very distinct bases and within different legal, economic, and social frameworks. Nevertheless, the effects were quite similar in many ways and the lives of policewomen resembled each other in certain characteristics more than they did their male colleagues. They often also shared values and culture with their male fellow officers. Yet, since such subcultures tend to be stereotypically macho, the women were often excluded and divided from or by the very occasions they sought to police.

Despite this marked resistance, policewomen in general can become confident and capable. The histories recounted in this study indicate that they learn resourcefully to use the existing system and its rules to help them: through professionalism, for instance, or they develop strategies of their own as the pioneers did. Again, while there were differences, it was clear that the force of voice and of transformation had been appreciated on both sides of the Atlantic. One of the ironic outcomes one can observe in the processes of adaptation which these women undergo is how relatively successful they are when compared with their male colleagues' reaction to them. None of the women whom I interviewed had worked in an organization where men were anything other than overwhelmingly dominant, at 85 per cent or more of total strength. Many had been, or still were, sole females. Yet they survived and even flourished, while their male colleagues could appear demoralized by this tiny influx.

An inescapable conclusion can be drawn from this research and related studies: some women wish to take part in the formal aspects of social control. They are comfortable with this role and enjoy their position. There may be consequential issues for the relevant agencies to face, but that suggests questions about the agencies. It cannot be argued that women are not capable of becoming police officers, or indeed other keepers of the peace. (There are other kinds of problems which I shall address in the next section.)

Police or similar organizations require both legitimacy and authority if they are to function properly in a democracy. In a tyranny they can use brute force, torture, and repression. There sometimes seems to be confusion about women, and members of other groups, sharing in these aspects of the institution, or even affecting it. Much authority is, of course, in these situations *symbolic*. Indeed it can be argued that Anglo-American policing is characterized by certain kinds of symbolic authority, as distinct from continental systems, based on the French model, which first used *secret* police. The famous British uniform, for example, was deliberately designed not to look like a military one (Styles 1987).

If authority is focused in symbols it should, in theory at least, be easier to transform a group whose members lack the requisite marks of affinity by attaching appropriate insignia of office. It is very instructive to compare the British and American cases over the matter of uniform to illuminate this point. American police officers of both sexes now wear the same uniform, with the occasional divergence, as I recorded above. This they recognized themselves as an important aspect not only of practical policing, but also of legitimacy and authority; wearing 'blues' and a badge were key to this and an issue of women's position in British policing which they frequently raised. Most of the British women complained about their uniforms, their objections centring on wearing skirts, their 'ridiculous' hats, bags, etc., but the underlying trend was to do with its 'misfit' status. Their uniforms did not carry a sufficiently clear message to the public about their status and powers. All problems of authority for women have not, of course, been solved in the USA: what they have done is to show that one barrier can be removed.

So far I have suggested some conclusions from and about women in policing. Wider questions do arise from looking at this topic. This is, first of all, because, while the police are distinct in certain ways, such as their legitimate use of force, they are not unique. Thus parallel cases suggest themselves as analogies and for analyses, such as prison guards or soldiers. Secondly, the police now share aspects of their role with more other organizations than ever before. There is a huge private security industry and many more 'private' places are policed by its members (Shapland 1989). More welfare workers, such as nurses or social workers, now have certain control powers. Increasingly, the police have to work with the latter because of changes in public policies. In consequence, it is important to consider the broader topics of women in control, and gender and control, and conclude our discussions with some conclusions about them.

Women in Control?

The answer to the question: 'are women now in control?' depends on the phrasing of it. There are women now quite widely employed and less widely deployed in positions of social control. Emphatically, however, they are not in charge of formal control agencies. Not yet anyway.

Different perceptions of what constituted control occurred throughout the literature and in much of this study. When posing questions about what Stan Cohen calls 'visions of social control', it is also essential to ask 'whose are the visions?' Cohen seems to suggest that only the powerful seek to establish and maintain order in society. Or rather he, along with a number of other scholars who have explored the history of 'social-control policy' (Cohen 1985: 15), are vague or coy about who exactly has brought about the historical transformations in the master patterns of deviancy control. There is a distinct lack of a 'sense of agency', of conscious actors and their complex and contradictory decisions (Ignatieff's study is an interesting exception, 1978). There are large sociological and historical issues which can be debated at length here.

As far as this discussion is concerned, I wish only to point out how the history and development of the participation of some women in the control process in two nations can illuminate both the debates and the concept itself. Women's roles have changed and grown. In the nineteenth century, groups of women took part increasingly in a range of activities to do with social control. Notably, they pursued and ran campaigns to change laws, alter public opinion, provide welfare and improve moral standards. They joined and often founded voluntary bodies which dispensed a variety of services as well as inventing an array of organizations and structures to do so. Much of this effort was produced by upper-class and middle-class women and directed at their poorer counterparts among the working class and the destitute. But it is dangerous to over-simplify. Working-class women also took part in missionary and welfare work and while clients could object to their treatment, they also praised what today seems 'maternalism' (Hahn Rafter 1983).

Women increasingly sought, won, and created wider roles for themselves in informal social control. They also became frustrated at their lack of political and formal powers. Their entry into policing was, initially, one aspect of campaigns to enhance their powers to protect themselves and their own sex. It was at once an expansionist and a protectionist move.

Since that early twentieth-century epoch, only two other steps of significance have been taken. First, women have a wider share and larger stake in the considerable range of control agencies which now exist. Secondly, they have been assimilated into the major institutions of formal control, although in some as a mere token presence. At this stage it remains an open question whether another breakthrough will ever occur. Whether, for instance, women will ever comprise half or more of a large police force, or indeed a government. It is not even clear that these are the goals of any group of women. Where there are groups dedicated to expanding women's role in such ways, they are much more likely to be aiming, still, at what can be called entryism and influence, not supremacy or dominance.

While this theme must remain in doubt there are at least two important conclusions to be drawn in this area. If women have, as I have argued, so long sought to be part of the social-control process, including its most 'masculine' apparatus, then notions about the oppression of women in our society have to be redrawn, or at least modified. Simple notions of patriarchal oppression are already heavily criticized (Scraton 1990; Sumner 1990). Even if we conclude that female 'controllers' are ineffective in the face of massed male power, we still need to understand their persistence in seeking such positions and their insistence that they are not ineffective but do in fact find and develop their own strategies and skills.

Such observations have wide implications. There have, for instance, been considerable debates about women in relation to the criminal-justice systems of both the USA and Britain in recent years (Smart 1977; Heidensohn 1985, 1986; Morris 1987; Daly 1989). These have focused on two main themes: on 'chivalry' and on victimization. The 'chivalry' debate concerns the degree to which the police, courts, and other agencies can be said to 'protect' women from the consequences of their own criminal behaviour. While some contributions (e.g. Eaton 1986) do consider whether the agent was male or female, many do not. Yet it should obviously be an important aspect of such studies to find out whether sex makes any difference on either side.

As far as victimization is concerned, this too has been over-simplified in some accounts as a matter of gendered oppression. Again this view has been gradually modified as more attention is given to female offenders (Allen 1986) and especially their use of violence (Heidensohn 1991b; A. Jones 1991; McDonald 1991). What has hardly been considered at all in this context is the *legitimate* use of physical force or even violence by women. Women, as Stanko has tirelessly pointed out (1990a, 1990b), are not merely passive victims of violence. They work out strategies of avoidance and resistance. Sometimes they fight back.

This then raises an enormous new range of problems. While I was completing this book a series of legal cases in Britain focused attention on the legal status of the use of such violence by women just as an earlier and notorious trial in New York had raised similar issues. Can it constitute legitimate self-defence? English law defines 'provocation' in ways which appear to put women at a disadvantage and 'disallows' their strategies. The relevance of this study to such highly-charged topics is to add some information to some of the wider considerations of context. Laws in such situations are very culturally bound. They and their interpretations are based on premisses about 'reasonable men' (*sic*). What is lacking from much of the surrounding debate is an awareness that legitimate use of force and violence by women has been extremely constrained and that this may be changing. Men, for instance, may box and wrestle and indulge in contact sports barred to women or socially taboo to them. That police and other women have learnt to handle many kinds of encounters is a dimension which should be added to this debate.

The key image of control in Foucault's work is the carceral archepelago, the remote gulag, cut off from society and the body politic. In Cohen's 'vision' it is more strikingly a net as well as a city. The net tangles and binds, entwining the deviant in its ever-widening meshes. Impressive and seductive as these are as metaphors for worrying features of contemporary problems, I find great difficulties with them, especially after completing this study. Both seem flawed, even in their own terms, because both describe something more sweeping and oppressive, a true Juggernaut, inexorably flattening all before it, a cross between a huge tank and an iron.

Yet none of these conveys the kind of historical complexity and present-day compromises which I have tried to describe. Women, often the focus of some of the most oppressive features of society, and nearly always the poorest and least powerful members of it, have sometimes chosen to resist and, occasionally, succeeded. They have also sought to join, change, and share in the agencies concerned. Although they have succeeded in doing all these, it is not clear even now that they are wholly accepted in these roles. Rather, it seems that the current male employees may voice values and beliefs which preclude women's membership, or only on terms set by the former. Most theorists of social control see it as controlled by élite groups for their own ends, almost never by men for theirs. Nor do they generally see the processes of control as the subject of interaction and negotiation. This again is obviously because it makes a great difference if one considers issues about the maintenance of order in terms of sex differences instead, for example, of class differences. It then becomes obvious that some women, at least, have considerable stakes in improving order, or more precisely in curbing the disorder of males. It might be helpful to rethink the problem of what I have called the male ownership of order in the light of this. In other words, what shapes the strong resistance to female police may be a reluctance to share power over order; it may also, and at the same time, be an unwillingness to allow women to police male *disorder*.

Gender and Control

'Gender', as in 'gender studies', 'sociology of gender', is quite often nowadays used instead of women. As Pateman sharply puts it: 'the term gender is now ubiquitous but frequently lies idle, used merely as an often not very apt synonym for women' (1988: 225). In other words, only women are perceived as having, or being, a gender, even though the whole point of the concept is that it expresses a duality; masculinity, and femininity are described in terms of their difference. One is nearly meaningless without the other.

One of the few authors to take such issues seriously and to attempt both an analysis of 'gender order' and to propose strategies for altering it, begins by focusing on power, particularly as demonstrated in both legitimate and illegal forms. 'The main axis of the power structure of gender is the general connection of authority with masculinity,' but, 'the authority of men is not spread in an even blanket across every department of social life.' Specifically, 'there is a "core" in the power structure of gender' and this in advanced capitalist societies consists *inter alia* of 'the hierarchies and work forces of institutionalized violence—military and paramilitary forces, police, prison systems' (Connell 1987: 109). Other parts of the 'core' include heavy industry and the state and most crucially 'working class milieux that emphasize physical toughness and men's association with machinery' (Connell 1987:

109). It is central to Connell's thesis that gender power relations have changed considerably in modern capitalist societies, with traditional domestic patriarchy being displaced 'by masculinities organized much more around technical rationality and calculation' (1987: 131).

While he consistently stresses the importance of history and of the social construction of gender order, Connell does not provide an entirely satisfactory explanation of what he calls 'a central fact', that of 'the control of the means of violence by some men rather than by any women' (1987: 153). He offers a partial answer by insisting that while state apparatuses can be oppressive of women, as indeed can other institutional forms, nevertheless

the main objects of physical repression are men. . . . The state both institutionalizes hegemonic masculinity and expends great energy in controlling it. The objects of repression, e.g. criminals, are generally younger men themselves in the practice of violence, with a social profile quite like that of the immediate agents of repression, the police or the soldiers. (1987: 128)

We have, of course, already seen many times that this is a distorted view of policing, albeit one often supported by many police officers and enshrined in the traditional police culture. In this subtle and thoughtful study, Connell does not explore these contradictions fully, but he does extend the debate considerably by stressing the variety and 'historicity' of gender and gender roles. Modern societies are, he argues, more dominated by gender relations than many communities were in the past or than they need to be.

He concludes with proposed strategies for changing gender order, considering both the abolition of gender and 'its reconstitution on new bases'. The second is his preference, even though he acknowledges that 'a great deal of our culture's energy and beauty, as well as its barbarism, has been created through and around gender relations' (1987: 288). Radical alliances will be, he argues, the bases for this restructuring as they have to some extent already become. Connell's is an important study because he does try both to question many assumptions about gender as well as to explain their origins. This approach certainly provides a framework for further exploration, but it does not provide some key answers which I have sought all through this book. Yet he does provide some key guide-lines, albeit only sketchily, in his presentation of the state and the street as areas of most pronounced masculine dominance of males and hence, presumably, the insistence on excluding women. What Connell does not have scope to explore are the tantalizing questions about why, when women have been incorporated into many activities, their participation has so fiercely been resisted here. These issues must remain, for the present, as addressed but not explained. They await further exploration.

While there have been some attempts, then, to redress this in studying men and masculinity, these have not yet gone very far in areas such as the study of social control. Pieces of a mosaic are already revealed but layers of sand conceal the rest. I think it possible, for example, and timely to advance a series of propositions about gender and control which would be worth testing and exploring.

The first is that gender divisions are central to social control, indeed perhaps their most integral and abiding features. The behaviour most completely learnt and adhered to is that of sex roles. These are also the most fully underpinned by informal sanctions and support. Take, for instance, the argument that much of the delinquent activity of adolescent males is just 'natural' masculine exuberance.

This is not, of course, to say that gender is rigid and that no one ever deviates from prescribed roles. Neither proposition is true. Indeed, ideas of appropriately masculine and feminine behaviour have altered during the past two centuries. Such alterations do not always occur in a symmetrical fashion. For instance, femininity, it can be argued, has expanded for most of the present century without many comparable shifts in notions of masculinity. Dress codes for women, for instance, now include in western societies almost every possible type of clothing once thought masculine. Hence, as we have seen, the unisex (i.e. men's) uniform worn by all US police officers. Men are still subject to a narrower range of acceptable wear so that male nurses, for example, do not wear 'female' clothing.

As I trust this instance shows, I am *not* arguing that institutionalized sexism is ubiquitous in agencies of the criminal-justice system. (Gelsthorpe (1989) has shown that this is not the case.) Rather, I suggest that gender divisions are universal and that they form part of the processes of control. Their various interactions are complex but profound. Thus all societies regulate sexuality and have rules about gender-appropriate sexual behaviour. While women may face heavier sanctions for breaking some rules—prostitutes are more likely than their clients to be punished—there are exceptions. Male homosexuality has been more rigorously controlled than female in western societies.

If gender is a feature of control, it follows that changes in gender roles have consequences for control agencies. That is clearly what happened in the early twentieth century in our example of women in policing. Women began to use a new freedom in a very conventionally masculine institution. What many of the women really wished to confront was the double standard of morality for men and women upheld by just such agencies. It is hardly surprising that entry proved problematic.

My second proposition is that social control is itself likely to be gendered. By this I mean that the social-control system, or the agencies which form parts of it, may have forms or styles, as well as personnel, which are gendered. I agree with Tamar Pitch, for instance, that social control in a number of post-war western societies has become 'feminized'. This means that certain organizations and issues have operated in less confrontational, less informal, and more negotiated ways. There is an ocean of research on the police which suggests that their culture is overwhelmingly masculine. This is unfortunately kept as a land-locked mass of water. It is not on the whole suggested that the system might change. Indeed much effort has gone into pointing out how functional it is.

While it may be difficult and perhaps even inappropriate to argue against individual agencies, such as the police, being gendered, I suggest that serious issues are raised by the predominance of one or other gender in the system as a whole. Amongst the most important of these are representative bureaucracy, effectiveness, and legitimacy. Any control agency will have difficulties if its staff do not 'represent' the local community. Moreover, if they do not draw on all that community's talents, they will be less effective. This was long seen at its most absurd in the height requirements of Anglo-American policing, which only gave the selectors choice among tall men. Most crucial of all these is legitimacy. Significantly, the police's legitimacy has diminished with some groups in modern times and it is especially clear that women are wary of the criminal-justice system and have lost faith in its ability to protect them from crime and its consequences.

Too often in sociological analysis, gender is equated with sex-role stereotype. Narrow, rigid definitions of gender are assumed to be predominant and even inevitable. But this is not an essential feature of a modern society; on the contrary, flexibility and change are possibly and surely desirable. Stereotypes simplify but they can also cause atrophy and fossilization. Gender stereotypes, for example, seem to lie at the heart of some troublesome deviant behaviour: such as domestic violence and football hooliganism. It would seem fairly obvious that such problems can only be touched by the pooling of all kinds of gendered or neutral responses.

Just to give one example. It was policy for quite a long time in Britain to subject young male delinquents to the rigorous penal discipline of a quasi-military kind (Manning 1985 (ed.). It was gradually realized, however, that their treatment was unsuitable and, in this form at least, it ceased. What has hardly happened yet is the full logical continuance of this pattern. If the socialization of girls is apparently so much more successful than that of boys, then surely something might be learned from how they are prepared for the world and life.

Towards the Future

I have tried in this book to tell the story of women in policing within the context of social control today. Inevitably questions about gender and about policing were raised too. Since it involved a comparison of women and policing in different but related societies, many aspects of both of these also featured. All this had to be seen in retrospect. To conclude, I should now like to speculate a little on the likely future of this most sensitive and central area of society.

Some feminists have expressed anxieties about women in positions of control (Enloe 1988; Cain 1991). The key to their argument is that power corrupts, or indeed it is already corrupted by its associations and women should have nothing to do with it. Enloe argues this with particular force about the military (1988), but Cain has also suggested it in relation to such people as social workers.

Other writers on such themes have tackled much broader criticisms. Stiehm has, for instance, argued strongly for a larger role for women in the military. She suggests that 'Speculation would be fruitful, too. What if women were given the Air Force and the other three services were left to men?' (1989: 237). Her purpose is both to challenge existing policies on the recruitment and deployment of women in the USA military on rational and democratic grounds and also to challenge feminists who reject women's participation. In doing so she asks a series of provoking questions which are highly relevant to women's role in policing and in other agencies:

Questions asked about women should also be asked about men . . . it might be . . . valuable to reflect on men's disability—their apparent incapacity to assimilate women or even to accommodate to their presence. I would recommend a shift to the investigation of *men's* limitations and to the study of the military as a male, rather than a human, or national institution. (1989: 239; original emphasis)

Stiehm argues that these are key problems that feminists, as well as military men, must engage with: 'this is intellectual work that *women* must engage in because men are invisible to most men qua men' (1989: 241; original emphasis). Much of what Stiehm has to say about women in the military can be said with even greater force about policing and related activities. Policemen and women are officers of the *peace* by title and convention; in practice their daily routine comprises much that is mundane and peaceable: only occasionally do violence and drama intrude. The relevance of Stiehm's challenging approach is that she accepts nothing as given even in the most unconventional, non-traditional of occupations for women. Following this course in considering gender and control enables us too to consider the unthinkable.

Earlier I cited M. Young's suggestion to a group of colleagues that 'there was no logical reason why the existing male/female ratios could not be reversed (i.e. about 10,000 men and 111,000 women' (1991: 234). Young notes first their 'blank response' and later 'a worried . . . "[that] would mean changing not just the police but the whole of the world . . . "' (1991: 234). He concludes that there are still 'substantial barriers' to surmount and, rather disappointingly, goes on to resurrect other very old friends 'the drunks and the disagreeable' (1991: 235) as evidence of female limitations. What would have been much more stimulating would have been Young's own considered response to his point.

After all, as I trust I have shown in this monograph, there are no rational reasons why men should dominate policing, nor so totally dominate formal social control. They are widely judged not to being doing it very well and to be getting worse. Since they are themselves the sex more likely to be involved in delinquency and crime there are good a priori grounds for *not* preferring them.

Now, I am not proposing Young's sex role reversal as a serious future plan. It does, however, provide a valuable vignette to explore some important issues about gender and control. Should one group, men, so dominate policing, and in such a masculine way? What are the consequences to society of their doing so? What would happen if their freehold ceased? The *Guardian* newspaper once suggested that the police should be recruited from among the nation's grandmothers. This may seem bizarre, but the 'new police' themselves were a peculiar and contested innovation when they first patrolled the streets of London.

Going back to first principles, or primary assumptions at least, in an exercise like this lets us examine just what is central about our notions of control and what is historical accumulation. It is obvious that there is far more of the second than the first. This brings us right back to some aspects of the postmodern condition we noted at the outset. Ours is a contingent and somewhat arbitrary world in which it is encouraging to find patterns and trends and to do so should always be accompanied by wariness. Amongst other things in this study I have tried to suggest that, within a large-scale masculine-gendered control enterprise, women have established their own activities against all the odds, and sustained them. The question now is: what happens next?

It is possible to reply in two ways. There is a neat list of points to be made about policy and policy changes. I have, I hope, made clear that comparing British and American experience is highly illuminating on this topic. The American approach is more open to development, more soundly based, and more confident. At its best it is exemplary and shows what can be done with class actions, affirmative action, and conditionally allocated government funds. British experience reveals that one can get quite a long way without most of these, but this also suggests that therefore far more might be achieved with a good mixture of the two.

At the most fundamental and yet highly symbolic level, US experience shows that women and men can wear the same uniforms without a massive breakdown in public order. British experience shows that women officers do not need guns as 'equalizers'. There are, however, much wider issues to face.

Policing, and social control generally, could become much more neutral, or more gender neutral. Police forces of the twenty-first century might not only be more genuinely mixed, they might also be far less macho in culture. There are serious questions to consider here as the policing of more plural and complex societies emerges as a difficult and threatening political conundrum. Should police officers, to reverse an ancient cliché, be recruited so young? Indeed, higher educational requirements in both societies are increasing age at entry already.

A second possible scenario is that control agencies continue along, or are even enforced on, gender-divided lines. A butch police force will still pursue its enquiries along its freemasonic lines. On separate, diverging lines will be other agencies. These will be, like social work, nursing, and education, 'feminine' professions, and they will all have to work on numerous social problems in uneasy multi-agency alliances. They will certainly misunderstand each other often, and co-operation of a few staff will be seen as sell-out by their colleagues. Such a plural solution may be preferable to a more total, corporate, and integrated approach.

A final version of the future might be embodied in gender-segregated institutions for the *clients* of control. Abolition of prisons for women, for instance, has been advocated several times in the late twentieth century (Heidensohn 1975; Carlen 1990). While there could hardly be such polarity in other parts of the criminal-justice system, there could certainly be some polarizing in such services. Most pressures to criminalize certain actions will bring more *men* into contact with formal control: such as rape in marriage, wife-beating, child sex abuse, even serious fraud. Male homosexual behaviour might be targeted again as moral panic rises about AIDS and HIV infection. In a dystopian future, this could lead to gender-segregated services in which men man those for the burgeoning numbers of males, or women do so because of their supposed lack of moral taint.

In short, in order to prepare for the future we need to think carefully about what legacies we shall carry forward into it and what we can safely discard. It is an unwise sociologist who tries to foresee the future. Nevertheless, I should like to venture one prediction. It is based on my observation of the history recounted in this book. As the nineteenth century turned into the twentieth century groups of women took a new place for themselves within the systems of control of two societies. These movements linked and learned from each other.

Much of the motivation which kept them alive over several decades was deep dissatisfaction with the world in which they lived, 'protected' by the stronger, superior sex. They knew all too well the realities of poverty, neglect, abuse, beatings, and double standards. They tried to protect their own sex and to remake society in a more moral fashion.

As another century ends there are clear signs of another era of deep concern among and for women about the moral state of society and how this specifically affects them. It is women who fear crime most. They are the victims of beatings, abuse, and sexual crimes. Men suffer these things too. There is, however, a major difference. Moral symmetry is lacking. Women are beaten and attacked. With a relatively few exceptions they do not abuse and attack. Some of the conditions, therefore, for female-led moral protest and protection exist in both Britain and the USA at the end of the twentieth century as they did at its beginning. It might very well not happen. Women are not much more in control at this stage than they were when the history unfolded here began. They are, however, much freer, have greater economic and political power, and are already inside, if not on top of, key control agencies. Women are not in control. They might begin to ask men why.

APPENDIX

The Research Study

The Police Officers

The interviews which form the core of Chapters 4 and 5 and are also drawn on in Chapters 6 and 7 were conducted in Britain and the USA during 1988 over a period of ten months. As my account in the text suggests, the female officers to whom I talked were located by personal contacts. Once I had made initial links it was not difficult to make others and the officers seemed willing to talk to me. Most of my interviews in Britain were conducted before I went to the USA to interview there, but several did take place afterwards.

Interviews in the USA had all to be planned in advance. I first established links through a British officer who put me in touch with an American counterpart and she in turn gave me some names and addresses. In all these cases, as in Britain, I wrote to each of the officers, setting out the aims of the study and asking for her co-operation. This was often followed up by a telephone call. After each interview I wrote to each subject in person thanking her for her help. In this way I ensured that everyone who took part knew what the project involved and who and where I was. No one raised any doubts about the purpose of the study and there were clear signs of interest and enthusiasm.

During the same period when the US interviews took place, I also collected material for a report for the Police Foundation on equal opportunities for women in policing. This was published in the following year (Heidensohn 1989*b*). In order to write this project, I collected material from all the police departments I visited. These included statistical tables, policy statements, circulars, and manuals of advice, and other data. I also discussed this topic with senior officers and senior lay officials and with staff at the Police Foundation in Washington, DC, and at the Police Executive Research Forum (PERF) in Washington. While this project and the research study were separate activities, obviously the information and comments I obtained informed my understanding of policing and equal-opportunities issues in the USA. These discussions were not tape-recorded, although I made notes at the time and wrote these up afterwards.

During the time I was with the US police I observed many encounters and situations which involved female officers. For instance, I attended roll call, went on patrol, attended police social clubs, visited officers in police precincts and in their own homes and in correction facilities to which they took detainees. I also saw police officers at work in back-room jobs.

In Britain my observations were less varied, although I did see women officers in police stations, in police training and organizational settings, and in their own homes. I have not used any of these observations *directly* as I did the interviews with the women, although they did affect my understanding of the work and role of the former. One interview in Britain, for instance, took place in a police station. A male officer came in and interrupted the interview; it was clear that he did so to check me out and also to find out what the woman was doing. She handled this with good humour and was not put out in any way, as the taped record shows. This encounter suggested a number of insights into the relations between male and female officers.

On several occasions I was asked by both fellow researchers and by (male) police officers if I would be interviewing men as well as women. That the question was posed was in itself interesting. It was never my intention to do so and it may be worth setting out my reasons. I do *not* believe that it is impossible or inappropriate for women to undertake research on men or vice versa, although I recognize that this is a viewpoint held strongly by some of my colleagues. There are, however, in my view, circumstances in which the social position of the interviewer may have an impact and elicit certain kinds of responses. In this instance it was, I believe, distinctly to my advantage to be a woman interviewing these women. I am sure that they were franker with me, felt relaxed, and were very forthcoming and said that they had enjoyed the interviews.

There was, as I have indicated in the text, a distinction between the British and American social reaction to me. All the British officers could obviously place me in my academic and research background and no doubt observe that I was white, middle-aged, and middle class. One did invite me to meet her first on neutral ground in a public place; she then arranged for our interview to take place in her own home and was both frank and very friendly in her approach.

In the USA officers were also extremely friendly, open, and welcoming. It was, however, harder for them to place me in the same way that their British counterparts could. Several assumed that I must be a serving or a former police officer although most recognized the legitimate interest of a 'criminal justice' academic in women in policing. There was in one or two places an assumption that I was identified with British police and British police policies and practices. I was questioned, for example, about the fact that British officers are unarmed and that women wear a different uniform from the men.

Despite these minor differences in reception, I was able to establish very considerable rapport with the US officers, who showed eagerness to take place in the study, responded fully to questions, and gave far more, and more interesting information than my initial outline questionnaire alone would have elicited. In the main text I have indicated the importance of the group sessions which the officers themselves initiated and which both aided me considerably and helped to create or develop bonds between them. Morash and Haarr (forthcoming) have documented an extensive development of this kind in their work on women officers in Detroit who formed themselves into a network with the avowed aim of providing female solidarity and improving the image of policewomen.

I doubt very much whether I could have achieved the same degree of rapport with male officers had I interviewed them for the same study. Further, I am sure that their responses would have been affected by the knowledge that I was primarily interested in their female colleagues. Indeed, many male officers whom I met while conducting the research offered their views of women in the police even without my asking them. On the other hand it was very apparent that my respondents felt pleased that they were the sole focus of my project. In fact, some adverse comments were made about the evaluation studies which did of course compare male and female performance, one officer insisting that the 'wrong kinds' of comparison were made. Another opposed the notion of comparing males and females on male performance norms.

A much more difficult aspect of the interview situation for me to read is the question of race. Black women formed a significant proportion of the US group and there were also Hispanic women among them. They appeared to have exactly the same friendly rapport as the white women and their comments were often the most insightful. Indeed several of their accounts describe situations in which race and gender were both determining factors. Some of the most blatant harassment from superiors had been experienced by black officers. Equally, however, they had developed some of the most formidable and skilful techniques for dealing with difficulties. Since there were signs of some racial divisions in some of the agencies I visited, and these were mentioned by some interviewees, there may be limitations on both the group of women and their response to me. Those whom I did meet and interview were, as I have suggested, extremely open and frank and raised issues about race and racism themselves.

The Security Guards

I had originally intended to include a larger sample of women in security positions in my study. In the event this proved to be too difficult to achieve for the significant reason that these are jobs in which few staff stay for long. Eventually I contacted and interviewed three women who had worked for at least two years in security. It is worth pointing out that they all subsequently left these posts and went to work elsewhere. All were British. While their experiences cannot be, therefore, used as a full-scale comparison with the policewomen, there were some notable differences, which I have pointed out in the text. However, what is also important to record is that they differed more from each other in many of their attitudes than did the women police. One guard, for instance, had worked in security for many years and in a number of settings and had clearly developed, at one stage, a very controlling personality and manner and considerable contempt for 'the punters'. Indeed this was so marked that she could no longer watch any sports or games, attend pop concerts, etc. with the general public. Unless she could have private facilities, such as a box, she would no longer attend these.

Another, on the other hand, took a much more business like approach to her work and believed that she and other women had a distinctive contribution to make to security work. While her job was fairly complex and security problems had grown worse recently, she had not been alienated from her clients as her colleague had. The three interviews with security officers were notable for the focus on actual control situation—of managing fights, crowds, clubs—far more than those with the police. They appeared, although the numbers are of course tiny, to engage in more confrontational situations than did the police. This is perhaps not surprising as their role was specifically geared to deal with order situations. Notably, they were not involved in the same amount of paperwork as the police and they were unlikely to have to attend court.

Interview Schedule

At each interview I asked questions about the following points, or checked that the subjects gave responses on these points. Very often they gave accounts unprompted, which covered these issues. This illustrates two significant methodological points. First, that these women, working as they did as women in a traditionally masculine occupation, had a well-developed sense of gender awareness and had considered their own histories in the light of this. They were thus what I have described elsewhere as 'knowing' women (Heidensohn 1992). They also, and this was obviously specific to being members of a non-traditional occupation, had clearly-presented and well-thought-out reasons for joining the police. These would have been very well rehearsed on their application to and on joining the police. As I show in the text, the women had often had to persist in their applications as, indeed, some of them described. Further, once they had joined, they frequently had to argue and justify the case for their continuance. Such experiences may not be unique to women: men may sometimes have to make the same case to family and friends. They are, however, far less likely to have to do so *within the police organization itself* as many of these women had to. Their responses were, then, the product of processes of thought, negotiation, and self-construction. Obviously, the number of times these subjects will have previously given such accounts varies greatly. This is not always simply a matter of years in service. Some clearly had much more confrontational personal styles; others joined police organizations as 'pioneers' or 'true firsts' and had gained, as Chapters 4 and 5 show, very acute perceptions about their roles and positions.

None of this makes their responses invalid. It was frequently apparent that these were not just glib. One woman told me personal details of her life which she usually kept silent about, in order to explain the pattern of her career. In the group interviews, as the sections of quoted dialogue show, there was often some debate and disagreement. In any case, what these replies do give are the responses these women gave me to a series of questions which combined the familiar and the unfamiliar and which all had to do with their own roles in policing. The point was not to seek any dark hidden truth but to listen to how they described their experiences, their strategies for dealing with them, and their war stories. I found them worth hearing and worthy of attention. It is for the reader to judge if that claim is justified.

The Questions

1. What is your background?
2. How did you choose policing as a career?
3. How did you enter policing? Can you describe your career so far?
4. Can you describe your present position?
5. What is a typical day like?
6. Is this a typical job?
7. Have you ever had to manage difficult situations?
8. What did they involve? What did you do?
9. What strategies did you adopt? What were your thoughts at the time? What lessons do you think you learned?
10. Do you like your job?
11. Are there differences between you and your male colleagues?
12. Are there similarities between you and your male colleagues?
13. Do you think women have distinctive styles of policing?
14. Can women manage violent encounters? Can they do so as well/badly/in the same way that men do?
15. How important is physique to a police officer?
16. Did you have any specific training as a woman officer? Do you have any specially-relevant knowledge e.g. martial arts training?
17. When you are not working, how do you manage such situations as a fight in a pub, trouble at a party?

18. Are certain situations different? Racially mixed encounters? Drunks? Groups of the same sex or mixed sex groups?

It will be apparent that while I ensured that answers were given to these questions (quite often I used the list as a checking device during the interview, coming back to a topic if I felt the response was not full enough), much of the information given to me went considerably beyond the points outlined here. The material ranged much more widely, usually because the officer herself chose to tell her story in that way or because in a group session, her fellow officers encouraged her to do so.

While I picked out the central themes and concepts which I highlighted in Chapters 4 and 5, this was done after careful analysis of the interviews. Where a respondent mentioned something of importance of her, I reran tapes and reread transcripts to see if her response was mirrored by others. Thus, for example, the young officer who had made the traffic stop in Chapter 4 was the first from whom I heard a description of a 'transformation scene'.

BIBLIOGRAPHY

ADLER, Z. (1982), 'Rape: The Intention of Parliament and the Practice of the Courts', *Modern Law Review*, 45.

—— (1987), *Rape on Trial* (Routledge: London).

—— (1990), *A Fairer Cop*, US Police Record on Equal Opportunities, Wainwright Trust Study Tour Report No. 1 (Wainwright Trust: London).

AHERN, J. F. (1972), *Police in Trouble: Our Frightening Crisis in Law Enforcement* (Hawthorne: New Jersey).

ALEXANDER, C. S. (1980), 'Blaming the Victim: A Comparison of Police and Nurses', *Women and Health*, 5/1.

ALLEN, MARY S. (1925) *The Pioneer Policewoman* (Chatto and Windus: London).

ALLEN, H. (1986), *Justice Unbalanced* (Open University Press: Milton Keynes).

ASHTON, N. L., *et al.* (1982), 'Helping Behaviour in Police Officers and Reasons for Choice of Career', *Psychological Reports*, 51/3(ii): 1126.

ATKINS, S., and HOGGETT, B. (1984), *Women and the Law* (Blackwell: Oxford).

Audit Commission (1990), *Police Papers: Effective Policing Performance Review in Police Forces* (Audit Commission: London).

BAHM, C. (1984), 'Police Socialization in the 80s', *Journal of Political Science and Administration*, 12/4: 390–4.

BAKER, M. (1987), *Cops* (Abacus: London).

BANKS, O. (1981), *Faces of Feminism* (Martin Robertson: Oxford).

BANKSTON, W. B., THOMPSON, C. V., JENKINS, Q. A., and FORSYTH, C. J. (1990), 'The Influence of Fear of Crime, Gender and Southern Culture on Carrying Firearms for Protection', *Sociological Quarterly*, 31/2: 287–307.

BANTON, M. (1964), *The Policeman in the Community* (Tavistock: London).

BARTLETT, H. W., and ROSENBLUM, A. (1977), *Policewoman Effectiveness* (Civil Service Commission/Denver Police Department: Denver, Colo.).

BAYLEY, D. H. (1977a), 'The Limits of Police Reform', in Bayley (1977b) (ed.).

—— (1977b) (ed.), *Police and Society* (Sage: Beverly Hills, Calif.).

—— (1985), *Patterns of Policing: A Comparative International Analysis* (Rutgers Univ. Press: New Brunswick, NJ).

—— and GAROFALO, J. (1989), 'The Management of Violence by Police Patrol Officers', in *Criminology*, 27/1: 1–22.

BELL, D. J. (1982*a*), 'Policewomen: Myths and Reality', *Journal of Police Science and Administration*, 10/1: 112–23.

—— (1982*b*) 'Police Uniforms Attitudes and Citizens', *Journal of Criminal Justice*, 10/1: 45–56.

BITTNER, E. (1967), 'The Police on Skid Row: A Study of Peace-keeping', *American Sociological Review*, 32/5: 699–715; in Bittner (1990*a*).

—— (1970), 'The Functions of the Police in Modern Society', National Institute of Mental Health, Crime and Deliquency Issues (Centre for Studies of Crime and Deliquency); in Bittner (1990*a*).

—— (1990*a*), *Aspects of Police Work* (Northeastern Univ. Press: Boston).

—— (1990*b*), 'Florence Nightingale in Pursuit of Willie Sutton', in Bittner (1990*a*) and originally in H. Jacob (1974) (ed.), *The Potential for Reform of Criminal Justice* (Sage: Berkeley, Calif.).

BLAND, L. (1985), 'In the Name of Protection: The Policing of Women in the First World War', in Brophy and Smart (1985) (eds.), *Women in Law* (Routledge: London).

BLOCH, P., and ANDERSON, D., *et al.* (1973), *Policewomen on Patrol: Major Findings: First Report*, (Police Foundation: Washington, DC).

—— (1974*a*) *Policewomen on Patrol: Final Report Methodology, Tables and Measurement Instruments* (Police Foundation: Washington, DC).

—— (1974*b*) *Policewomen on Patrol: Final Report* (Police Foundation: Washington, DC).

BLOM COOPER, L. (1985), *A Child in Trust: Report of the Inquiry into the Death of Jasmine Beckford* (Brent Borough Council).

BORITCH H., and HAGAN, J. (1990), 'A Century of Crime in Toronto: Gender, Class, and Patterns of Social Control, 1859 to 1955', *Criminology*, 20/4: 567–99.

BOWLES, G., and DUELLI KLEIN, R. (1983), *Theories of Women's Studies* (Routledge: London).

BOX, S. (1983), *Power, Crime and Mystification* (Tavistock: London).

—— (1987), *Recession, Crime and Punishment* (Macmillan: Basingstoke).

BOYLE, C. NINA. (1915), *The Vote*, 9 Apr.: 727.

BREWSTER, C., and TEAGUE, P. (1989), *European Community Social Policy Its Impact on the UK* (Institute of Personnel Management: London).

BROGDEN, M. (1987), 'The Emergence of the Police: The Colonial Dimension', in *British Journal of Criminology*, 27/1: 4–15.

BROOKSHIRE, JAN (1980), 'Police Training: A Personal Challenge to the Female Officer', *The Police Chief*, 47/10.

BROWN, A. (1988), *Watching the Detectives* (Hodder & Stoughton: London).

BROWN, J., and CAMPBELL, E. (1991), 'Less than Equal', *Policing*, 7, Winter 324–33.

BROWN, MICHAEL (1981), *Working the Street: Police Discretion and th*

Dilemmas of Reform (Russell Sage Foundation: New York).

BROWNMILLER, S. (1975), *Against Our Will: Men, Women and Rape* (Penguin: Harmondsworth).

BRYANT, L., DUNKERLEY, D., and KELLAND, G. (1985), 'One of the Boys?' *Policing*, 1/4, Autumn.

BULMER, M. (1986), *Neighbours: The Work of Philip Abrams* (Cambridge Univ. Press: Cambridge).

BURGESS, R. G. (1984), *In the Field: An Introduction to Field Research* (Allen & Unwin: London).

CAIN, M. (1973), *Society and the Policeman's Role* (Routledge: London).

—— (1979), 'Trends in the Sociology of Police Work', *International Journal of the Sociology of Law*, 7/2.

—— (1989) (ed.), *Growing up Good* (Sage: London).

—— (1990), 'Realist Philosophy and Standpoint Epistemologies: A Feminist Criminology as a Successor Science', in Gelsthorpe and Morris (1990) (eds.).

—— (1991), Paper Delivered to International Feminist Conference on Women, Law, and Social Control (Montreal).

California Highway Patrol (1976), Women Traffic Officer Report: Final Report. Sacramento/Calif. and Department of California Highway Patrol.

CAMPBELL, A. (1984), *The Girls in the Gang* (Blackwell: Oxford).

CARLEN, P. (1983), *Women's Imprisonment* (Routledge: London).

—— (1990) *Alternatives to Women's Imprisonment* (Open University Press: Milton Keynes).

—— and WORRALL, A. (1987) (eds.), *Gender, Crime and Justice* (Open University Press: Milton Keynes).

CARRIER, J. (1988), *The Campaign for the Employment of Women as Police Officers* (Avebury/Gower: Aldershot).

CASTLES, S., with BOOTH, H., and WALLACE, T. (1984), *Here for Good* (Pluto: London).

Centre for Police Studies (1989), *The Effect of the Sex Discrimination Act on the Scottish Police Service* (University of Strathclyde: Glasgow).

CHARLES, M. T. (1981), 'The Performance and Socialization of Female Recruits in the Michigan State Police Training Academy', *Journal of Police Science and Administration*, 9/2.

—— (1982), 'Women in Policing: The Physical Aspect', *Journal of Political Science and Administration*, 10/2: 194–205.

CHATTERTON, M. (1983), 'Police Work and Assault Charges', in Punch (1983) (ed.).

—— (1989), 'Managing Paperwork', in Weatheritt (1989) (ed.).

CHUNN, D., and GAVIGNAN, S. (1988), 'Social Control: Analytical Tool or Analytical Quagmire?', *Contemporary Crises*, 12/2: 107–24.

CLARKE, R. V., and HOUGH, M. (1984), *Crime and Police Effectiveness*,

Home Office Research Study, No. 79 (HMSO: London).

COHEN, A. (1992), *Masquerade Politics* (Univ. of California Press: Berkeley Calif.).

COHEN, R. (1987), *The New Helots* (Gower: Aldershot).

COHEN, S. (1985), *Visions of Social Control* (Polity Press: Oxford).

—— and SCULL, A. (1983) (eds.), *Social Control and the State* (Blackwell: Oxford).

COLMAN, A. M. (1983), 'Attitudes of British Police Officers: A Rejoinder', *Sociology*, 17/3: 388–92.

CONNELL, R. W. (1985), 'Theorising Gender', *Sociology*, 19/2: 260–73.

—— (1987), *Gender and Power* (Polity Press: Oxford).

CORRIGAN, P. (1979), *Schooling the Smash Street Kids* (Macmillan: London).

COWLEY, J. A. (1982), *Assessment of Affirmative Action in Criminal Justice Agencies: An Executive Summary*, (National Institute of Justice: Washington, DC).

CRITCHLEY, T. (1978), *A History of Police in England and Wales* (Constable: London).

CROMPTON, R., and MANN, M. (1986) (eds.), *Gender and Stratification* (Polity Press: Oxford).

CROUCH, B. M. (1985), 'Pandora's Box: Women Guards in Men's Prisons', *Journal of Criminal Justice*, 13/6, Nov.–Dec.

—— and ALPERT, G. P. (1982), 'Sex and Occupational Socialization Among Prison Guards: A Longitudinal Study of Criminal Justice and Behaviour', 9/2, June.

CUMMING, E., CUMMING, I., and EDEL, L. (1965), 'Policeman as Philosopher, Guide and Friend', *Social Problems*, 17: 276–86.

DALY, K. (1989), 'Criminal Justice Ideologies and Practices in Different Voices: Some Feminist Questions about Justice', *International Journal of the Sociology of Law*, 17: 1–18.

—— and CHESNEY-LIND, M. (1988), 'Feminism and Criminology', *Justice Quarterly*, 5/4.

DAVIS, M., with RUDDICK, S. (1989), 'Los Angeles: Civil Liberties between the Hammer and the Rock', *New Left Review*, 37–60, June.

DAY, P., and KLEIN, R. (1987), *Accountabilities: Five Public Services* (Tavistock Press: London).

DEEM, R. (1978), *Women and Schooling* (Routledge: London).

DEVAULT, M. (1990), 'Talking and Listening from Women's Standpoint: Feminist Strategies for Interviewing and Analysis', *Social Problems*, 37/1: 96–116.

DOBASH, EMERSON R., and DOBASH, R. (1979), *Violence Against Wives* (Open Books: London).

DOBASH, R., and DOBASH, R. E. (1981), 'Community Response to Violence against Wives: Charivari, Abstract Justice and Patriarchy', *Social Problems*, 28/5.

DONZELOT, J. (1985), *The Policing of Families* (Hutchinson: London).

DOWNES, D., and ROCK, P. (1988), *Understanding Deviance* (2nd edn., Clarendon Press: Oxford).

—— (1991), 'The New Audit', Preface in N. Fielding (1991).

DRIVER, E., and DROISEN, A. (1989) (eds.), *Child Sexual Abuse* (Macmillan: Basingstoke).

DURKHEIM, E. (1949), *Division of Labour in Society* (Free Press: New York).

EATON, M. (1986), *Justice for Women?* (Open University Press: Milton Keynes).

EDOBOR, PATRICK IGBINOVIA (1987), 'African Women in Contemporary Law Enforcement', *Police Studies*, 10, Spring.

EDWARDS, J. (1987), *Positive Discrimination, Social Justice, and Social Policy*, (Tavistock Press: London).

EDWARDS, S. (1981), *Female Sexuality and the Law*, (Martin Robertson: Oxford).

—— (1984), *Women on Trial* (Manchester Univ. Press: Manchester).

—— (1990), *Policing Domestic Violence* (Sage: London).

EMMISON, M., and WESTERN, M. (1990), 'Social Class and Social Identity: A Comment on Marshall *et al.*', *Sociology*, 24/2: 241–53.

ENLOE, C. (1988), *Does Khaki Become You?* (Pandora: London).

ETTRIDGE, R., HALE, C., and HAMBRICK, M. (1984), 'Female Employees in All-Male Correctional Facilities', *Federal Probation*, 48/4, Dec.

FEINMAN, C. (1986), *Women in the Criminal Justice system* (2nd edn., Praeger: New York).

FIELDING, N. G. (1988a), 'Competence and Culture in the Police', *Sociology*, 22/1: 45–65.

—— (1988b), *Joining Forces: Police Training, Socialization and Occupational Competence* (Routledge: London).

—— (1989), 'Police Culture and Police Practice', in M. Weatheritt (1989) (ed.).

—— (1991), 'Conflict and Change in Britain Series', *The Police and Social Conflict: Rhetoric and Reality* (Athlone Press: London).

—— and FIELDING, J. (1991), 'Police Attitudes to Crime and Punishment: Certainties and Dilemmas', *British Journal of Criminology*, 31/1: 39–53.

FINCH, J. (1984), '"It's Great to Have Someone to Talk to": The Ethics, and Politics of Interviewing Women', in C. Bell and H. Roberts (1984) (eds.), *Social Researching, Policies, Problems and Practices* (Routledge: London).

FOUCAULT, M. (1967), *Madness and Civilisation* (Tavistock Press: London).

—— (1977), *Discipline and Punish* (Allen Lane: London).

FOX, L. (1952), *The English Prison and Borstal System* (Routledge: London).

FRAZER, E. (1988), 'Teenage Girls Talking About Class', *Sociology*, 22/3: 343–58.

FRIEDMANN, R. (1986), 'Transformation of Roles for Israeli Police Officers: Perceptions of a Community Oriented Role', *Police Studies*, 9/2, Summer.

FRIEDSON, E. (1973) (ed.), *The Professions and Their Prospects* (Sage: London).

FUCHS EPSTEIN, C. (1988), *Deceptive Distinctions* (Yale University Press: New Haven, Conn.).

GARLAND, D. (1985), *Punishment and Welfare* (Gower: Aldershot).

—— (1990), *Punishment and Modern Society: A Study in Social Theory* (Clarendon Press: Oxford).

GESLTHORPE, L. (1989), *Sexism and the Female Offender* (Gower: Aldershot).

—— (1990), 'Feminist Methodologies in Criminology: A New Approach or Old Wine in New Bottles', in Gelsthorpe and Morris (1990) (eds.).

—— and MORRIS, A. (1988), 'Feminism and Criminology in Britain', *British Journal of Criminology* 28/2: 223–41.

—— —— (1990) (eds.), *Feminist Perspectives in Criminology* (Open University Press: Milton Keynes).

GIDDENS, A. (1989), *Sociology* (Polity Press: Oxford).

GOLDEN, KATHRYN, (1981), 'Women as Patrol Officers: A Study of Attitudes (of male officers)', *Police Studies*, 4, Fall.

—— (1982), 'Women in Criminal Justice: Occupational Interests', *Journal of Criminal Justice*, 10: 147.

GRAEF, R. (1990), *Talking Blues: The Police in their Own Words* (2nd edn., Fontana: London).

GREGORY, J. (1987), *Sex, Race and the Law* (Sage: London).

GRIMES, A. P. (1967), *The Puritan Ethic and Woman Suffrage* (Oxford Univ. Press: Oxford).

GRIMSHAW R., and JEFFERSON, T. (1987), *Interpreting Policework* (Allen & Unwin: London).

HAGAN, J., SIMPSON, J. H., and GILLIS, A. R. (1979), 'The Sexual Stratification of Social Control: A Gender-based Perspective on Crime and Delinquency', *British Journal of Sociology*, 30/1: 25–38.

HAHN RAFTER, N. (1983), 'Chastizing the Unchaste: Social Control Functions of a Women's Reformatory 1894–31', in Cohen and Scull (1983) (eds.).

HALSEY, A. H., HEATH, A. F., and RIDGE, J. M. (1980), *Origins and Destinations* (Blackwell: Oxford).

HAMMERSLY, M. (1990), 'What's Wrong with Ethnography? The Myth of Theoretical Description', *Sociology*, 24/4: 597–615.

HANMER, J., and SAUNDERS, S. (1984), *Well-founded Fear* (Hutchinson: London).

—— RADFORD, J., and STANKO, E. (1989), *Women, Policing and Male Violence* (Routledge: London).

Harding, S. (1987) (ed.), *Feminism and Methodology* (Indiana Univ. Press: Boston).

Hatty, S. (1984), 'Women in the Prison System: Proceedings', *Australian Institute of Criminology*.

Heal, K., Tarling, R., and Burrows, J. (1985) (eds.), *Policing Today* (HMSO: London).

—— and Laycock, G. (1986) (eds.), *Situational Crime Prevention: From Theory into Practice* (HMSO: London).

Hearn, J. (1982), 'Notes on Patriarchy, Professionalization and the Semiprofessions', *Sociology*, 16/2.

—— (1987), 'Notes on Patriarchy, Professionalization and the Semi Professions', *Sociology*, 16/2: 184–203.

Heidensohn, F. (1968), 'The Deviance of Women: A Critique and an Enquiry', *British Journal of Sociology*, 19/2: 160–75.

—— (1975), 'The Imprisonment of Females', in S. McConville (1975) (ed.), *The Use of Imprisonment* (Routledge: London).

—— (1985), *Women and Crime* (Macmillan: London).

—— (1986), 'Models of Justice: Portia or Persephone? Some Thoughts on Equality, Fairness and Gender in the Field of Criminal Justice', *International Journal of the Sociology of Law*, 14.

—— (1987), 'Women and Crime: Questions for Criminology', in Carlen and Worrall (1987) (eds.).

—— (1989*a*), *Crime and Society* (Macmillan: Basingstoke).

—— (1989*b*), *Women in Policing in the USA* (Police Foundation: London).

—— 'Equal Opportunities in Law Enforcement: Experiences in the USA', *Occupational Psychologist*, 11.

—— (1991*a*), 'Introduction: Convergence, Diversity and Change', in Heidensohn and Farrell (1991*c*) (eds.).

—— (1991*b*), 'Sociological Perspectives on Female Violence', paper given at Conference on Perspectives on Female Violence, St George's Hospital Medical School, London.

—— (1992), 'From Being to Knowing: Some Reflections on the Study of Gender in Contemporary Society', Paper delivered at the Centre international de criminologie comparée, University of Montreal, February.

Heidensohn, F., and Farrell, M. (1991*c*) (eds.), *Crime in Europe* (Routledge: London).

Hernandez, E. (1982), 'Females in Law Enforcement, Feminity, Competence, Attraction, and Work Acceptance', *Criminal Justice and Behaviour*, 9/1: 13–34.

Hewitt, S. (1985), *A Lesser Life* (Michael Joseph: London).

Higgins, J. (1980), 'Social Control Theories of Social Policy', in *Journal of Social Policy*, 9/1: 1–25.

Higgs, Milton C., *et al.* (1974), *Women in Policing: A Manual* (Police Foundation: Washington, DC).

264 BIBLIOGRAPHY

HM Chief Inspector of Constabulary (1989), *Annual Report*, HC 524 (HMSO: London).

—— (1990), *Annual Report*, HC 412 (HMSO: London).

HMSO (1989), *Report of Her Majesty's Inspector of Constabulary* (Home Office: London).

HOBBS, D. (1988), *Doing the Business* (Oxford Univ. Press: Oxford).

HOCHSCHILD, A. P. (1973), 'Making it: Marginality and Obstacles to Minority Consciousness', in *Annals of the New York Academy of Science*, 208: 79–82.

HOCHSTEDLER, ELLEN (1984), 'Impediments to Hiring Minorities in Public Police Agencies', *Journal of Police Science and Administration*, 12/2.

HOLDAWAY, S. (1979) (ed.), *The British Police* (Edward Arnold: London).

—— (1983) (ed.), *Inside the British Police* (Blackwell: Oxford).

—— (1989), 'Discovering Structure: Studies of the British Police Occupational Culture', in M. Weatheritt (1989) (ed.).

—— (1991a), *Recruiting a Multiracial Police Force* (HMSO: London).

—— (1991b), 'Race Relations and Police Recruitment', *British Journal of Criminology* 31/4: 365–82.

HOMANT, R. (1983), 'The Impact of Policewomen on Community Attitudes toward Police', *Journal of Police Science and Administration*, 11/1: 16–22.

Home Office (1990), *Ethnic Minority Recruitment into the Police Service*, Circular 33.

—— (1991), *Criminal Statistics 1990* (HMSO: London).

HOPKINS, E. (1884), *An English Woman's Work among Workingmen*.

HORNE, P. (1980), *Women in Law Enforcement* (2nd edn., Thomas: Springfield, Ill.).

—— (1985) 'Female Correction Officers: A Status Report', *Federal Probation*, 4g/3: 46–54.

HOUGH, M. (1985), 'Organisation and Resource Management of the Uniformed Police', in Heal *et al.* (1985) (eds.).

—— (1987), 'Thinking about Effectiveness', in Reiner and Shapland, (1987).

—— and MAYHEW, P. (1983), *The British Crime Survey*, Home Office Research Study, No. 76, (HMSO: London).

HUNT, J. (1984), 'The Development of Rapport through the Negotiation of Gender in Fieldwork among Police', *Human Organization*, 43/4.

HUTZEL, E. L. (1933), *The Policewoman's Handbook* (Columbia Univ. Press: New York).

IGNATIEFF, M. (1978), *A Just Measure of Pain* (Pantheon: New York).

JANOWITZ, M. (1975), 'Sociological Theory and Social Control', *American Journal of Sociology*, 81/1: 92–108.

JOHNSON, T. J. (1972), *Professions and Power* (Macmillan: London).

JOHNSON, T., MISNER, G., and BROWN, L. (1981), *The Police and Society* (Prentice Hall: Englewood Cliffs, NJ).

JONES, A. (1991), *Women who Kill* (Gollancz: London).

JONES, C. (1985), *Patterns of Social Policy: An Introduction to Comparative Analysis* (Tavistock Press: London).

JONES, D. (1982), *Crime, Protest, Community and Police in Nineteenth Century Britain* (Routledge: London).

JONES, S. (1986), *Policewomen and Equality* (Macmillan: London).

JURIK, N. C. (1985) 'An Officer and a Lady: Organizational Barriers of Women Working as Correctional Officers in Men's Prisons', *Social Problems* 32: 301–5.

KAY LORD, L. (1986), 'A Comparison of Male and Female Peace Officers' Stereotypic Perceptions of Women and Women Peace Officers', *Journal of Police Science and Administration*, 14/2.

KEELER, R. (1981), 'Female Guards Face Problems', *Empire State*, Report 7.

KELLING, G. (1986), 'Neighbourhood Crime Control and the Police: A View of the American Experience', in Heal and Laycock (1986) (eds.).

KENNEDY, D., and HOMANT R. (1981), 'Nontraditional Role Assumption and the Personality of the Policewoman', *Journal of Police Science and Administration*, 9/3: 346–55.

—— —— (1984), 'Battered Women's Evaluation of the Police Response', *Victimology*, 9/1.

KERSTEIN, A. (1982), 'Crime Prevention Assistants: The Bridge Between Recruitment and Training of Female Officers', *Police Chief*, 49/8: 8.

KINSEY, R. (1984), *Merseyside Crime Survey: First Report, Nov. 1984* (Merseyside County Council: Liverpool).

—— LEA, J., and YOUNG, J. (1986), *Losing the Fight against Crime* (Blackwell: Oxford).

KIRP, D., YUDOF, M. G., and STRONG, FRANKS M. (1986), *Gender Justice* (Univ. of Chicago Press: Chicago).

KIZZIAH, C., and MORRIS, M. (1977), *Evaluation of Women in Policing Program, Newton Massachusetts* (Approach Associates: Oakland, Calif).

KLOFAS, J., and TOCH, H. (1982), 'The Guard Subculture Myth', *Journal of Research in Crime and Delinquency*, 19: 238–54.

LEES, S. (1986), *Losing Out: Sexuality and Adolescent Girls* (Hutchinson: London).

LEIMEN, S. (1984), *Black Police: White Society* (New York Univ. Press: New York).

LESTER, D., GRONAN, F., and WOUDRACK, K. (1982), 'The Personality and Attitudes of Female Police Officers: Needs, Androgyny and Attitudes toward Rape', *Journal of Police Science and Administration* 10/3: 357–60.

LEVI, M., and JONES, S. (1985), 'Public and Police Perceptions of Crime Seriousness in England and Wales', in *British Journal of Criminology* 25/3.

LOCK, J. (1979), *The British Policewoman: Her Story* (Hale: London).

LUCAS, N. (1986), *WPC 'Courage'* (Weidenfeld & Nicholson: London).

LUHMANN, N. (1981), *Gesellschaftsstruktur und Semantik*, ii (Suhrkamp: Frankfurt).

McBARNET, D. (1979), 'Arrest: The Legal Context of Policing', in Holdaway (1979) (ed.).

McCORMACK, R. J. (1986), *Corruption in the Subculture of Policing* (Fordham Univ. Press, New York).

McDONALD, E. (1991), *Shoot the Women First* (Fourth Estate: London).

McKENZIE, I. K., and GALLAGHER, G. P. (1989), *Behind the Uniform: Policing in Britain and America* (Harvester Wheatsheaf: Hemel Hempstead).

McMAHON, M. (1990), 'Net-Widening: Vagaries in the Use of a Concept', *British Journal of Criminology*, 30/2: 121–49.

MAHAJAN, A. (1982), *Indian Policewomen: A Sociological Study of the New Role* (Deep & Deep: New Delhi).

MALSEED, J. (1987), 'Straw Men: A Note on Ann Oakley's Treatment of Textbook Prescriptions for Interviewing', *Sociology*, 21/4: 629–31.

MANNING, N. (1985) (ed.), *Social Problems and Welfare Ideology* (Gower: Aldershot).

MANNING, P. (1977), *Police Work* (MIT Press: Cambridge, Mass.).
Metropolitan Police/Equal Opportunities Commission (1990), *Managing to Make Progress: A Report of a Collaborative Exercise between the Metropolitan Police and the Equal Opportunities Commission*.

MARK, R. (1978), *In the Office of Constable* (Collins: London).

MARSHALL, P. (1973), 'POLICEwomen on Patrol', *Manpower*, 10/5.

MARTIN, S. E. (1979), 'POLICEwomen and PoliceWOMEN: Occupational Role Dilemmas and Choices of Female Offenders', *Journal of Police Science and Administration*, 2/3: 314–23.

—— (1980), *Breaking and Entering* (Univ. of California Press: Berkeley, Calif.).

—— (1989), *Police Foundation Reports: Women on the Move: A Report on the Status of Women in Policing* (Police Foundation: Washington, DC).

—— (1990), *On the Move: The Status of Women in Policing* (Police Foundation: Washington, DC).

—— (1991), 'The Effectiveness of Affirmative Action: The Case of Women in Policing', *Justice Quarterly*, 8/4.

MAWBY, R. I. (1990), *Comparative Policing Issues* (Unwin Hyman: London).

MAYER, J. A. (1983), 'Notes towards a Working Definition of Social Control in Historical Analysis', in Cohen and Scull (1983) (eds.).

MAYNARD, M. (1990), 'The Reshaping of Sociology: Trends in the Study of Gender', *Sociology*, 24/2: 269–91.

MILLAR, J., and GLENDINNING, C. (1989), 'Gender and Poverty', *Journal of Social Policy*, 18/3: 363–83.

MILLER, W. R. (1977), *Cops and Bobbies* (Univ. of Chicago Press: Chicago).

MILTON, C. H. (1972), *Women in Policing* (Police Foundation: Washington, DC).

MISHKIN, B. D. (1981), 'Female Police in the US', *Police Journal*, 54/1.

MITCHELL, J. (1971), *Women's Estate* (Penguin: Harmondsworth).

—— and OAKLEY, A. (1986) (eds.), *What is Feminism?* (Blackwell: Oxford).

MONKKONEN, E. H. (1981), *Police in Urban America 1860–1920* (Cambridge Univ. Press: Cambridge).

MORASH, M., and GREENE, J. R. (1986), 'Evaluating Women on Patrol: A Critique of contemporary Wisdom', *Evaluation Review*, 10/2, Apr.

—— and HAARR, 'Gender, Workplace Problems and Stress in Policing', *Criminology,* (forthcoming).

MORGAN, R., and SMITH, D. J. (1989), *Coming to Terms with Policing* (Routledge: London).

MORRIS, A. (1987), *Women, Crime and Criminal Justice* (Blackwell: Oxford).

MORRISON, C. M. (1984), 'A Sociological Analysis of the British Police in the Media', unpublished Ph.D. thesis, University of Aberdeen, Apr.

MORRISON, P. (1991), 'Women make Better Cops L.A. Probers Find', *Los Angeles Times Service*, 14 July.

MUSHENO, M., and SEELEY, K. (1986), 'Prostitution and the Women's Movement', *Contemporary Crises*, 10/3: 237–55.

OAKELY, A. (1974), *The Sociology of Housework* (Martin Robertson: London).

—— (1980), *Women Confined: Towards a Sociology of Childbirth* (Martin Robertson: Oxford).

—— (1981), 'Interviewing Women: A Contradiction in Terms', in H. Roberts (1981) (ed.).

—— (1987), 'Comment on Malseed', *Sociology*, 21/4: 632.

OPCS (1991), *Social Trends 1990* (HMSO: London).

OSBORNE, J. A. (1987), 'Myths Regarding Female Correctional Officers', *Free Inquiry in Creative Sociology*, 15/1, May.

OWINGS, C. (1925), *Women Police: A Study of the Development and Status of the Women Police Movement* (Bureau of Social Hygiene: Hitchcock, NY).

PARTON, N. (1985), *The Politics of Child Abuse* (Macmillan: London).

PATEMAN, C. (1988), *The Sexual Contract* (Polity Press: Oxford).

Pennsylvania State Police (1974), *Pennsylvania State Police Female Trooper Study* (Hamsburg, Pa.).

PERF (Police Executive Research Foundation) (1988), Washington, DC, Personal communication from the Director, May.

PETRIE, G. (1971), *A Singular Iniquity: The Campaigns of Josephine Butler* (Macmillan: London).

(Philadelphia) (1978), 'The Study of Police Women Competency in the Performance of Sector Police Work in the City of Philadelphia', Phase I, State College, Pa.; Bartell Associates.

PHILIPS, D. (1977), *Crime and Authority in Victorian England: The Black Country 1835–1860* (Croom Helm: London).

—— (1983), 'A Just Measure of Crime, Authority, Hunters and Blue Locusts: "The Revisionist" Social History of Crime and the Law in Britain 1780–1850', in Cohen and Scull (1983) (eds.).

PIKE, M. S. (1985), *The Principles of Policing* (Macmillan: London).

PITCH, T. (1985), 'The Feminization of Social Control', *Research in Law, Deviance and Social Control*, 7, Autumn.

POTTS, L. W. (1981), 'Equal Employment Opportunity and Female Criminal Justice Employment', *Police Studies*, 4, Fall.

—— (1983), 'The Police and Determinants of Rape Prosecutions: Decision-Making in a Nearly Decomposable System', *Police Studies*, 6/4.

—— (1983*b*), 'Female Professionals in Corrections: Equal Employment Opportunity Issue', *Federal Probation*, 47/1, Mar.

PROCHASKA, F. K. (1980), *Women and Philanthropy in Nineteenth-Century England* (Clarendon Press: Oxford).

PUNCH, M. (1979), *Policing the Inner City* (Macmillan: London).

—— (1983) (ed.), *Control in the Police Organization* (MIT Press: Cambridge, Mass.).

—— (1985), *Conduct Unbecoming: The Social Construction of Police Deviance and Control* (Tavistock Press: London).

—— and NAYLOR, T. (1973), 'The Police: a Social Service', *New Society*, 24.

RADFORD, J. (1989), 'Women Policing: Contradictions Old and New', in Hanmer, Radford, and Stanko (1989) (eds.), *Women, Policing and Male Violence* (Routledge: London).

RADZINOWICZ, L. (1948–69), *A History of English Criminal Law*, i–vi (Stevens: London).

RAMAZANOGLU, C. (1989), 'Improving on Sociology: Problems in Taking a Feminist Standpoint', *Sociology*, 23/3: 427–42.

REEVES, J. B., and AUSTIN, S. F. (1985), 'Exploring Differential Occupational Stress and the Male Sex Role', *Free Inquiry in Creative Sociology*, 13/1, May.

REINER, R. (1985), *The Politics of the Police* (Wheatsheaf: London).

—— (1988), 'British Criminology and the State', *British Journal of Criminology*, 28/2: 268–89.

—— (1989), 'The Politics of Police Research in Britain', in M. Weatheritt (1989) (ed.).

—— (1991), *Chief Constables* (Oxford Univ. Press: Oxford).

—— and Shapland, J. (1987) (eds.), 'Introduction: Why Police?', *British Journal of Criminology*, 27/1 (Special Issue on Policing in Britain): 1–4.

REISER, S. (1982), 'The Israeli Police', *Police Studies*, 5: 27–35.

REISS, A. J. (1971), *The Police and the Public* (Yale Univ. Press: New Haven, Conn.).

REITH, C. (1956), *A New Study of Police History* (Oliver & Boyd: London).

REMMINGTON, PATRICIA W. (1981), *Policing: The Occupation and the Introduction of Female Officers* (Atlanta Study) (Univ. Press of America: Lanham, MD.

RENDALL, J. (1985), *The Origins of Modern Feminism: Women in Britain, France and the US 1780–1860* (Macmillan: London).

REUSS-IANNI, E. (1983), *The Two Cultures of Policing: Street Cops and Management Cops* (Transaction Books: New York).

ROBERTS, H. (1981) (ed.), *Doing Feminist Research* (Routledge: London).

ROBINSON, C. D., *et al.* (1987), 'The Origin and Evolution of the Police Function in Society: Notes Towards a Theory', *Law and Society Review*, 21/1: 109–53.

ROCK, P. (1983), 'Law, Order and Power in Late Seventeenth Century and Early 18th Century England', in Cohen and Scull (1983) (eds.).

—— (1988), 'The Present State of Criminology in Britain', *British Journal of Criminology*, 28/2: 188–200.

—— (1991), personal communication.

RODGER, J. J. (1988), 'Social Work as Social Control Re-examined: Beyond the Dispersal of Discipline Thesis', *Sociology*, 22/4.

ROSENBAUM, D. (1986) (ed.), *Community Crime Prevention* (Sage: Beverley Hills, Calif.

Royal Commission on the Police (1962), Final Report, Cmnd. 1728 (HMSO: London).

RUSSELL, G. W., *et al.* (1988), 'Male Responses to Female Aggression', *Social Behaviour and Personality*, 16/1: 51–9.

RYAN, M., and WARD, T. (1989), *Privatization and the Penal System* (Open Univ. Press: Milton Keynes).

SAMPSON, A., STUBBS, P., SMITH, D., PEARSON, G., and BLAGG, H. (1988), 'Crime, Localities and the Multi-Agency Approach', *British Journal of Criminology* 28/6: 478–93.

SCARMAN, Lord (1981), *The Brixton Disorders, 10–12 April 1981*, Cmnd. 8427 (HMSO: London).

SCRATON, P. (1985), *The State of the Police* (Pluto: London).

—— (1987), *Law, Order and the Authoritarian State* (Open Univ. Press: Milton Keynes).

—— (1990), 'Scientific Knowledge or Masculine Discourses? Challenging Patriarchy in Criminology', in Morris and Gelsthorpe (1990) (eds.).

—— and GORDON, P. (1984) (eds.), *Causes for Concern* (Penguin: Harmondsworth).

SCULL, A. (1977), *Decarceration: Community Treatment and the Deviant: A Radical View* (2nd edn., Polity Press: Oxford, 1984).

SCULL, A. (1981), 'Progressive Dreams, Progressive Nightmares: Social Control in Twentieth-Century America', *Stanford Law Review*, 33: 301–16.

SEIDLER, V. (1990) (ed.), *Male Orders* (Routledge: London).

SHAPLAND, J. (1989), paper given at British Criminology Conference, Bristol Polytechnic.

—— and HOBBS, D. (1989), 'Policing Priorities on the Ground', in Morgan and Smith (1989) (eds.).

—— and VAGG, J. (1987), 'Using the Police', *British Journal of Criminology* 27/1: 54–64.

—— —— (1988), *Policing by the Public* (Routledge: London).

SHARPE, J. A. (1988), 'The History of Crime in England 1300–1914', in *British Journal of Criminology*, 28/2: 254–68.

SHERMAN, L. (1975), 'Evaluation of Policewomen on Patrol in a Suburban Police Department', *Journal of Police Science Administration*, 3: 434–8, Dec.

—— (1977), 'Policewomen Around the World', *International Review of Criminal Policy*, 33.

SICHEL, J., *et al.* (1977), *Women on Patrol: Pilot Study of Police Performance in New York City* (Vera Institute, New York).

SIEGEL, M. (1980), *Cops and Women* (Tower Publications: New York).

SINFIELD, A. (1978), 'The Social Division of Welfare Revisited', *Journal of Social Policy*, 7/2.

SKOLNICK, J. (1966), *Justice without Trial* (Wiley: New York).

SLIWA, L. (1986), *Guardian Angels* (Sidgwick & Jackson: London).

SMART, C. (1977), *Women, Crime and Criminology* (Routledge: London).

—— (1990), 'Feminist Approaches to Criminology or Postmodern Woman Meets Atavistic Man', in Gelsthorpe and Morris (1990) (eds.).

SMITH, B. (1960), *Police Systems in the US* (2nd edn., Harper & Bros.: New York).

SMITH, D., and GRAY, J. (1983), Policy Studies Institute, *Police and People in London*, 1–4, (Police Studies Institute: London).

SMITHIES, E. (1982), *Crime in Wartime* (Allen & Unwin: London).

SNORTUM, J. R., and BEYERS, J. C. (1983), 'Patrol Activities of Male and Female Officers as a Function of Work Experience', *Police Studies*, 6/1.

SOUTHGATE, P. (1981), 'Women in the Police', *The Police Journal*, 54/2.

—— and EKBLOM, P. (1984), *Contacts between Police and Public: Findings from the British Crime Survey*, Home Office Research Study, 77 (HMSO: London).

SPENDER, D. (1980), *Man Made Language* (Routledge: London).

STACEY, M., and PRICE, M. (1981), *Women, Power and Politics* (Tavistock Press: London).

STALKER, J. (1988), *Stalker* (Penguin: Harmondsworth).

STANKO, E. (1985), *Intimate Intrusions* (Routledge: London).

—— (1990*a*), *Everyday Violence* (Pandora: London).

—— (1990b), 'When Precaution is Normal: A Feminist Critique of Crime Prevention', in Gelsthorpe and Morris (1990) (eds.).

STANLEY, L., and WISE, S. (1983), *Breaking Out* (Routledge: London).

STEAD, P. J. (1977), 'The New Police', in Bayley (1977) (ed.).

STEDMAN-JONES, G. (1977), 'Class Expression versus Social Control? A Critique of Recent Trends in the Social History of Leisure', in Cohen and Scull (1983) (eds.).

STEEDMAN, C. (1984), *Policing the Victorian Community: The Formation of English Provincial Police Forces 1856–1880* (Routledge: London).

STEEL, B. S., and LOVRICH, N. P. (1987), 'Equality and Efficiency Trade-Offs in Affirmative Action: Real or Imagined? The Case of Women in Policing', *Social Science Journal* (Fort Worth), 24/1.

STEFFENSMEIER, D. J. (1979), 'Sex Role Orientation and Attitudes toward Female Police', *Police Studies*, 2/1, Spring.

STENSON, K., and COWELL, D. (1991) (eds.), *The Politics of Crime Control*, introduction (Sage: London).

STERLING, B. S., *et al.* (1982), 'Perceptions of Demanding versus Reasoning Male and Female Police Officers', *Personality and Social Psychology Bulletin*, 8/2: 336–40.

STEVENS, JAMES W., and ALDRICH, P. S. (1985), 'The Integration of Women into W. German and US Police Service', *International Journal of Comprehensive and Applied Criminal Justice*, Spring–Winter.

STIEHM, J. (1989), *Arms and the Enlisted Woman* (Temple Univ. Press: Philadelphia).

STORCH, R. D. (1977), 'Police Control of Street Prostitution in Victorian London: A Study in the Contexts of Police Action', in Bayley (1977) (ed.).

STYKES, R. E. (1977), 'A Regulatory Theory of Policing: A Preliminary Statement', in Bayley (1977) (ed.).

STYLES, J. (1987), 'The Emergence of the Police: Explaining Police Reform in Eighteenth Century and Nineteenth Century England', *British Journal of Criminology*, 27/1: 15–23.

SULTON, C., and TOWNSEY, R. (1981), *A Progress Report on Women in Policing* (Police Foundation: Washington, DC).

SUMNER, C. (1990), 'Foucault, Gender and the Censure of Deviance', in Gelsthorpe and Morris (1990) (eds.).

THANE, P. (1982), *Foundations of the Welfare State* (Longman: London).

—— (1992), 'Gender and Social Welfare in Britain, 1880s–1940s', *Geneses, Sciences Sociales and Histoire*.

TICE, D., and BAUMEISTER, R. (1985), 'Masculinity Inhibits Helping in Emergencies: Personality Does Predict the Bystander Effect', *Journal of Personality and Social Psychology*, 49/2: 420–8.

TOWNSEY, R. D. (1982), 'Black Women in American Policing: An Advancement Display', *Journal of Criminal Justice*, 10/6.

VAN WINKLE, M. C. (1925), preface to C. Owings, *Women and Police* (Hitchcock: New York).

VAN WORMER, K. (1981), 'Are Males Suited to Police Patrol Work?', *Police Studies*, 3: 41–4, Winter.

VEGA, M., and SILVERMAN, I. J. (1982), 'Women Police Officers as Viewed by their Male Counterparts' (based on a survey of three Law Enforcement Agencies in the Tampa Bay area of Florida), *Police Studies*, 5, Spring.

VILO, G., LONGIURE, D., and KENNEY, J. (1983/4), 'Can Police Deter Rape: Two Views Preventing Rape: An Evaluation of a Multifaceted Program', *Police Studies*, 6/4, Winter.

WADDINGTON, P. A. J. (1982), '"Conservatism, Dogmatism and Authoritarianism in British Police Officers": A Comment', *Sociology*, 16/4: 591–4.

WALBY, S. (1988), 'Gender Politics and Social Theory', *Sociology*, 22/2.

—— (1989), 'Theorising Patriarchy', *Sociology*, 23/2: 213–34.

WALKER, R. (1985), 'Racial Minority and Female Employment in Policing', *Crime and Delinquency*, 31/4: 555–72.

WALSH, A. (1984a), 'Gender Based Differences: A Study of Probation Officers Attitudes about, and Recommendations for, Felony Assault Cases', *Criminology*, 22/3: 371–88.

—— (1984b), 'Gender Based Differences: A Study of Probation Officers Attitudes about and Recommendations for Felony Sexual Assault Cases', *Criminology*, 22/3: 371–87.

WARNER, R., STEEL, B. S., LOVRICH, N. P. (1989), 'Conditions Associated with Representative Bureaucracy Cases of Women in Policing', *Social Science Quarterly*, 70/3: 562–79.

WARREN, C. (1981), 'New Forms of Social Control: The Myth of Deinstitutionalization', *American Behavioural Scientist*, 24/6: 724–40.

WEATHERITT, M. (1989) (ed.), *Police Research: Some Future Prospects* (Avebury: Aldershot).

WEBER, M. (1948), 'The Sociology of Charismatic Authority', in H. H. Gerth and C. Wright Mills (1948) (eds.), *From Max Weber* (Routledge: London).

WELLS, A. S., (1929), 'Reminiscences of a Police Woman', in *Police Reporter*, 23–8, Sept.

—— (1932), 'Twenty two Years a Police Woman', in *The Western Woman*, 7: 15–16, July–Sept.

WESTLEY, W. (1970), *Violence and the Police: A Sociological Study of Law, Custom Morality* (MIT Press: Cambridge, Mass.).

WEXLER, J. G., (1985), 'Role Styles of Women Police Officers', *Sex Roles*, 12/7–8: 749–56.

—— and QUINN, V. (1985), 'Considerations in the Training and

Development of Women Sargeants' *Journal of Police Science and Administration*, 13/2.

—— et al. (1983), 'Sources of Stress among Women Police Officers'. *Journal of Police Science and Administration*, 11/1: 46–53.

WILDING, P. (1982), *Professional Power and Social Welfare* (Routledge: London).

WILLIAMS, F. (1989), *Social Policy: A Critical Introduction* (Polity Press: Oxford).

WILLIAMS, H. (1989), 'Introduction: Women on the Move', Police Foundation Reports (Washington, DC).

WILSON, J. Q. A. (1968), *Varieties of Police Behaviour: The Management of Law and Order in Eight Communities* (Harvard Univ. Press: Cambridge, Mass.).

—— and KELLING, G. (1982), 'Broken Windows: The Police and Neighbourhood Safety', *Atlantic Monthly*, Mar.

WINNAND, K. E. (1986), 'Police Women and the People they Serve', *Police Chief*, 53.

WYLES, L. (1951), *A Woman at Scotland Yard* (Faber: London).

YIN, R. K. (1986), 'Community Crime Prevention: A Synthesis of Eleven Evaluations', in D. Rosenbaum (1986) (ed.).

YOUNG, D-J. (1985), 'Women in Policing: A Comparative Study of the US and the Republic of China (Taiwan)', *Police Studies*, 8, Fall.

YOUNG, M. (1991), *An Inside Job* (Clarendon Press: Oxford).

ZIMMER, L. (1986), *Women Guarding Men* (Univ. of Chicago Press: Chicago).

ZUPAN, L. (1986), 'Gender-Related Differences in Correctional Officers' Perceptions and Attitudes', *Journal of Criminal Justice*, 14/4, July–Aug.

INDEX